Napkin Folding

Napkin Folding

Surinder Kumar Rai

RANDOM

RANDOM PUBLICATIONS

NEW DELHI (INDIA)

Napkin Folding

ISBN 978-93-5111-257-0

Published in 2014 in India by

RANDOM PUBLICATIONS

4376-A/4B, Gali Murari Lal, Ansari Road
New Delhi-110 002
Phone : +91-11-43580356, +91-11-23289044
e-mail: randomexports@gmail.com, sales@randompublications.com, info@randompublications.com

Reprinted 2026

Type Setting by : Keystoneprintads, Delhi-110051

Preface

This book gives its readers an introduction to Napkin Folding. An overview of napkins, napkin etiquette and holder is provided. Elements and dimensions of napkin style, colour, material, care and cleaning are covered. An overview of contemporary napkin folding styles and techniques is done. The subject areas of table setting and decorating are covered. Details of table manners, table setting and dining etiquettes are described. An overview of Origami, as an art of folding, is made.

Napkin folding actually is the art of folding table napkins for neatness and beauty uses. Its purpose is to add a creative package for the table setting but in the sense that it does not diminish its true purpose as a protection for our clothing. It can also be used as a face or lip wiper whenever the situation calls for it. Napkins are used to enhance to the decoration of the dining table. Napkins folded in various forms can help to make any dinner table enjoyable and festal. No matter how simply or complexly done, elegant and creative napkin folds transform meals into celebrations. From quick-and-easy folds to very intricate napkin creations, this book offers step-by-step directions and illustrations of more than 50 types of napkin folds. Napkin folding is most commonly encountered as a table decoration in fancy restaurants. Typically, and for best results, a clean, pressed, and starched square cloth (linen or cotton) napkin is used.

Napkin folding has a centuries old history and dates back to the times of Louis XIV of France. Napkin folding is adaptable. The size of your finished creation will depend on the original size of the napkin. Luncheon napkins are approximately 17 inches square; dinner napkins are a bit larger, at 20 inches square. The square shape, not the size, is the essential factor. Woven napkins of natural fibers, such as cotton and linen, retain their creases and are less likely to fall apart once constructed. It is also possible to create attractive results with heavy-gauge paper napkins. Some patterns are simple and require a minimum of folds to create the design; others, more complex, may require a little practice. The versatile lotus flower fold serves as part of the place setting, to be unfolded for use at the table. It can sit under an appropriate-sized dish as a decorative holder or used as a thermal vessel for keeping bread warm.

Folds show up better with solid-color napkins but, for a special twist, use two napkins of contrasting or complementing colors in a fold design. Beginners and those using fabrics that balk at retaining folds can apply spray starch to the folds and iron the design in place. For a more permanent arrangement -- one that is decorative and not intended for use as a napkin -- you can apply fabric stiffener.

Surinder Kumar Rai

Acknowledgement

I feel extremly delighted and honored to present this book entitled Napkin folding. From quick-and-easy folds to very intricate napkin creations, this book offers step-by-step directions and illustrations of many types of napkin folds. The book has easy to follow instructions and well-drawn pictures which make it easy to understand how to fold the napkins.

The concept of this edited book is given by Prof. Girja Shankar Sharma and we are thankful for his valuable inspiration and suggestions received by us from time to time. I would like to convey my sincere thanks to all students, teacher, research scholars and other writers for their contributions in providing a valuable knowledge platform.

I will always be thankful to SamataAggarwal for her Inspiration, support and blessings from the core of my heart, Further, I am also thankful to Kishore Chandra and Surendra Singh for their valuable suggestions. I convey my sincere thanks to all the members of the editorial Board for their continuous support during the course of editing of the book.

I would like to thank to my father Shri Khetrapal Prasad and Mother Smt. Kanti Prasad for being sources for necessary motivation in the making of this book. At the end, I express my deep sense of gratitude for my younger brother Shri Dinesh Prasad & wife Smt. Sobha Prasad for their constant support.

And lastly I would like to thank Random Publications for publishing this book.

Surinder Kumar Rai

Contents

1

Napkin

Folded Napkin

A napkin, or face towel (also in Canada (some parts), the United Kingdom, Australia, New Zealand and South Africa: serviette) is a rectangle of cloth used at the table for wiping the mouth and fingers while eating. It is usually small and folded, sometimes in intricate designs and shapes. The word comes from Middle English, borrowing the French *nappe*—a cloth covering for a table—and adding *-kin*, the diminutive suffix.

In the United Kingdom and Canada both terms, *serviette* and *napkin*, are used. In the UK, napkins are traditionally *U* and serviette *non-U*. In certain places, *serviettes* are those made of paper whereas *napkins* are made of cloth. The word *serviette* in lieu of the term *napkin* is not typically used in American English, though, as discussed is not unheard of in Canadian English and Canadian French. In Canada the term was used until the late 70's and very early 1980's to mean a paper napkin, though very few people use it today, but instead use "napkin". In Australia, 'serviette' generally refers to the paper variety and 'napkin' refers to the cloth variety. Conventionally, the napkin is often folded and placed to the left of the place setting, outside the outermost fork. In an ambitious restaurant setting or a caterer's hall, it may be folded into more or less elaborate shapes and displayed on the empty plate. Origami techniques can be used (replacing the traditional paper method with the serviette/napkin) to create a 3D design e.g. a crane (bird). A napkin may also be held together in a bundle (with cutlery) by a napkin ring. Alternatively, paper napkins may be contained with a napkin holder.

Napkins were used in ancient Roman times. One of the earliest references to table napkins in English dates to 1384–85.

Summaries of napkin history often say that the ancient Greeks used bread to wipe their hands. This is suggested by a passage in one of Alciphron's letters (3:44), and some remarks by the sausage seller in Aristophanes' play, *The Knights*.

The bread in both texts is referred to as *apomagdalia,* which simply means bread from inside the crust known as *the crumb,* and not special "napkin bread". The use of paper napkins is documented in ancient China, where paper was invented in 2nd century BC. Paper napkins were known as *chih pha,* folded in squares, and used for the serving of tea. Textual evidence of paper napkins appears in a description of the possessions of the Yu family, from the city of Hangzhou.

A BRIEF HISTORY OF NAPKIN FOLDING

The use of the napkin in Europe began in 1400 on the tables of royalty, where they started to use napkins made from warm or even perfumed cloth. At the beginning of the 1800s, napkins became part of the bourgeois lifestyle, mostly to protect the sumptuous dresses of the period during meals. This is the era when the folding of napkins as decoration for dining tables began. The art really took off around 1880 with the incoming prosperity of the Industrial Revolution.

Mrs Beeton's book of Household Management, published in 1861, had an extensive reference section on napkin folding. These designs have now become classics and are still used today. Some of them, with modified instruction are featured in Luigi's book.

The First and Second World Wars were periods of interlude in terms of the development of these decorations. At the beginning of the 1950s, with the war over, decorations and creativity flowed again reviving the art of folded napkins as a means of expression. This is when the development of very elaborate and complex napkin folds took place. The James Ginder book on Napkin Folding, first published in 1978 by Virtue in over 54 languages, has been my inspiration and my guide through my career — not always very easy to follow but the only one available at the time.

Since the early 1980s we have become more reluctant to use napkin folding as part of the table preparation on the grounds of hygiene. With no practice there is no training and napkin folding has seen a decline in application in favour of a new style of table setting. A new trend of minimalism has been embraced. Elaborate napkin folding went out of favour and a new term "simplicity in style" has been has adopted. This new minimalist trend is very popular today with many fine dining operations.

Even so, we still use fancy napkin folds — particularly for weddings and special occasions where the "Fare la bella figura" is of great importance and considered a valuable asset.

There is no doubt that the development of napkin folding has been greatly influenced by Origami, the ancient Japanese art of paper folding. We would go as far as saying that it is an extension of this noble art, after all it does give the same pleasure and satisfaction to the creator.

LINEN NAPKINS – THE HISTORY

In historical terms, the appearance of linen napkins for dining took some time to develop.

First, the the table had to be invented: Early Egyptians used stone pedestals with trays on top to raise food and drinks off the floor and the Chinese made small tables for writing and painting.

However, the concept of using a table to serve and eat food is believed to have begun with the ancient Greeks, who used small individual tables set in front of them, the first T.V. trays! The Romans advanced that concept by using large tables made from marble or exotic woods of citrus trees. With the appearance of the dining table came the need to protect it, and various table coverings came into use.

TABLECLOTHS AS NAPKINS

Tablecloths not only protected these prized tables, they offered a way for diners to remove the crumbs or grease from their fingers between bites. Since forks and knives were also yet to be developed, people ate with their hands.

To clean them, they used whatever was within reach. Sometimes this was their shirts, but if the host were kind enough to drape the table in a cloth, so much the better. Often, the tablecloth became so disgustingly dirty that it had to be changed between courses. As linen was not cheap, keeping an adequate supply of linens on hand could present a challenge to all but the wealthiest of families.

THE BIRTH OF LINEN NAPKINS

Around the dawn of the Middle Ages, someone had the idea to provide long cloths that would stretch the entire length of the table and would be shared by many diners. An example of this is found in the painting "The Last Supper," by Dieric Bouts (1425–1475).

The first individual linen napkins were brought into style around the 16th Century. They were larger than those in use today, measuring around 45 inches square, but they offered ample room for the guest to find a clean spot while eating an entire meal with his hands.

By the 17th century, royalty accepted the use of the fork and napkins began to shrink in size, as being neat and tidy was strictly emphasized. By the beginning of the 18th century linen napkins had become staples in most linen closets.

There was one curious fact about the use of napkins, however, that persisted for the next two centuries: Napkins were not laundered between meals. In fact, they might be used for several days before they were washed. Each family member had their own napkin, and at the end of the meal, individuals placed his or her napkin in its special spot. Napkin rings made this process easier, keeping the used napkins organized so each person could find their napkin.

STYLES AND COLORS

Early on, table linens were not thought of as a style or decorative aspect of the home. Most table linens were natually colored or white as there made of hemp or linen. It was difficult to find dyes that would withstand the rough conditions napkins endured during laundering. Dyes were made from vegetable and animal extracts. During the Victorian era (1837-1901) things began to change. Chemists formulated new and inexpensive dyes in many bright and water resistant colors. This allowed table linens to be dyed in a wider range of colors to match the home's decor. In the 21st Century napkins come in many different fabrics colors and sizes. Napkin rings are no longer used to identify which napkin goes to who but are used as decorative accessories.

PAPER NAPKINS

HISTORY

As early as 1887, John Dickinson used paper napkins at his company's party in the United States. The first American company to introduce paper napkins was Scott Paper, but that did not occur until 1931. Other paper products, including tissues and paper towels, were also introduced around this time, but using paper napkins did not become popular in the United States until the 1950s.

BENEFITS

Paper napkins are convenient because they eliminate the need to wash napkins, and they guarantee that the user will have a clean napkin. They are also lightweight and easy to pack when eating on the run. Thicker paper napkins are easiest to fold. Paper napkins come in a wide variety of sizes, patterns and styles.

DISADVANTAGES

Paper napkins consume natural resources and pollute landfills, when cloth napkins could do the job. Napkins bleached with chlorine may contain dioxins and other toxins. Additionally, some paper napkins are thin, tear easily, may not absorb well, and may be abrasive to the skin.

ENVIRONMENTALLY CONSCIOUS

You can take steps to minimize environmental waste. Limit the number of napkins you use, and those that are put on the table but not used should be reserved for later use. If food spills, wipe it up with a sponge instead of paper napkins or towels. Choose paper napkins that come in bulk since the packaging is greener than purchasing more packages in a smaller size. Look for paper napkins that are unbleached and made from recyclable material. Use the smallest napkin size that will efficiently do the job.

FUN FACTS

The average person uses six paper napkins daily. However, using cloth napkins is only greener if the napkins are used more than once and washed with a regular laundry load. Laundry loads just for napkins can waste water and detergent.

DISPOSABLE NAPKINS

PAPER NAPKINS

Manufactured in several sizes and in a variety of colours and extraordinary designs and patterns. A small size, 16cm square, is normally used in fast food outlets. Medium sized napkins, 33cm square, are for general purposes and the large size, 40cm square, are for restaurant use. There is an extra large size, 48cm square, usually called a dinner napkin but these are not always readily available in the retail market. A name or corporate logo is often found on white or single colour napkins. They can also be printed with a name and date of a special occasion or event.

The quality of a paper napkin is defined by its "ply". The term ply defines layers and the thickness of the paper napkin — therefore the more ply, the thicker the napkin. Small napkins are usually one ply, medium are one or two ply and large napkins are usually two or three ply. It is possible occasionally to find four ply on large and extra large napkins. The feel of the napkin could be soft or embossed; the embossing provides extra thickness while still maintaining the two ply structure.

EMBOSSED NAPKIN

Very popular in the United States and some parts of Europe, these napkins are made of compressed paper — very similar to the domestic kitchen towel. They are extremely absorbent and perfect for occasional spillage. Unlike paper napkins, they are not defined with the word "ply" being of compressed paper construction. Like paper napkins, they come in a multitude of colours and patterns. Sizes: normally 33cm and 40cm square. Because of their spring effect, they are only suitable for simple designs of napkin folding.

AIRLAID NAPKINS

This is the latest in "Compressed Paper" technology. There is no way to adequately describe this type of napkin, which is not strictly paper and technically not linen either. However, this innovative contemporary material, known in the trade as "Airlaid", is well suited for anyone who requires a more refined product than ordinary paper napkins or for when the use of linen napkins is just not practical solution.

Different manufacturers of Airlaid (also described as "Formed Fabric" or "Compressed Paper Napkins") use different methods of processing at the manufacturing stage. Therefore these napkins, unlike paper napkins, are defined more by the manufacturer's brand name rather than the type or way in which there are constructed. The sizes of these napkins are usually 33cm and 40cm square. Some manufacturers produce a 48 cm square, but again this is not always easily available for the domestic market. The cost per unit of this type of napkin is a factor that one really needs to take into account, against linen napkins and 3ply paper napkins. As all cases there are advantages and disadvantages on the choice of Airlaid napkins.

NAPKIN DISPENSER

Napkin dispenser is a container that holds paper napkins in eating joints or in house. It can either be functional with a handle or manually. These dispensers are common in fast food restaurants that keep paper napkins for the convenience of the customers. For cloth napkins, these dispensers are not suitable. Stainless steel, wood and plastic are some of the common materials used in manufacturing these napkin dispensers. The main feature of these holders or dispensers is to snug the napkins in such a way that they should not come out.

HISTORY OF NAPKIN DISPENSERS

Scott Paper Company is the inventor of the paper napkins that led to the popularity of the napkin dispenser in 1930. During 19th century, the wrought iron and ring napkin holders were a commonly used item in most of the households and even a daily job for blacksmiths. However, mechanically manufactured holders were also available at that time but handmade items excelled in the design and creativity.

Plastic colored napkin holders were very popular in 1950-1970 and were known as Vintage napkin holders. These holders were either made of solid plastic or transparent material. Large quantity production of such holders was the evidence of their popularity in households. However, non-plastic holders were also use to manufacture but in very small quantities.

DESIGN, CONSTRUCTION AND FUNCTION OF NAPKIN DISPENSERS

The napkin holder or napkin dispenser is specifically designed to hold the paper napkins, generally, by sandwiching the napkins in between two surfaces or in a container. There are two designs of the dispensers; vertical and horizontal and both have the same function. They can even be placed on table top as a piece of decoration. In olden times, woodsmiths and metalsmiths were famous for making several kinds of napkin dispensers, but with advancement in technology the machine made holders are gaining popularity.

The basic design and construction of dispensers include a hard material; hence metal and wood are considered the best raw materials. Hardwood or plywood are the strong and durable materials used in the production. For metallic dispensers, stainless steel or chrome-finished metal is widely used.

Wrought iron is often used instead of steel sheet. Operation of napkin dispenser is quite easy and it is usually kept on the table top in restaurants and in even homes. It is quite easy to dispense napkins from the dispenser. Napkins are held in such a way that a single napkin slides from the holder at a time. Fe napkin dispenser use napkin rolls instead of individual napkins. These roll napkin dispensers make use of a sharp cutter to tear the napkin from the roll. They are usually installed near the counter for convenience of the customers.

WHAT IS NAPKIN DECOUPAGE

Napkin decoupage is the craft of applying large pieces or cutouts from paper napkins to a project surface. This surface may be wood, glass, metal, cardboard or another material. Each napkin piece or cutout is coated with a liquid decoupage medium before it's applied to anything. Final coats of a clear protective finish are used to protect the napkin-decoupaged surface. The paper napkins used for this type of decoupage may be full or cocktail sized; they also may be used alone or in combination with other types of paper in a project.

Crafters who do decoupage work with paper napkins tend to seek out interesting napkin designs found in food specialty and gift shops as well as other stores. The motifs and designs printed on paper napkins range from whimsical to elegant. For example, picnic paper napkins may have cartoon-like drawings of a chef barbecuing a steak, while those meant for a party or luncheon might feature photographic images of beautiful rose buds.

Since such a large range of design options is available, napkin decoupage can be used for many types of craft projects. For instance, paper napkin cutouts of colorful butterflies and flowers could be applied to a plain baby crib to add some design interest. The same types of cutouts could also be used in napkin decoupage to create pictures for the walls. While any type of napkin cutouts can be applied to wood plaques before coating with a clear varnish or polyurethane, they could also be matted and framed as a print or photograph would be. Strips from around the edges of the napkins can be used to border pictures or other projects as well. Purchasing paper napkins in packages also can help ensure the same basic pattern and colors are used in making sets of pictures or other items.

Other than using cutouts, completely covering the surface with napkins may also be done in this form of decoupage. Since only the front of printed napkins may have a picture or pattern, while the backs might be a solid color, both parts could be combined to cover an entire plate, box or even a chair. For example, an inexpensive folding metal-framed chair can get a new design with napkin decoupage. Strips of the paper napkins must be carefully wrapped around the chair legs, and after the entire chair is covered with napkin strips and/or cutouts, it's important to use a good clear coating to protect the finished project from the wear and tear of repeated use.

2

Tissue Paper

Tissue Paper Sheet

Tissue paper or simply tissue is a lightweight paper or, light crêpe paper. Tissue are made from recycled paper pulp.

PROPERTIES

Key properties are: Absorbency, basis weight, thickness (bulk), brightness, stretch, appearance and comfort.

PRODUCTION

Tissue paper is produced on a paper machine that has a single large steam heated drying cylinder (yankee dryer) fitted with a hot air hood. The raw material is paper pulp. The yankee cylinder is sprayed with adhesives to make the paper stick. Creping is done by the yankee's *doctor blade* that is scraping the dry paper off the cylinder surface. The crinkle (crêping) is controlled by the strength of the adhesive, geometry of the doctor blade, speed difference between the yankee and final section of the paper machine and paper pulp characteristics. The highest water absorbing applications are produced with a through air drying (TAD) process. These papers contain high amounts of NBSK and CTMP. This gives a bulky paper with high wet tensile strength and good water holding capacity. The TAD process uses about twice the energy compared with conventional drying of paper.

The properties are controlled by pulp quality, crêping and additives (both in base paper and as coating). The wet strength is often an important parameter for tissue paper.

APPLICATIONS

HYGIENIC TISSUE PAPER

x tissue paper is commonly used for facial tissue (paper handkerchiefs), napkins, bathroom tissue and household towels. Paper has been used for hygiene purposes for centuries, but tissue paper as we know it today was not produced in USA before the mid-1940s. In Western Europe large scale industrial production started in the beginning of 1960s.

THE INDUSTRY

Out of the world's estimated production of 21 million tonnes of tissue, Europe produces approximately six million tonnes.

The European tissue market is worth approximately 10 billion Euros annually and is growing at a rate of around 3%. The European market represents around 23% of the global market. Of the total paper and board market tissue accounts for 10%. In North America, people are consuming around three times as much tissue as in Europe.

In Europe, the industry is represented by The European Tissue Symposium (ETS), a trade association. The members of ETS represent the majority of tissue paper producers throughout Europe and about 90% of total European tissue production. ETS was founded in 1971 and is based in Brussels since 1992.

SUSTAINABILITY

The paper tissue industry, along with the rest of the paper manufacturing sector, has worked hard to minimise its impact on the environment. Recovered fibres now represent some 46.5% of the paper industry's raw materials. The industry relies heavily on biofuels (about 50% of its primary energy) and it is highly energy-efficient. Its specific primary energy consumption has decreased by 16% and the specific electricity consumption has decreased by 11%, due to measures such as improved process technology and investment in combined heat and power (CHP). Specific carbon dioxide emissions from fossil fuels decreased by 25% due to process-related measures and the increased use of low-carbon and biomass fuels. Once consumed, most forest-based paper products start a new life as recycled material or biofuel EDANA, the trade body for the non-woven absorbent hygiene products industry (which includes products such as household wipes for use in the home) has reported annually on the industry's environmental performance since 2005. The industry's impact on the environment is, in fact, relatively small. For example, less than 1% of all commercial wood production ends up as wood pulp in absorbent hygiene products.

In addition, the industry contributes less than 0.5% of all solid waste and around 2% of municipal solid waste (MSW) compared with paper and board, garden waste and food waste which each comprise between 18 and 20 percent of MSW. There has been a great deal of interest, in particular, in the use of recovered fibres to manufacture new tissue paper products. However, whether this is actually better for the environment than using new fibres is open to question. A Life Cycle Assessment study indicated that neither fibre type can be considered environmentally preferable. In this study both new fibre and recovered fibre offer environmental benefits and shortcomings.

Total environmental impacts vary case by case, depending on for example the location of the tissue paper mill, availability of fibres close to the mill, energy options and waste utilization possibilities. There are opportunities to minimise environmental impacts when using each fibre type.

When using recovered fibres, it is beneficial to:

- Source fibres from integrated deinking operations to eliminate the need for thermal drying of fibre or long distance transport of wet pulp,
- Manage deinked sludge in order to maximise beneficial applications and minimise waste burden on society; and
- Select the recovered paper depending on the end-product requirements and that also allows the most efficient recycling process.

When using new fibres, it is beneficial to:

- Manage the raw material sources to maintain legal, sustainable forestry practices by implementing processes such as forest certification systems and chain of custody standards; and
- Consider opportunities to introduce new and more renewable energy sources and increase the use of biomass fuels to reduce emissions of carbon dioxide.

When using either fibre type, it is beneficial to:

- Improve energy efficiency in tissue manufacturing;
- Examine opportunities for changing to alternative, non fossil based sources, of energy for tissue manufacturing operations

- Deliver products that maximise functionality and optimize consumption; and
- Investigate opportunities for alternative product disposal systems that minimize the environmental impact of used products.

The Confederation of European Paper Industries has published reports focusing on the industry's environmental credentials. In 2002, it noted that "a little over 60% of the pulp and paper produced in Europe comes from mills certified under one of the internationally recognised eco-management schemes". There are a number of 'eco-labels' designed to help consumers identify paper tissue products which meet such environmental standards. Eco-labelling entered mainstream environmental policy-making in the late seventies, first with national schemes such as the German Blue Angel programme, to be followed by the Nordic Swan (1989). In 1992 a European eco-labelling regulation, known as the EU Flower, was also adopted. The stated objective is to support sustainable development, balancing environmental, social and economical criteria.

TYPES OF ECO-LABELS

There are three types of eco-labels, each defined by ISO (International Organization for Standardization).

Type I: ISO 14024

This type of eco-label is one where the criteria are set by third parties (not the manufacturer). They are in theory based on life cycle1 impacts and are typically based on pass/fail criteria. The one that has European application is the EU Flower.

Type II: ISO 14021

These are based on the manufacturers or retailers own declarations. Well known amongst these are claims of "100% recycled" in relation to tissue/paper.

Type III: ISO 14025

These claims give quantitative details of the impact of the product based on its life cycle. Sometimes known as EPDs (Environmental Product Declarations), these labels are based on an independent review of the life cycle of the product. The data supplied by the manufacturing companies are also independently reviewed. The most well known example in the paper industry is the Paper Profile. You can tell a Paper Profile meets the Type III requirements when the verifiers logo is included on the document.

3

Facial Tissue

A Box of Tissues

Facial tissue and paper handkerchief refers to a class of soft, absorbent, disposable papers that is suitable for use on the face. They are disposable alternatives for cloth handkerchiefs. The terms are commonly used to refer to the type of paper tissue, usually sold in boxes, that is designed to facilitate the expulsion of nasal mucus from the nose although it may refer to other types of facial tissues including napkins and wipes.

Facial tissue is often referred to as a "tissue", or by the genericized trademark "Kleenex" which popularized the invention and its use.

MANUFACTURE

Facial tissue and paper handkerchiefs are made from the lowest basis weights tissue paper (14 18 g/m). The surface is often made smoother by light calendering. These paper types consist usually of 2–3 plies. Because of high quality requirements the base tissue is normally made entirely from pure chemical pulp, but might contain added selected recycled fibre. The tissue paper might be treated with softeners, lotions or added perfume to get the right properties or "feeling". The finished facial tissues or handkerchiefs are folded and put in pocket-size packages or a box dispenser.

HISTORY

Facial tissue has been used for centuries in Japan, in the form of washi (˜aŽ†) or Japanese tissue, as described in this 17th-century European account of the voyage of Hasekura Tsunenaga:

- "They blow their noses in soft silky papers the size of a hand, which they never use twice, so that they throw them on the ground after usage, and they were delighted to see our people around them precipitate themselves to pick them up."

In 1924 facial tissue as it is known today was first introduced by Kimberly-Clark as Kleenex. It was invented as a means to remove cold cream. Early advertisements linked Kleenex to Hollywood makeup departments and sometimes included endorsements from movie stars (Helen Hayes and Jean Harlow) who used Kleenex to remove their theatrical makeup with cold cream. It was the customers that started to use Kleenex as a disposable handkerchief, and a reader review in 1926 by a newspaper in Peoria, Illinois found that 60% of the users used it for blowing their nose.

Kimberly-Clark also introduced pop-up, colored, printed, pocket, and 3-ply facial tissues.

4

Paper Towel

A Roll of Paper Towels on a Wooden Stand

A paper towel (also called kitchen roll or the kitchen paper) is an absorbent textile made from paper instead of cloth. Unlike cloth towels, paper towels are disposable and intended to be used only once. Paper towels soak up water because they are loosely woven which enables water to travel between them, even against gravity. Paper towels can be individually packed (as stacks of folded towels or held coiled). Paper towels have almost the same purposes as conventional towels, such as drying hands, wiping windows, dusting and cleaning up spills.

HISTORY

Early Paper Towels

In 1907 the Scott Paper Company of Philadelphia, Pennsylvania introduced paper towels to help prevent the spread of colds from cloth towels in restrooms. Popular belief is that this was partly by accident and was the solution of what to do with to a railroad car full of long paper rolls meant for toilet paper that was unsuitable to cut into rolls of toilet paper. In 1919, William E. Corbin, Henry Chase, and Harold Titus began experimenting with paper towels in the Research and Development building of the Brown Company in Berlin, New Hampshire. By 1922, Corbin perfected their product and began mass-producing it at the Cascade Mill on the Berlin/Gorham line. This product was called Nibroc Paper Towels (Corbin spelled backwards). In 1931, the Scott Paper Company of Philadelphia, Pennsylvania introduced their paper towel for kitchens. They are now the leader of the manufacture of paper towels.

PRODUCTION

Paper is made from either virgin or recycled paper pulp which is extracted from wood or fiber crops. They are sometimes bleached during the production process to make the color more white. It is not uncommon for rolls of paper towels to include intricate colored images on each square (such as flowers or teddy bears). Resin size is used to improve the wet strength. Patterns of shapes such as circles or diamonds are often imprinted into the paper towels to help it hold moisture. Manufacturers use the pattern of the material, microscopic spaces within the pattern, and a type of cellulose in the fibres in order to maximize absorption. Most rolls are manufactured with two layers of paper, but different types can have more layers. They are classified by their key properties such as strength, absorbency, weight, and thickness. Paper towels are packed individually and sold as stacks, or are held on a continuous roll, and come in two distinct classes, domestic and institutional. A 2007 study shows the consumption of paper towels and other tissue products is highest in the United States of America at around 24 kilograms per capita, with consumption higher than in Europe, and more than 500 times higher than in Latin America.

MARKET

Tissue products including paper towels are split into "at home" and "away from home" markets, with about two-thirds of North American consumption at home. As a percent of total tissue products, the "away from home" segment uses a third more paper towels. The growth in "away from home" use of paper towels has been reduced by switch from folded towels to roll towel dispensers, which reduces the amount of paper towels used by each patron.

Within the forest products industry, paper towels are a major part of the "tissue market", second only to toilet paper. Consumption of paper towels and other tissue products is highest in the United States of America, with consumption 50% higher than in Europe, and nearly 500% higher than in Latin America.

Marc Jacobs, the creative director for Louis Vuitton and head designer for Marc Jacobs and diffusion line Marc by Marc Jacobs, designed an innovated coat that mix advance technology with posh style. For his 2014 Resort Line, Marc Jacobs designed a raincoat made entirely of paper towels.

5

About Napkins

Today, discriminating hosts and hostesses have a wide variety of napkin products from which to select. For formal dining, there is the cloth napkin, the paper napkin being reserved for more informal settings.

Cloth napkins come in several sizes, each size tailored to a specific use. A beverage napkin, used when serving drinks and hors d'oeuvres, like most cloth napkins, is square, about five inches to each side. A luncheon napkin is a couple of inches larger, and a dinner napkin larger still. The theory, evidently, is that the more food and drink that is served, the more potential there is for spillage, so the bigger the napkin must be to catch it.

Cloth napkins may be purchased in a rainbow of colors and a variety of fabrics, imprinted with custom designs and monograms, and can even come with matching tablecloths. However, a high-thread-count, white, linen or linen-cotton mix damask napkin is still considered the zenith of elegance.

Though a wedding reception should be considered a formal occasion, only the very wealthy can afford to have a catered meal for scores of guests, one that is served on fine place settings where cloth napkins have been set out. An acceptable cost-cutting compromise for big celebrations including weddings is to use a paper napkin whose size, heft, and finish resemble a cloth napkin. They can be ordered embossed with the bride and groom's monograms or otherwise tailored to the buyer's specifications.

NAPKIN ETIQUETTE

Whether the napkin is cloth or paper, when in polite company, a napkin is to be used with a measure of etiquette, so as not to offend other diners through a display of boorishness. (You're excused from these rules only when the napkin you are offered is one of those flimsy little paper things that pop out of tabletop dispensers – the kind of "napkin" you cannot place on your lap expecting it to not blow away within 20 seconds; even here, however, try to keep boorish behavior in check.)

- *Rule* 1: When you're given a napkin, use it. Don't let it sit beside your plate. It was given to you for wiping your face when you need to and to protect your lap from spills. Leaving it beside your plate marks you as a slob.
- *Rule* 2: Wait for the host to pick up and unfold his napkin before you do the same with yours.
- *Rule* 3: If the napkin is larger than your lap, fold it such that it just covers your lap.
- *Rule* 4: In polite society, movements at the dinner table tend to be small, so don't make any ostentatious displays like wildly shaking the napkin to open it. Just unfold it. And when you wipe your mouth, don't use the napkin as you would a wash cloth during your morning shower; gently dab at your mouth.
- *Rule* 5: Don't wait for the food to be served before you open your napkin. Should your napkin still be sitting on the table when the food arrives, the server may have to create space to set your plate.
- *Rule* 6: Should you have to leave the table during the meal, leave

the napkin, loosely folded, on your seat or on the table to the left of your plate. Also put the loosely folded napkin to the left of your plate when you're done eating, never on the plate.

- *Rule* 7: The place for a napkin? In your lap. It is not tucked into your pants, nor does it belong tucked into your shirt collar. However, if you are in a milieu where that kind of behavior is acceptable, don't be afraid to go along. For example, diners from Southern Italy (or southern New Jersey) have long known that a bowl of spaghetti topped with marinara sauce can be better enjoyed when you don't have to worry about the red stuff splattering on your shirt. Many Italian and Italian-American diners therefore tuck the napkin into their collars as a matter of course. Feel free to do the same. Live! Enjoy!

But what about that waiter who carries a napkin draped over one arm? In part, it's practicality. It's readily available to mop up any accidental spills or other messes at your table. But the practice dates back a couple of hundred years in France; that was how waiters carried the napkins they would distribute to diners. Napkins have been in use for thousands of years.

It's possible that cavemen at their wooly mammoth barbeques wiped the grease from their mouths using the animal's pelt... and then rubbed it in their hair to get that suave, slicked-back look. But we don't really know that. What we do know is that, by the Bronze Age, it's likely something like a napkin was in use in many parts of the world. The first recorded use of the napkin was by the Romans.

When that hearty eater, Buffetus Allucaneatus, reached for his napkin at the Roman dinner table, he didn't find a cloth. What he used was some wadded up unbaked dough, which he pressed to his face. That removed whatever bits and morsels of food were sticking to it. Later, if he wished, he could bake and eat his napkin, morsels and all.

With the fall of Rome, Europe entered that slovenly, napkin-less period of the Dark Ages, with its uncouth barons and unwashed princesses wiping their hands on their tunics and mopping their faces with their shirttails and cuffs. We don't know how knights encased in steel armor managed to wipe off their mouths.

By the time of the Renaissance, the French had a single, large communal napkin about the size of a table cloth which everyone at the table used. It may have been the precursor of the table cloth. It got smaller and smaller over the years until everyone had his own napkin. By the 1700's, the French aristocracy had even promulgated rules of napkin etiquette, some of which we still use today throughout the Western world; e.g., we don't blow our nose into our napkin. Or anyone else's napkin, either.

CLOTH AND LINEN NAPKINS

Is it ostentatious to use a cloth napkin rather than a paper one at every meal? Maybe, but who cares? It's a touch of luxury.

The fanciest napkins are those made from damask cloth. Damask, which takes its name from the city of Damascus, Syria, used to refer to a method of weaving cloth in which threads of one type of fabric – say, silk – would be woven with threads of another, such as flax.

This is still done, though the term damask also now applies to textiles with just the look of this type of weave; this is something that can now be achieved using a single type of thread such as cotton or linen. Brown when they come off the loom, but then bleached white, linen damask napkins are the crème de la crème of face-and-hand wipers. The best of these employ something called a double-damask weave, a heavier fabric that is especially responsive to making fancy folds.

CLEANING NAPKINS

One objection to using cloth napkins that invariably arises is the problem of food or lipstick stains. Probably the best suggestion when it comes to tough food stains like barbeque sauce or wine is to avoid using your best white cloth napkins when you are serving foods or beverages that stain. Use paper those nights or some less fancy, expendable cloth napkins, preferably in a dark color.

But, if it's too late and your best table linens are already stained and soiled, perhaps these tips will help:

1. Starching napkins when you wash and iron them not only makes them easier to fold; it also helps repel stains the next time they're used.
2. Glycerin removes lipstick stains.
3. For wine stains, wet them with water as soon as possible, then mound salt on both sides of the stain.
4. Supposedly, white wine poured on a red wine stain will remove it.
5. Wash all napkins as soon as possible after they are used.
6. Treat the stains with a prewash stain remover, then wash promptly.
7. Wash in warm or hot water using a powdered oxygen bleach and an enzyme-boosted detergent.
8. It may help to soak the napkins overnight in a mix of just enough water to cover them, one cup of laundry detergent, and one cup of dishwasher detergent. Wash the next morning.
9. After washing, dry the napkins on a clothes line to let the sun bleach away stains.
10. When all else fails, soak white napkins in strong bleach solution.

At some point, something like a strong grease stain will fail to yield to any kind of attack.

That's the time to reflect upon the verity that the world and all therein is ephemeral, and every napkin has to meet its ultimate fate: getting tossed or becoming a cleaning rag. Life is like that.

PAPER NAPKINS

Cloth napkins have been wiping off messy lips for centuries; paper napkins, however, didn't come along until 1887, when John Dickenson introduced them in the United States at his company's annual dinner. This happened at about the same time that facial tissue and toilet paper was being introduced. It was, in total, a veritable paper revolution. However, paper napkins did not become truly popular in American households until the 1950's. Now they are used to a far greater extent than cloth napkins, much to the dismay of both traditionalists and environmentalists. Paper napkins also became popular with expense-conscious restaurateurs, and not simply for their lower initial cost; they were found to be more convenient and to eliminate the costs of, day in and day out, sending cloth napkins out to be laundered and receiving them back into inventory. Equally important, with paper napkins there is never the possibility of giving a guest a napkin with a residual stain on it or, sin of all restaurant sins, giving a diner a used napkin. The fast food restaurants that began proliferating in the 1950's probably could not exist today without those wads of paper napkins clerks stuff by the handful in your takeout bags. (Hmmm, no more fast food without paper napkins, eh? Maybe that alone would be a good reason for banning them.)

Paper napkins come in a broad range of sizes, patterns, and quality. There are paper napkins with every kind of holiday design printed on them, colorful napkins for colorful parties, and even paper napkins that closely resemble cloth. You may order custom-designed paper napkins with the names and dates of the commemorative occasions you specify printed on them.

Paper napkin technology, ever advancing, has given us the paper napkin dispenser box and silver weights to keep the contents from catching a breeze and being blown out of their dispenser boxes – the perfect gift for the person who has everything, including a paper napkin fetish. Recent inventions include a napkin with a slightly adhesive surface that will not slip off your lap.

For home use, there's no denying paper napkins can be a convenience – as in those times when you discover, twenty minutes before your bridge party, all your cloth napkins are in the laundry hamper, unwashed. Paper napkins can be used for any formal occasion and even some formal occasions. It's generally okay to use them for classy wing-dings when the napkins are of such quality that they can almost pass for cloth. Also, paper napkins with color patterns are appropriate at any holiday celebration or other festive occasions, such as cook-outs, no matter whether the occasion calls for champagne or beer. Besides being versatile and making after dinner cleanup easier, paper napkins can – just like cloth napkins – be folded in into fancy shapes. In fact, paper napkins will hold their shape better when folded because the paper holds a crease better than the cloth; cloth napkins look better when the pattern features rounded folds rather than sharp corners. Make sure, when you're using a paper napkin for folding, that it's 3-ply and that you've got clean, dry hands before folding.

NAPKIN RINGS

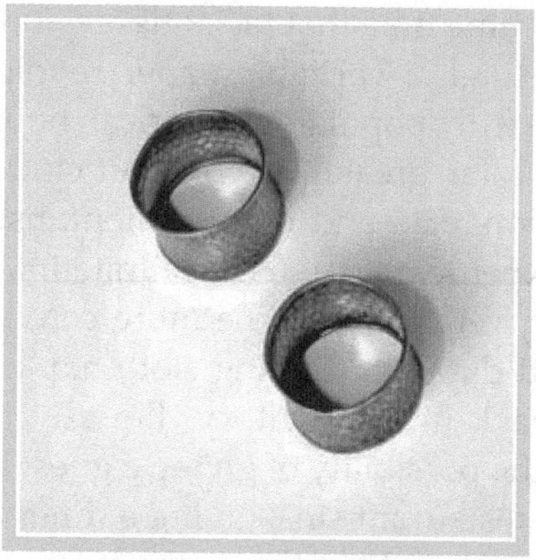

They can be as simple as strips of ribbon or as elegant as bejeweled silver rings or porcelain rings designed by Versace, but napkin rings, whatever their form, all have the same purpose – to bind a clean napkin, generally cloth, and keep it in place at each dinner place setting. The process of folding napkins renders them more attractive, but so do napkins rings, and with less time expended when a host is rushing to prepare for a sit-down affair.

Just so long as they will hold an entire napkin, rings can be made from nearly any kind of substance – paper, plastic, metal, wood, glass, ceramics, you name it. They can be purchased, generally in sets of four or eight, online, at antique stores, giftshops, and department stores. They can also be hand crafted at home. For instance, if you are handy at cutting glass, you can make attractive rings from the tops of long-neck beer bottles. Sculpey Clay can be used to bake in your home oven ceramic rings that you or your kids design yourselves. And you can keep your Uncle Finley out of trouble by having him whittle you some rings out of a chunk of walnut.

But, ever since napkin rings began being crafted in 1836, the most popular ones have been made of silver. (Napkin holders date back to the Middle Ages, but true rings did not emerge until much later.) These have recently found a good market with collectors.

Extremely ornate napkin rings made during the Victorian and art nouveau periods can be very ornate, the more valued ones designed by such silversmiths as Georg Jensen, Tiffany, Liberty, or Gorham – true works of art that bring high prices at auction. Birds, animals, and children were popular themes for the craftsmen. Rings were sometimes made in combination with other pieces such as vases, butter dishes, or salts and pepper shakers. It's rare, however, that such sets can be found today.

Some collectors specialize in various types of rings – those used by children (some featured letters of the alphabet or nursery rhymes), those bearing ornate engravings of the owners' names, "breakfast rings" – small rings used in Germany and Holland to hold paper napkins at breakfast, and many other varieties.

English rings are especially interesting because they are stamped with their date of manufacture and the city where they were made (usually Birmingham, London, Chester, or Sheffield). The really nice thing about these kinds of antiques is that they hold their value even while you can continue to use them at your dinner table.

Napkin rings fell out of use about the time paper napkins were becoming popular in the early 20th Century. But they were brought back into popularity through their use in the Eisenhower White House of the 1950's. Should you happen to be a guest at an occasion where napkin rings are being used, it's considered polite, when you are done eating, to place your used napkin back in the ring.

CUSTOM-MADE NAPKINS

Did You Know you can have Napkins Made for You just the Way you want them and at a Price that won't Break your Bank?

At ForYourParty, for example, you can design your own paper napkins. First, you select the size: cocktail (5" × 5"), luncheon (6.5" × 6.5"), guest towel (4.25" × 8"), dinner (8" × 8"), or a napkin wrapped in a paper napkin ring (6" × 1.5" high). Second, select a color from the 40 tints available. These include white and a linen-like white. Third, select the color you want any imprint to be. Fourth, specify the text (up to four lines) you want to have printed and indicate the type fonts you want to use. Next, select from a variety of graphic elements you may want to include – flowers, Christmas scenes, etc. Specify how you want the design formatted, and, finally, review the napkin in its entirety and change whatever you wish. The company promises to ship your order the following day. The price for this service runs from $24 to $50 for 50 napkins.

Many companies sell custom-made napkins on the internet. A number of them specialize. Outvite, for instance, produces custom napkins for gay and lesbian celebrations. American Yacht Supply produces napkins with a nautical theme. And Bennington Potters produces cloth napkins to match not just place mats they supply but also the stoneware table settings they make.

Maybe you're an artist and want to put your work onto napkins. Companies like Party Innovations will do that for you, charging you a one-time fee for making a plate of whatever you send them. You can use the plate over and over again with no extra charge.

6

How to Fold Napkins

Entertaining during the holidays means tables brimming with delicious dishes and adorned with festive trimmings. When setting a holiday table or for any other special occasion, an elegant or whimsically folded napkin can add some flair.

Consider five easy tips to spruce up your holiday table with creative napkin shapes:

1. *Cloth napkin sizes*: Square-shaped napkins provide a better medium for napkin-folding designs. Luncheon napkins typically are smaller than dinner napkins. Look for cloth luncheon napkins measuring 18-inches-by-18-inches or 20-inches-by-20-inches and cloth dinner napkins measuring 22-inches-by-22-inches or 24-inches-by-24-inches.
2. *Material*: Opt for sturdy linens such as a double-damask weave. According to the Napkin Folding Guide, damask weaving threads one type of fabric (such as silk) with another (such as flax) to create a "heavier fabric that is especially responsive to making fancy folds." A cotton or poly-cotton blend is also foldable-friendly, especially for less intricate folds such as a basic cone fold, silverware pouch fold or scarf fold.
3. *Preparation*: Before folding each napkin, it needs to be laundered, starched and ironed. Starching is a key component to preparing the cloth napkin prior to folding. The starch in the fabric makes it easier to create and hold the folds, ultimately allowing the napkin to keep its form when it is placed at the table setting. Refer to the tag on the napkin for laundering instructions.
4. Choosing your folds. Holiday table settings should be special. Consider five styles of napkin folds for your holiday table:
   - Scarf fold
   - Cone fold
   - Basic silverware pouch
   - Arrow fold

- Standing fan fold
- The scarf fold requires a napkin ring and allows you to show off your most festive holiday rings. To create the fold, simply lay the napkin flat, grasp it with your fingers at its center and insert it through the napkin ring. The cone fold requires a few more steps:
- Lay the napkin flat and fold in half with the open end facing away from you.
- Fold the left half over the right half.
- Turn the napkin so it resembles a diamond shape with the open end away from you.
- Fold the top layer of the open end toward you.
- Flip the napkin over.
- Fold the left side over about two-thirds and then do the same with the right.
- Tuck the corners into the left side to create the final cone shape.
- The folded napkin should have a slight pouch. Slip a candy cane or small silk floral inside before setting the napkin atop the dinner plate.

5. Creative touches. The basic silverware pouch fold allows you to slip the silverware into the napkin. You also can add a peppermint stick or sprig of holly for a Christmas dinner. The arrow fold shape looks similar to a paper airplane and is a great way to showcase napkins in rich seasonal colors. Likewise, the standing fan fold allows you to show off the print of the cloth.

CUFFED ROLL

CUFFED ROLL NAPKIN FOLD

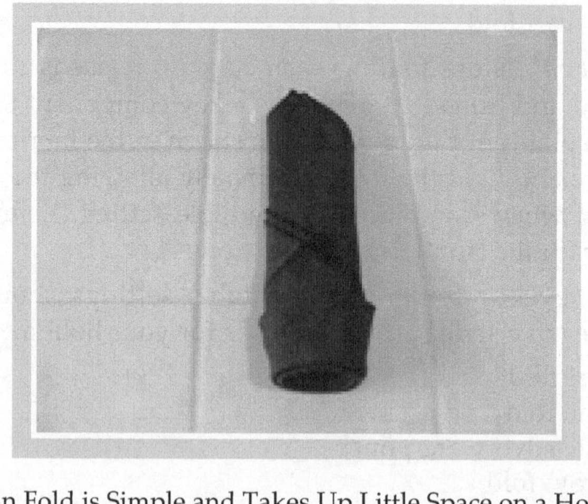

This Napkin Fold is Simple and Takes Up Little Space on a Holiday Table.

Lay the Napkin Out Flat on the Diagonal.

Fold the Bottom Half Up so the Fold is at the Bottom.

At the Bottom Edge, Fold Under about 1-2", toward the Back.

At One Side Begin Rolling the Napkin.

Continue Rolling all the Way Across.

At the Back, Secure the Left Point into the Folded Cuff.

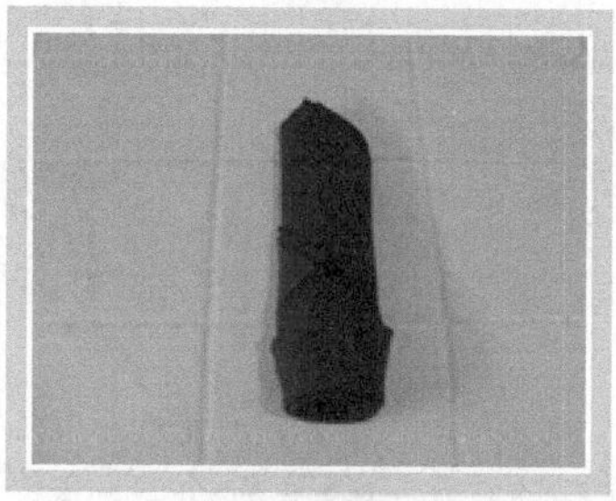

Finished Fold Turn the Napkin Over for the Finished Fold.

THREE POINT "HAT"

THREE POINT HAT NAPKIN FOLD

Here's an Easy Decorative Fold that's often Seen in Restaurants.

Lay the Napkin out Flat on the Diagonal.

Fold the Bottom Half Up so the Fold is at the Bottom.

Lift each of the 2 Side Points Up to the Top Center Point.

The Napkin Should Now Look Like this.

Turn the Napkin Over.

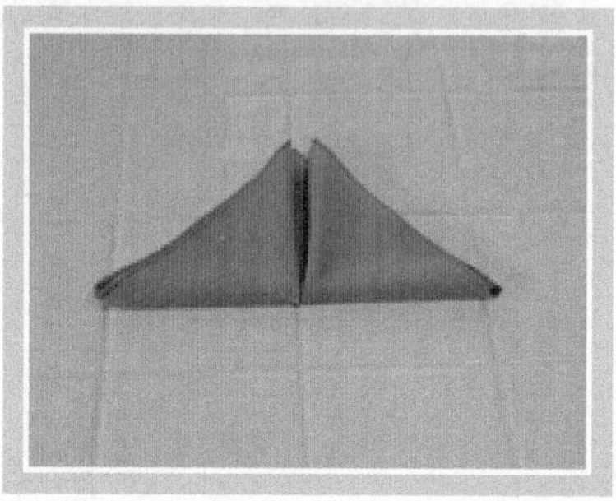

Fold the Bottom Half Up to form a Triangle. This will be the Front of the Napkin.

Turn the Napkin Over.

Bring the 2 Side Corners to the Center and Fold one Inside of the Other to Secure the Fold.

Again Turn the Napkin Over to the Front.

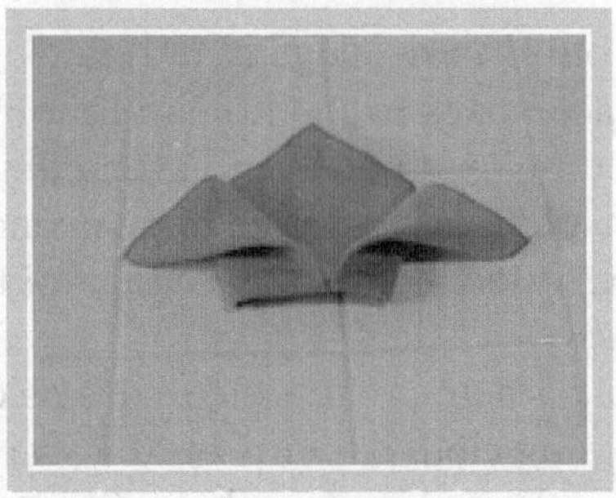

Finished Fold Down the 2 Ends to form the 3 Points.

7

Napkin Folding Techniques

The scarf napkin fold is easy, elegant and quick. Napkin folding or the art of napery can be traced back to the Roman Empire but we take many of our modern napkin folding techniques and etiquette from the French of the 1700's. The scarf napkin fold is a classic fold that anyone can create. A beautiful table set for eight, can be festooned with gracefully folded scarf-styled napkins in a matter of moments.

The scarf napkin fold is a drape-like fold that is held in place with a napkin ring or clip. When choosing cloth napkins for the scarf fold, consider using a quality cloth napkin in a design or color that will highlight a unique napkin ring. Unlike other more complicated napery techniques, the scarf fold can be achieved beautifully with a simple cotton napkin as well as a thicker damask napkin. Lightly starching your napkins before folding will help repel some stains and will allow the napkin to drape better through the napkin ring.

There are only three steps to create a scarf napkin fold:

- *Step* 1: Begin by setting your napkin design-side up on a flat surface. Most napkin folding techniques suggest putting the napkin face down but the scarf technique is the opposite because of how it is inserted into the napkin ring or clip. Run an iron lightly over the napkin to remove any creases or wrinkles.
- *Step* 2: Find the center of the napkin with your finger. Grasp the center area and pull the napkin upward from the table toward you, allowing the points to fall towards the table's surface. Have the napkin ring or clip ready in your other hand.
- *Step* 3:Insert the napkin into the napkin ring or clip so it is secured about halfway in the middle of the napkin. Arrange the folds to look pretty and flowing.

Napkin folding is easiest when you work with a square napkin. Many etiquette books suggest using a smaller napkin, a 17-inch-by-17-inch for lunch and a larger napkin, 20-inch-by-20-inch for dinners. Square crocheted or lace napkins can be an elegant choice for the scarf fold.

It is recommended to wash your napkins after each use. Be sure to treat any stains with a prewash stain remover. In some cases, fabric softener might waterproof the linens, so it is advised to avoid using these softeners. A mild detergent works for most fabrics. Launder the cloth napkins in a warm perma-press cycle with a cold-water rinse. Use nature to diminish residual stains. Line drying napkins allows the sun to bleach leftover stains. If you cannot line dry, set your dryer on a perma-press cycle for about ten minutes with an eight-minute cool down setting. Remove the napkins after drying and lay flat if still damp.

The scarf napkin fold is an ideal choice for the first time napkin folder. It is not complicated and can be done quickly when pressed for time. The scarf fold works great for anyone wanting to highlight unusual or stylish napkin rings. Use the scarf napkin fold to add another level of whimsy, fun or elegance for a casual weeknight meal or a formal dinner party.

NAPKIN FOLDING TECHNIQUES: ROLLING NAPKIN

Napkin folding is a simple, but elegant way to add flair to a table setting. In about twenty to thirty minutes, you can fold a place setting for eight to ten people. If you already have the napkins, this is also a free way to add an extra to the dining experience. It is generally associated with elegant restaurants, and is a skill that once learned, can be used repeatedly for either family dinners, dinner parties, weddings, or a special dinner with your spouse. Practice with one napkin for about 10 minutes before attempting to do an entire place setting, though.

If this is for a dinner party, try to fold these a few days in advance and then place them in a covered dish to avoid gathering dust. These directions are assuming a square, medium weight napkin, though they could be used with a heavier weight paper napkin as well.

First, clean the place you will be folding the napkin. Then, lay the napkin on the table so that two corners are even with your hands, and there is a point at the top and the bottom. Fold the bottom point to the top point to form a triangle with two layers of fabric that are connected at the bottom. It will resemble <^> in regards to the places you can and see two layers of fabric.

Decide if you are going to place the silverware in the napkin, or place the napkin on the plate. If you are placing the silverware in the napkin, follow directions immediately below. (If not, skip to the starred section below.)

Then, place the silverware on top, in the center below the point, if desired. The handles will be close to you on on the base of the triangle. The silverware will be visible, but if folded correctly will stay inside the napkin until unrolled by the guest.

Take the left corner and place the napkin over the silverware with the point under the silverware.

*If you are not using silverware, you will just tightly roll the left corner to the bottom middle of the napkin. * Last, take the right corner point and bring it around to the back of the napkin.

You will tuck this point into the back of the napkin between the top two layers. If done correctly, you will have a flat bottom with a double layered point that can stand upright or hold the silverware. If this isn't working, try starching the fabric, or try tightening the last two folds. If you stand this on the plates, it should go on the dinner plate in the center, or by the water glass.

NAPKIN FOLDING TECHNIQUES: SCARF NAPKIN

Neatly folded napkins add pizzazz and poise to any dining table, either for a party or a simple family gathering. Instead of merely tucking napkins under the fork or placing them atop the plate at each place setting, why not spice up your table with fancy folded napkins? The scarf fold is by far the simplest napkin folding technique of all to create. This elegant napkin folding design is quick and quite easy to manage.

What materials will you need to fold your napkins into scarf folds? Gather your materials for your scarf fold napkins before you begin. Cloth napkins work particularly well for producing the scarf fold. If your napkins are brand new and somewhat stiff, you may want to launder them first, so they will drape more softly. You will also need napkin rings or other ornamental fasteners.

How do you create the scarf fold with your napkins? First, fold a napkin into square quarters. Here's how: Place the napkin flat on a clean table, counter or other work surface. Fold the napkin in half, and create a crease on the fold. Fold the napkin in half again, to produce a small square. Hold the center point of the napkin, allowing the other edges to fall open slightly.

Place a napkin ring or another ornamental fastener over the folded point of the napkin. Slide this down at least a few inches to create the scarf fold. Gently arrange the open edges of the napkin to create decorative drapes, like a scarf.

Repeat the process with as many cloth napkins as you need for your party. Of course, paper napkins may also be used, but it can be difficult to create the draped, scarf-like effect with paper napkins.

Why not experiment with a variety of ornamental napkin fasteners? You can use a fancy or plain napkin ring, a piece of yarn or ribbon, a scarf clip, a stretchy hair scrunchy or even a rubber band to hold your scarf fold in place.

Use your imagination, and have fun with this. For various parties and special events, we have tucked all sorts of party favors into our scarf fold napkins. We have used toy jeweled rings for bridal showers, pacifier rings for baby showers and even notebook clips for back-to-school celebrations. We have tucked candy canes, lollipops, pretty pens, feathers, flowers, paper fans and other goodies into ribbons and rubber bands on scarf fold napkins. What a fun way to dress up a festive table with scarf fold napkins.

HOW TO FOLD NAPKINS FOR YOUR TABLE

The napkins were folded into pretty shapes, and added to the feeling of the setting. Have you ever seen a napkin folded so beautifully that you didn't want to use it? The napkin folds I have found and used are not complicated or hard, and you will be happy with the results.

Here's what you need:

- Cloth napkins, you pick out the colors for your setting.
- Simple or decorative napkin rings, or you can choose ribbon or a raffia bow.
- An iron, some folds look neater if you have an iron handy.
- Yourself and a little bit of time.

SCARF NAPKIN FOLD

- Use a napkin ring, ribbon, or raffia bow to secure this fold
- Iron napkins flat first to avoid folded creases
- Lay napkin flat and grasp center point.
- Holding the center, let the points fall into folds.
- Have napkin ring ready
- Insert into napkin ring.
- Arrange folds as desired

TRADITIONAL NAPKIN FOLD

- Use a napkin ring, ribbon, or raffia bow to secure this fold.
- Iron napkins flat first to avoid folded creases
- Fold napkin in quarters. Set on a diagonal with the folded center portion at the top.
- Make 2-4 small pleats on each side of the napkin, about 4" from the top.
- Have napkin ring ready
- Insert the top four inches of the napkin into napkin ring so the "wings" of the napkin can be spread out.
- Arrange folds as needed to be attractive.
- Rolling Napkin Fold

- You'll need a napkin ring, ribbon, or raffia bow to secure this fold.
- Fold napkin in quarters. Set on a diagonal with the folded center portion at the top and all open edges at the bottom.
- Begin rolling each side toward the center, making 2 long rolls (this will be the back).
- Have napkin ring ready.
- Insert the roll into a napkin ring and turn over so smooth side is up.

GOBLET FAN FOLD

- Have goblets already set out
- Lay the napkin flat.
- Begin accordion folding from the bottom, all the way up to the top. Make each fold about 3/4" – 1" wide.
- Fold the pleated napkin in half.
- Insert the napkin into the goblet, folding the first inch or so under to keep pleats secure.
- Unfold the pleats and shape into a fan. Interlock the two center pleats if needed to keep the fan intact.

KNOTTED NAPKIN FOLD

- Lay the napkin flat on a diagonal.
- Bring the top half down to form a triangle with the fold across the top.
- Beginning at the bottom, start rolling the napkin up.
- Roll all the way up to the folded edge.
- Fold roll in half in preparation for tying the knot.
- Loop end through and loosely tie a knot.

TAILORED NAPKIN FOLD

- Lay the napkin out flat.
- Fold the bottom half up so the fold is at the bottom.
- Fold again, so the napkin is folded in quarters.
- Take 2 of the 4 corners and fold them down at an angle.
- Roll or fold them under to make a fold about 1-2" wide.
- Fold the other 2 corners to the back, an inch or two above the first fold.

- Fold the pointed sides toward the back, forming the finished fold.
- Silverware can be inserted into the "pocket" if desired.

THE PYRAMID NAPKIN FOLD

This classy napkin folding technique is simple, fast, and can be made easily with most napkins. If the napkin being used is thin and flops easily then iron it with light starch prior to folding and it will turn out perfectly!

Lay the Napkin Face Down in Front of You.

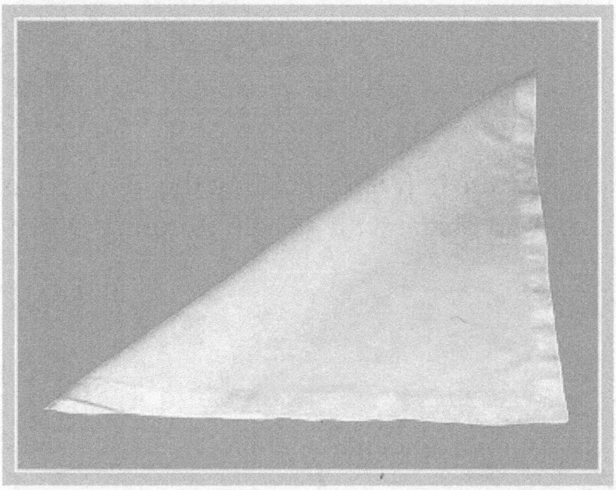

Fold the Napkin in Half Diagonally.

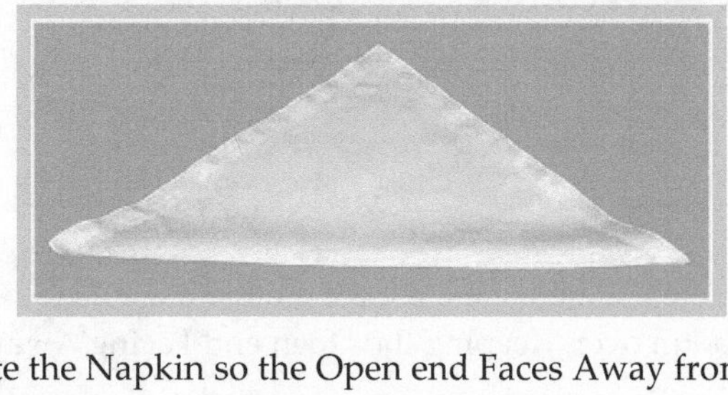

Rotate the Napkin so the Open end Faces Away from You.

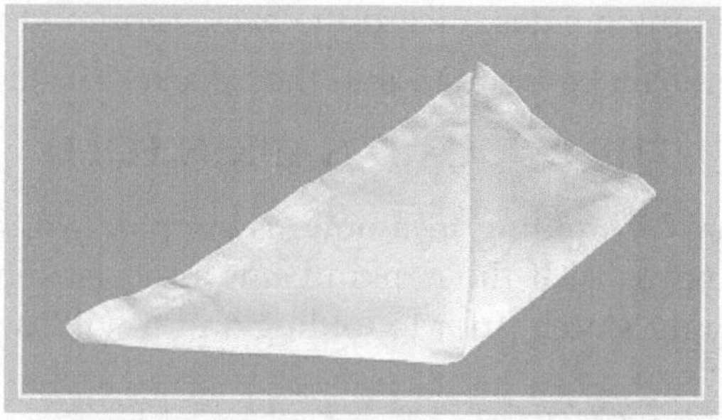

Fold the Right end Up to Meet the Far Corner, Ensuring the Edge of this New Fold Lays on the Centerline as Shown.

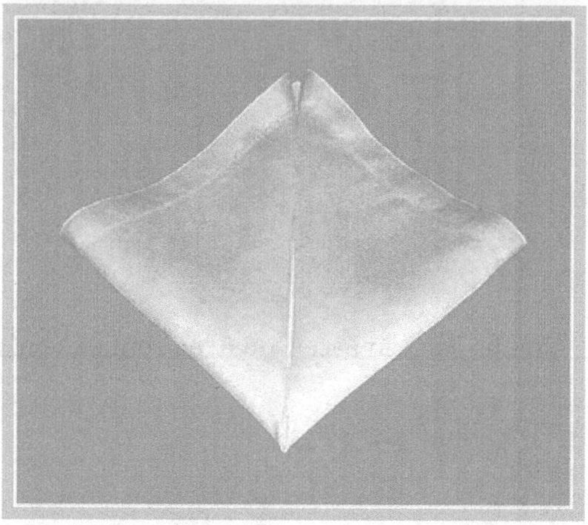

Repeat the Last Step with the Left Side, Folding the Left tip Up to the Far Corner, Creating a Diamond Shape with a Seam Running Down the Center.

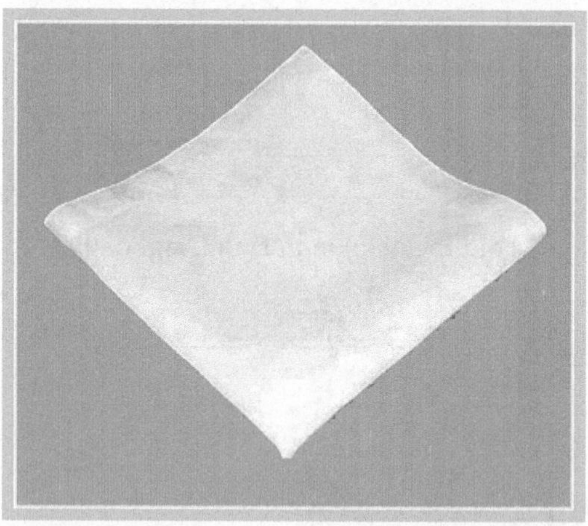

Turn the Napkin over, Keeping the Open end Facing Away from You.

Fold the Napkin in Half by Bringing the Farthest Point of the Diamond up and Back to the Nearest Point.

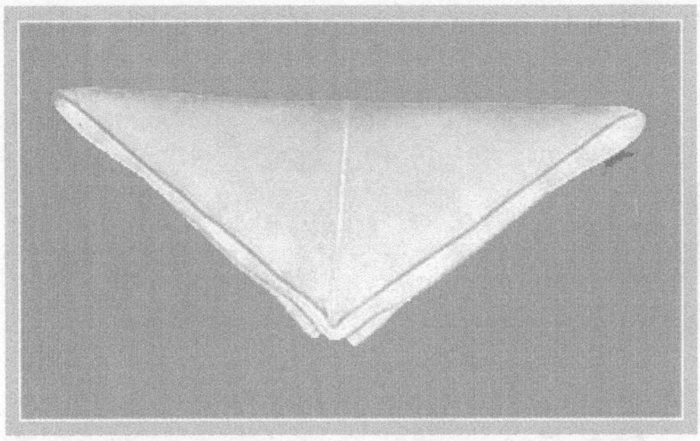

Turn the Napkin Over Again, this Time Keeping the Open end Facing Towards You.

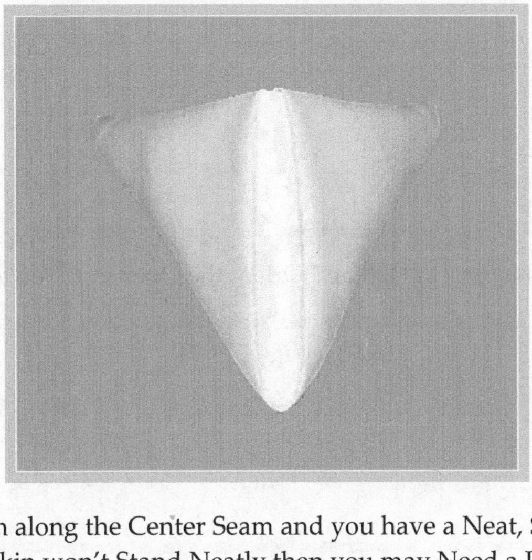

Fold the Napkin along the Center Seam and you have a Neat, Sturdy Pyramid. If your Napkin won't Stand Neatly then you may Need a Little Starch.

THE ARROW NAPKIN FOLD

This method of folding napkins is very simple and can be done with almost any napkin without a need for starch. It adds a flowing, elegant look to your table.

Lay the Napkin Face Down in Front of You.

Fold the Napkin in Half and Orient the Open end Towards You.

Fold the Far-right Corner over to the Center of the Side that is Closest to You. The edge of this fold should run down the center of the napkin.

Repeat the Last Step with the other Side, Folding
the Far-left Corner in to Rest along Side the Previous Fold.

Fold the Right-flap out Diagonally so that it's
Outer Edge Runs even with the Far Edge of the Napkin.

Repeat the Previous Step on the other Side, Folding
the Left-flap out Diagonally to Meet the Far Edge of the Napkin.

Slide the Left and the Right Sides Together, Allowing the Napkin to Bend at the Farthest Point. This Will Cause the Flat, Center Part to Bow. Pretty Easy, Huh?

THE BIRD OF PARADISE NAPKIN FOLD

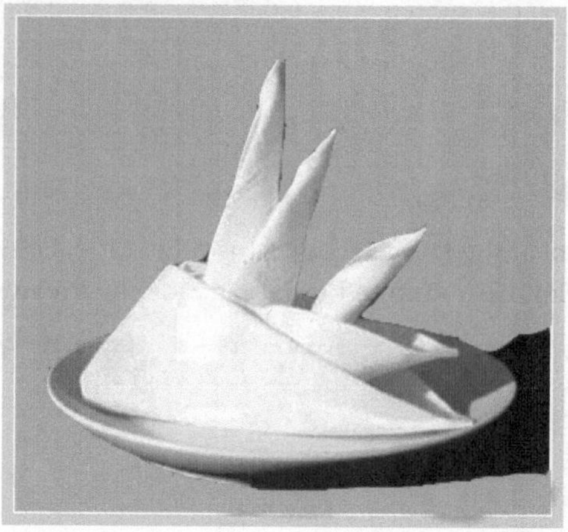

This is a classic and classy napkin folding technique that requires a stiff napkin. If you don't have any dinner napkins made of stiff linen then a light starching should fix you right up.

Lay the Napkin Face Down in Front of You.

Fold the Napkin in Half.

Fold the Napkin in Quarters.

Fold the Napkin in Half Diagonally, Creating a Triangle.

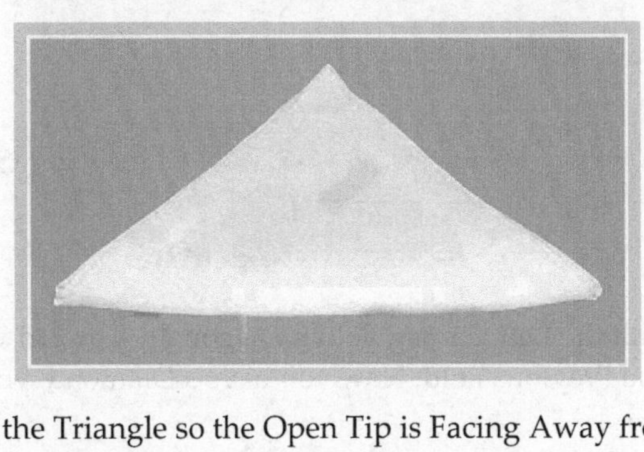

Orient the Triangle so the Open Tip is Facing Away from You.

Fold the Right Corner Diagonally Towards you - Laying it Down Along the Centerline of the Triangle, Making a New Tip Pointing Towards you. An Iron can make this Important Fold a Whole Lot Easier.

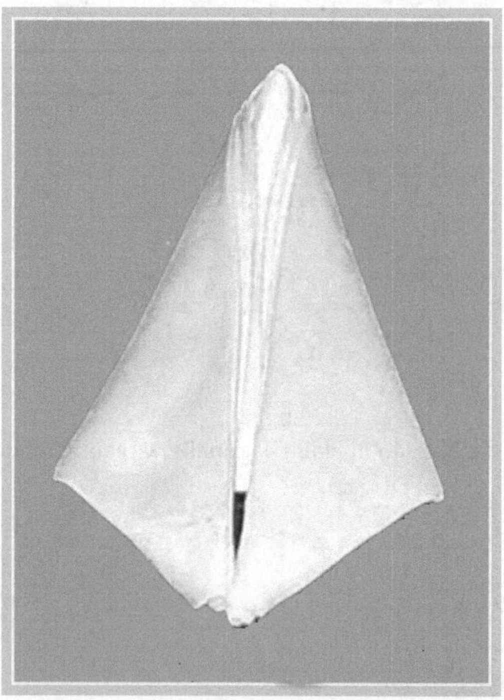

Do the Same with the Left Corner, Fold it Diagonally Toward you and Press it Down Next to the Previous Fold. Now you have a Diamond, you're Rich! Yay!.

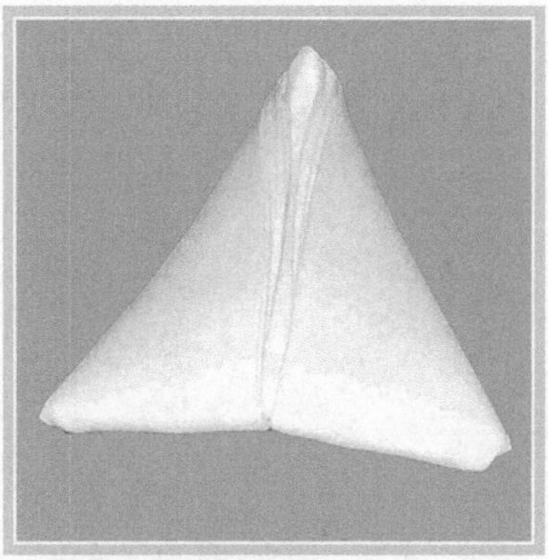

Fold the Two "Wings" that you Just Made in Folds 6 and 7 Under so that you have Your Original Triangle Shape Back Once again an Iron can make a World of Difference.

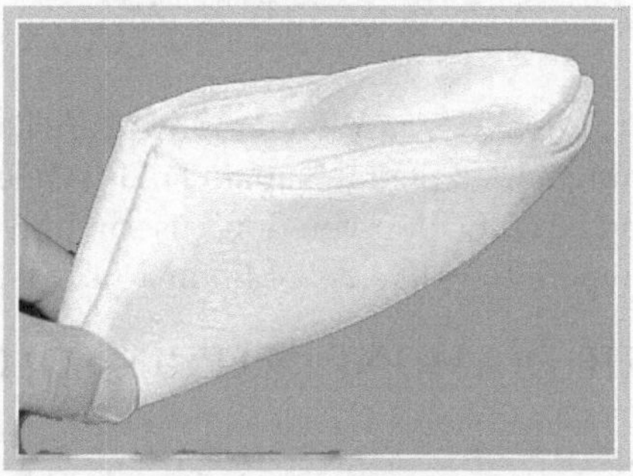

Fold the Triangle in Half by Bringing the Center Seam Towards you and Allowing the Ends to Fall.

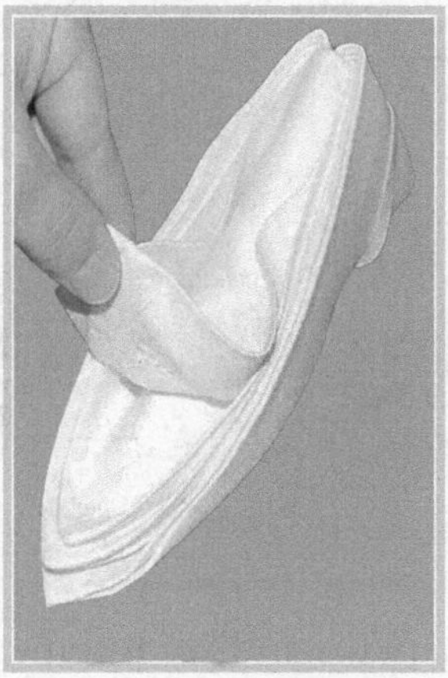

This Bird's almost Ready to Fly, but First you Must Give it Some Feathers. While Holding the Base Firmly to keep your Folds Together, Pull up the Four 'Flaps' Created by the Napkin's Corners.

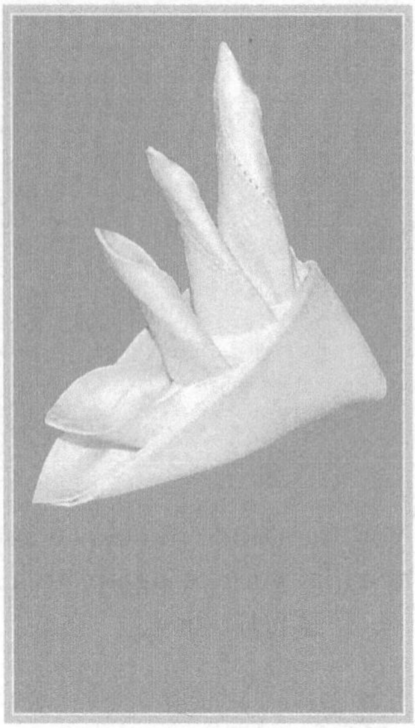

Pretty Cool Fold, isn't it? It makes you Wonder if there are People Sitting Around in Basements Performing Experimental Napkin Folds While the Rest of us are Sleeping. This Fold can be Difficult if you don't use an Iron or have a Fairly Stiff Napkin so be Prepared to put a Few Minutes into Making each One.

THE DIAMOND NAPKIN FOLD

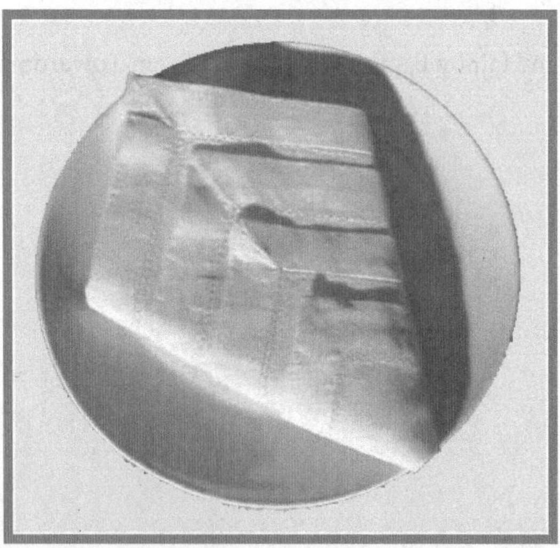

Got some really limp napkins and want something nice to make without eating up too much time? Then this one's for you, if you're using thick/stiff napkins then an iron will help.

Lay the Napkin Face-down in Front of You.

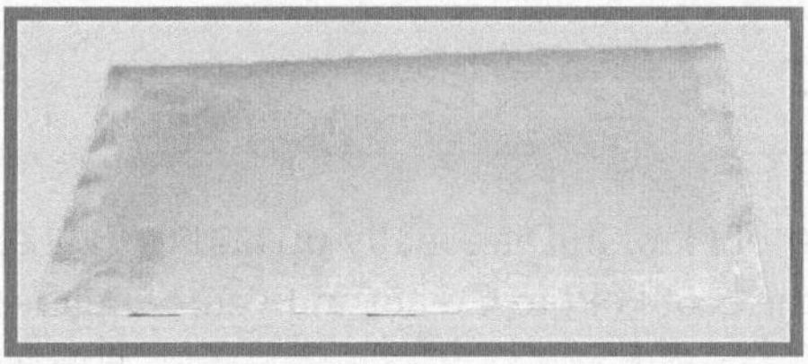

Fold the Napkin in Half and Orient the Open end Toward You.

Fold the Napkin into Quarters.

Fold the Top-most Layer of the Napkin in Half Diagonally - up and to the Left.

Fold the Next Layer of Napkin Diagonally up and to the Left, Stopping Slightly before the Last Fold to Create an Even, Staggered Effect.

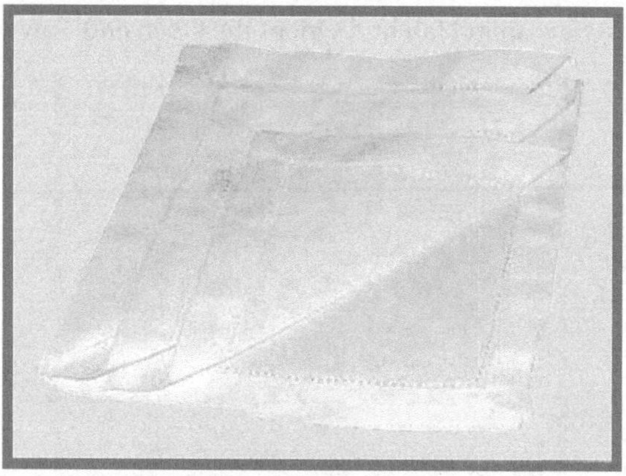

Repeat by Folding up the Next Layer of Napkin to a Point just before the Last One.

And One Last Time with One Last Layer. Keep them as Uniform as you Can.

Now Fold Both Sides of the Napkin Under and in to Create an Even, Staggered Diamond Effect on the Napkin. Press it Down as Flat as Possible and you're Ready for Guests Within 60 Seconds!

THE CONE NAPKIN FOLD

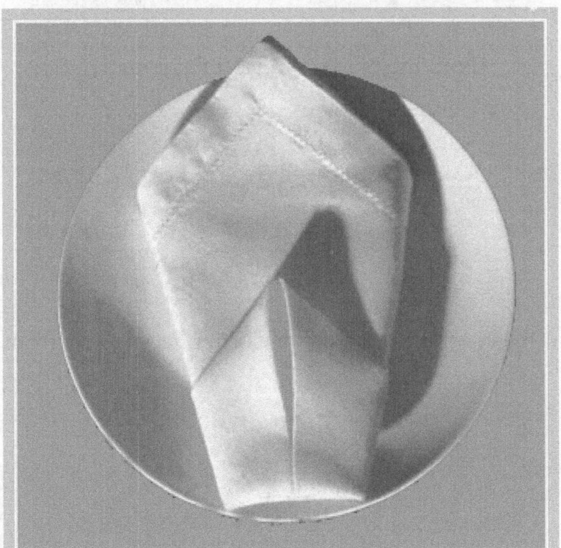

This nice napkin design originated from the napkin-worshiping indians native to Guam called the dirty-wipey-nappies...or not. An iron will be helpful.

Lay the Napkin Face Down in Front of You.

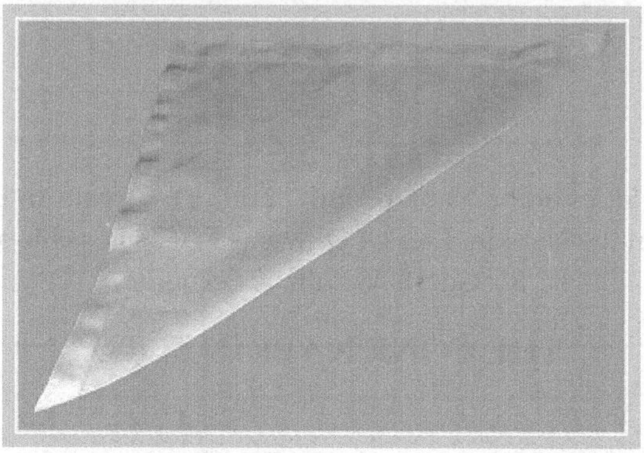

Fold the Napkin in Half Diagonally.

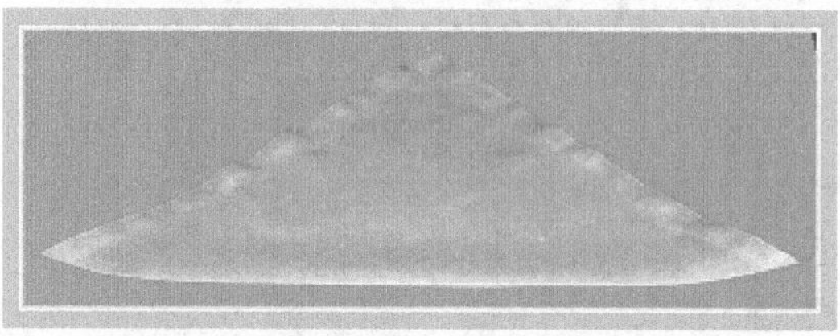

Orient the Napkin so the Open Corner Faces away from you.

Fold the Left-most Corner Diagonally so the Point Rests on Top of the Far Corner.

Repeat the Last Step with the Right Side,
Bringing this Fold Evenly along to the Last One.

Turn the Napkin over, Keeping the Open Ends Pointing away from You.

Evenly Fold the Bottom Third of the Napkin up and Press the it Down Well.
An Iron may be Needed Here.

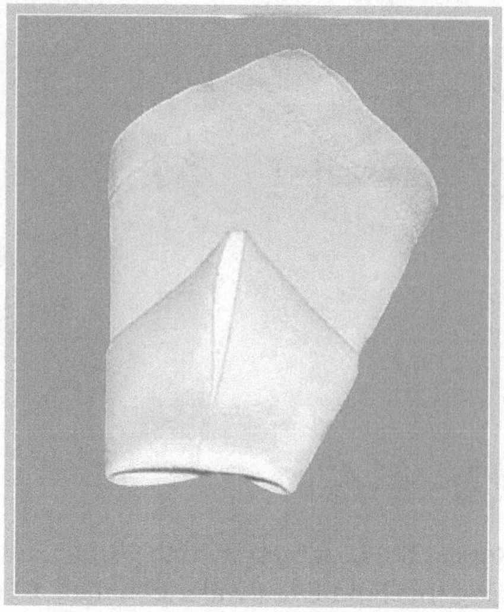

Fold Both the Left and Right Sides Back and Underneath the Napkin Evenly to Create the Finished Product Seen Here. That Looks so Nice I Bet you just Can't Wait to Smear Food on it!

THE FRENCH NAPKIN FOLD

Look at me, I'm sophisticated. Look at me, I'm elegant. Look at me, I'm going to be used to wipe someone's messy face! Sec re Bleu!

The french fold is a nice simple napkin fold that requires no special skills or tools (well.. hands are helpful).

Lay the Napkin Face-down in Front of You.

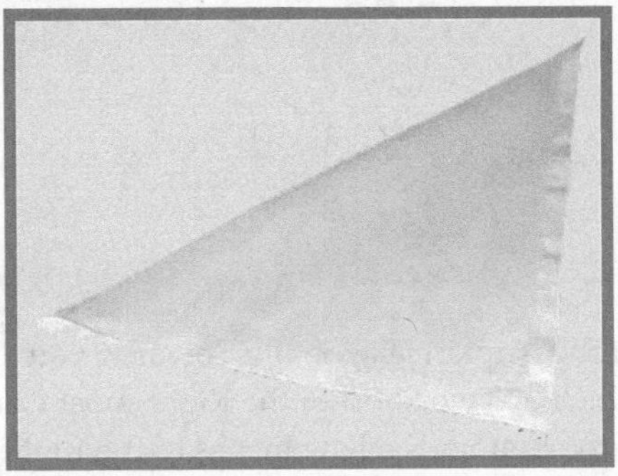

Fold the Napkin in Half Diagonally.

Orient the Napkin so the Long Side is on the Left.

Fold the Far Corner of the Napkin Diagonally Towards you and to the Right so that the Crease Falls an Inch or Two Short of the Right-most Corner and the Newly Formed Point at the Bottom is a Few Inches to the Right of the Left One.

Fold the Right-most Point Towards You, Pivoting at the Same Place the Last Fold Pivoted. Use the Finished Napkin to Drape the dinner Place. Very Classy and Uncomplicated.

THE BISHOP'S HAT NAPKIN FOLD

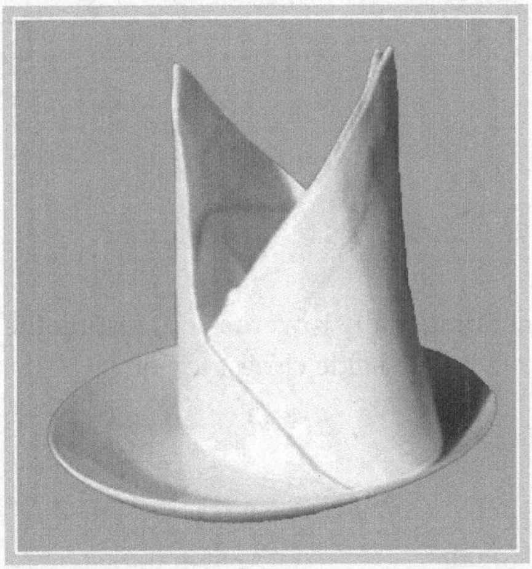

This is a classic dinner napkin fold, but it can be difficult to line up the corners in the cap. Some starch and an iron make it easier to be precise while folding this one....and yes I know it's not sitting in the center of the plate, next time I'll stay out of the cooking wine, I promise.

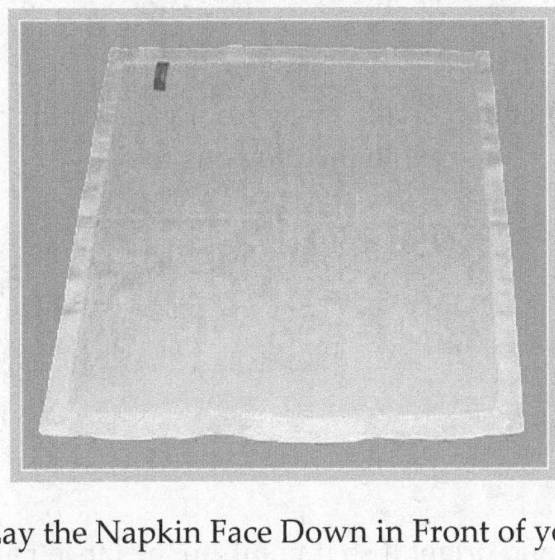

Lay the Napkin Face Down in Front of you.

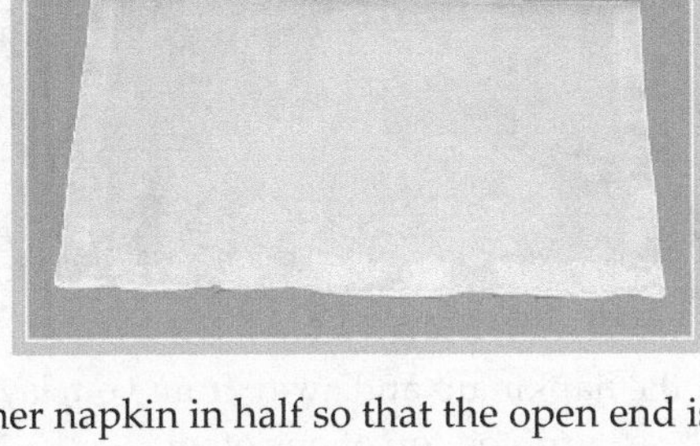

Fold the dinner napkin in half so that the open end is towards you.

Fold the far-right corner diagonally towards you, resting the point in the center of the side closest to you.

Fold the near-left corner diagonally away from you, resting it so that it lays right next to the previous fold.

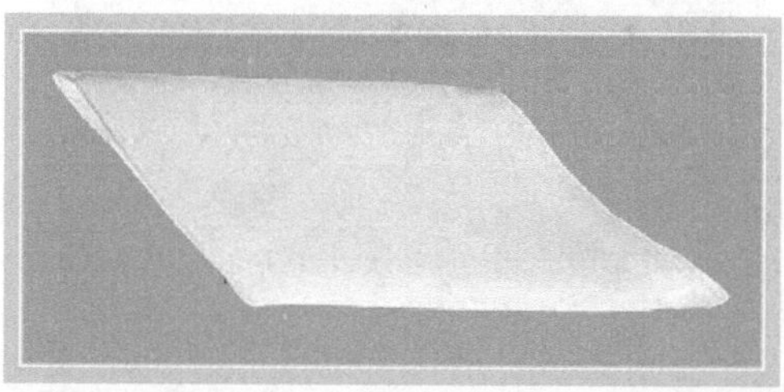

Flip the napkin over and orient it so it points to the far-left and to the near-right.

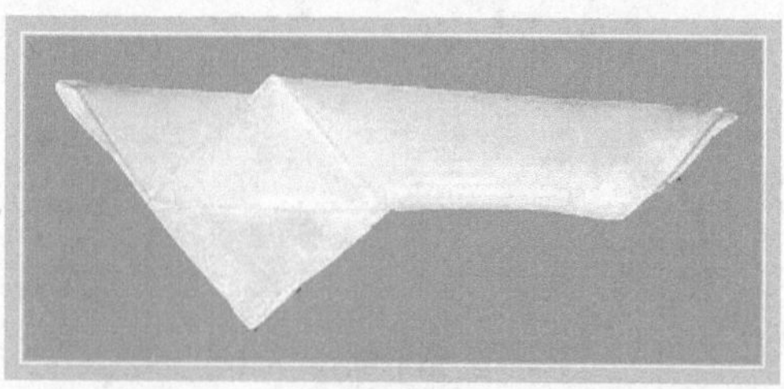

Fold the bottom half of the napkin up and away from you, laying it so the far edges run on top of one other.

Reach underneath of the napkin and pull out the flap on the right, making the near-side come to two points as seen in the picture.

Gently roll the left half of the left triangle over and tuck it's end underneath the right triangle.

Flip the napkin over, points pointing away from you.

Fold the right-triangle to the left, tucking it's end into the other triangle.

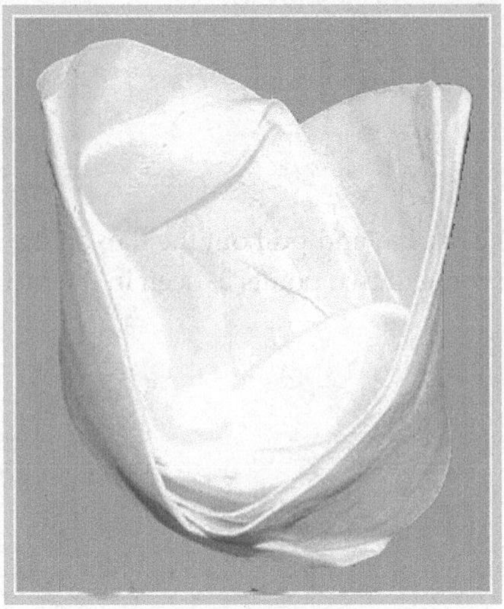

Open up the hat and press the material inside down to fill it out so that it becomes circular, this may take a little fidgeting.

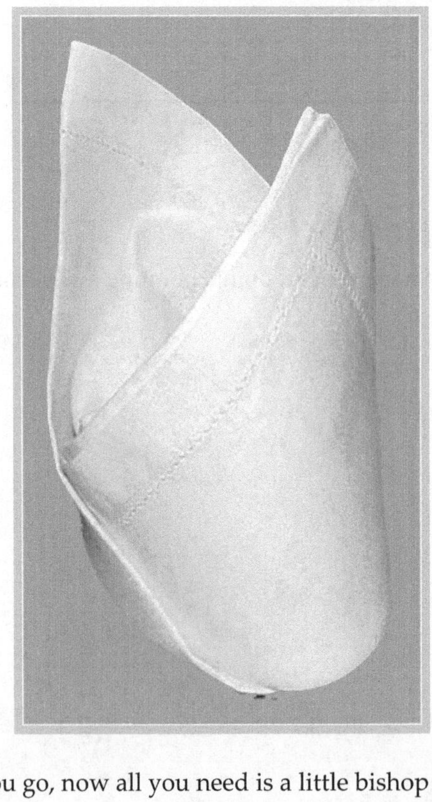

There you go, now all you need is a little bishop to wear it.

THE ROSEBUD NAPKIN FOLD

This sophisticated cloth napkin design benefits from stiff material or light starch. A hot iron will also make it easier to be exact.

Lay the napkin face-down in front of you.

Fold the napkin in half diagonally.

Orient the napkin so the open end points away from you.

Fold the far-right corner up diagonally so that the point rests on top of the far corner. The edge of this new flap should lay right on the center line.

Repeat step four on the other side, bringing the left-most corner up to meet the far corner, creating a diamond shape.

Flip the napkin over while keeping the open end pointing away from you.

Fold the bottom of the napkin up about 3/4's of the way as shown and press the fold down well.

Flip the napkin over.

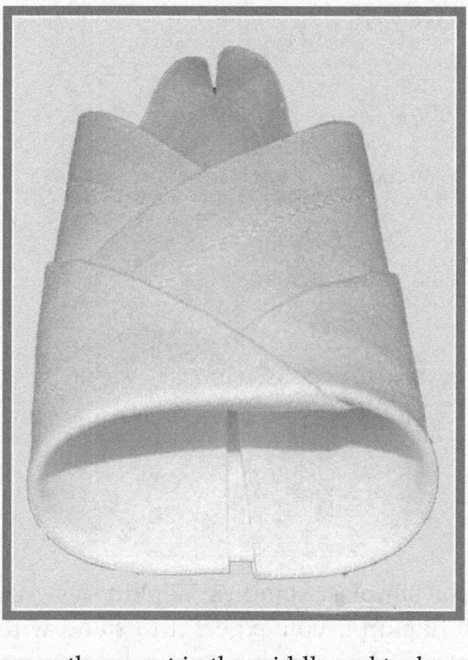

Curl both sites up so they meet in the middle and tuck one into the other.

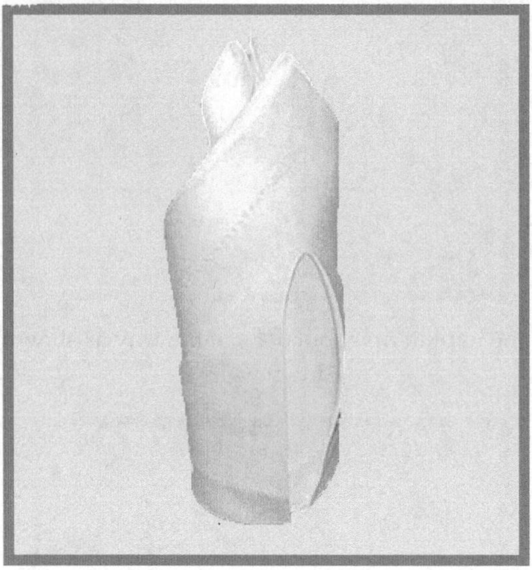

Stand it up and straighten it out. If you have trouble keeping the points even, break out the iron and back track to the folds that mess up your alignment. Is it me or do these look like Egyptian headgear?

THE SAIL NAPKIN FOLD

This is one of the simplest standing napkin designs there are, but you will still need a stiff napkin if you expect it to stand without flopping over. Who'd have thought you'd be starching your dinnerware?

Lay the napkin face-down in front of you.

Fold the napkin in half and orient the open end towards you.

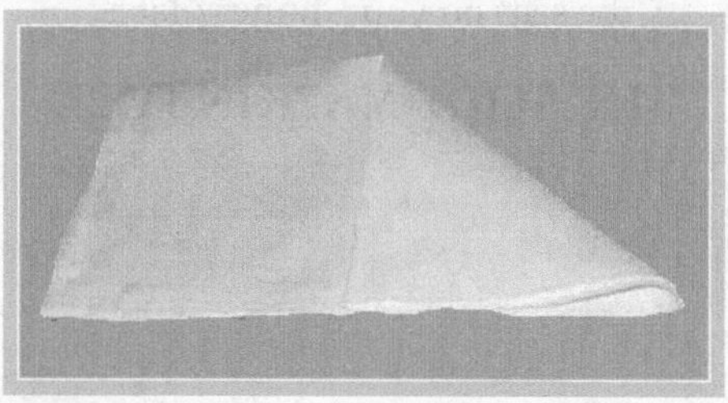

Fold the far-right corner diagonally to the center of the side that is closest to you. The edge of this flap should run down the center of the napkin.

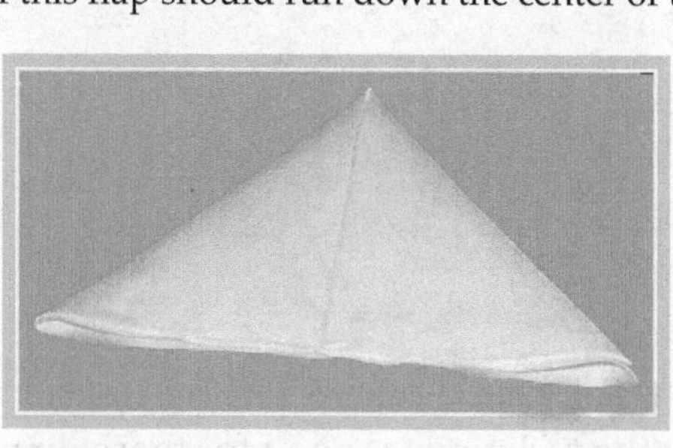

Repeat the last step with the other side, folding the far-left corner diagonally to rest right along side the previous fold.

Fold the napkin in half by bringing the center seam up from the work surface and allowing the ends to fall backwards. Smooth down the folds so it stands nicely and whala! A fast and easy standing-fold for your dinner party. Now you can sail across the seas on your dinner plates.

THE SLIDE NAPKIN FOLD

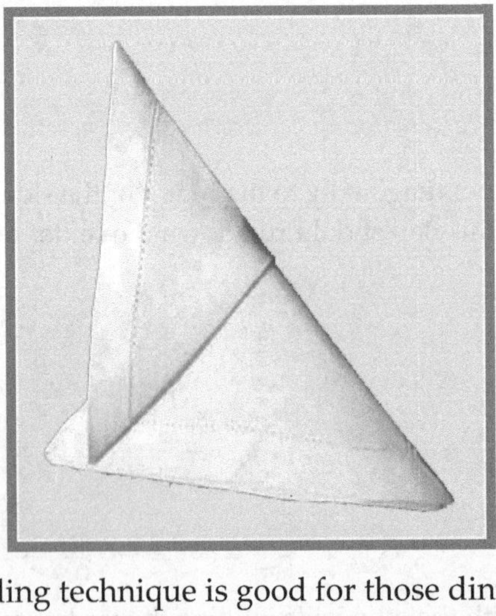

This napkin folding technique is good for those dinners where you want something fancy, but not too complex. This requires either stiff material or starch.

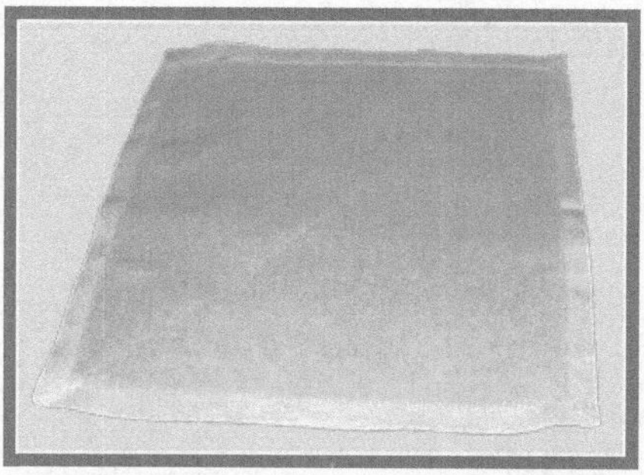

Lay the napkin face-down in front of you.

Fold the napkin in half and orient the open end towards you.

Fold the napkin into quarters.

Orient the napkin so that the open end is pointing away from you.

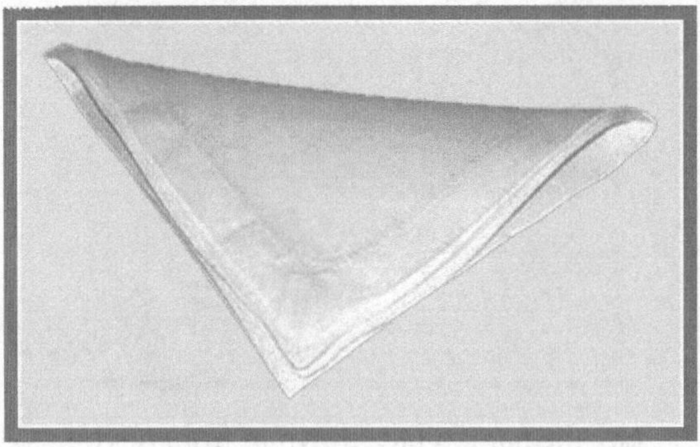

Fold the napkin in half by bringing the far end up to the front. Press this fold down well.

Take the top-layer of napkin and fold it back, making a crease about 1/2"-1" before the top.

Flip the napkin over, keeping the single-layer tip pointing away from you

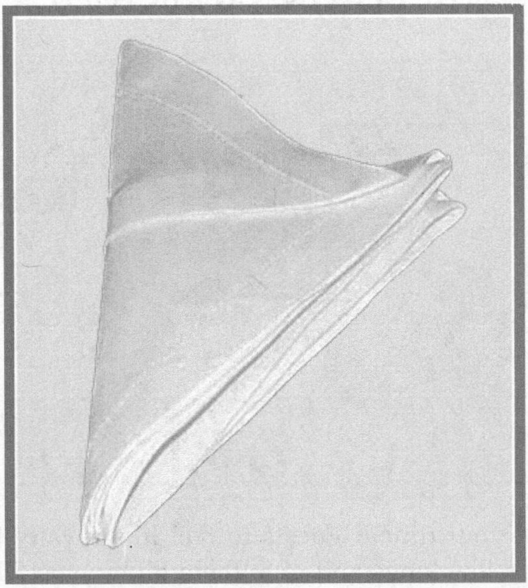

Fold the napkin in half from left to right and press the fold down well.

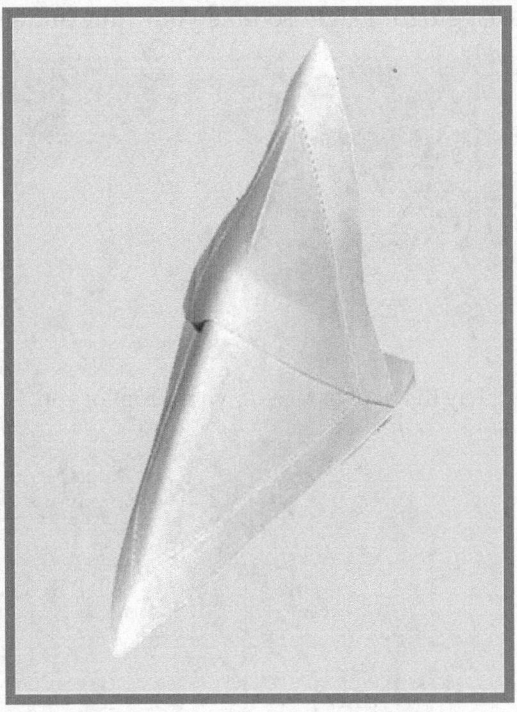

Open and stand - Very nice!

THE CROWN NAPKIN FOLD

Do you want your dinner guests to feel like royalty but have no red carpet? Treat them like kings and give them all crowns! Then you can use this napkin to wipe the cheese out of that introduction.

This napkin folding design just doesn't work well without a little starch in the cloth, if it's sagging it's ugly so take your time and get it right.

Lay the napkin face-down in front of you.

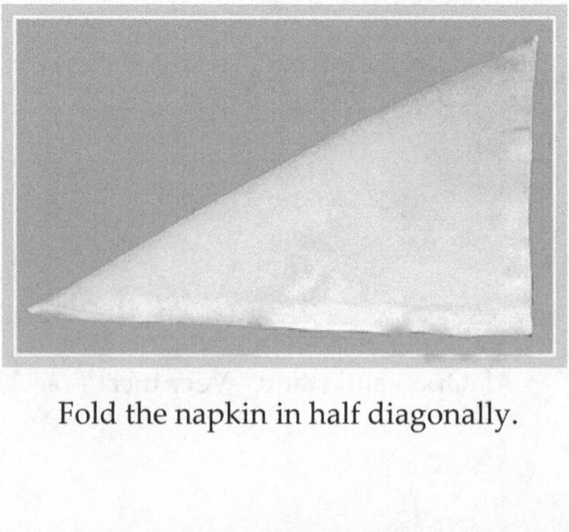

Fold the napkin in half diagonally.

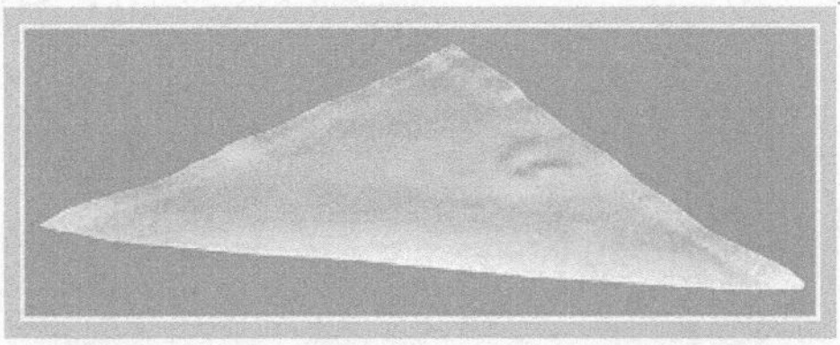

Orient the napkin so the open ends are pointing away from you.

Fold the right-corner up so that the point rests directly on top of the middle-corner. The edge of this new flap should lay on the center line of the napkin.

Repeat step four on the other side, bringing the left-most corner up to meet the middle-corner, creating a diamond shape.

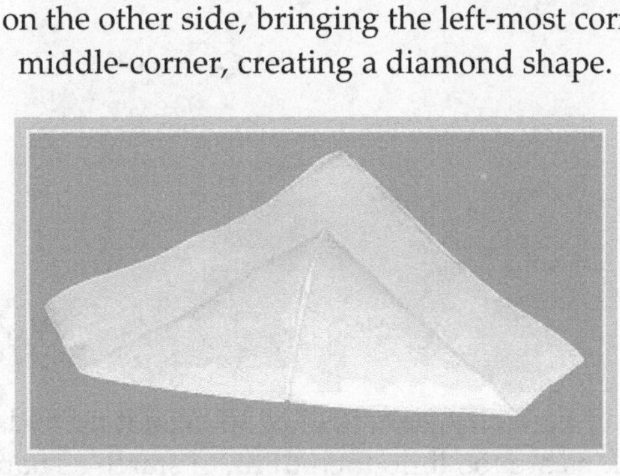

Fold the bottom of the napkin up about 2/4's of the way and press this fold down well.

Fold the smaller triangle down so the point rests on the near edge of the napkin. Press.

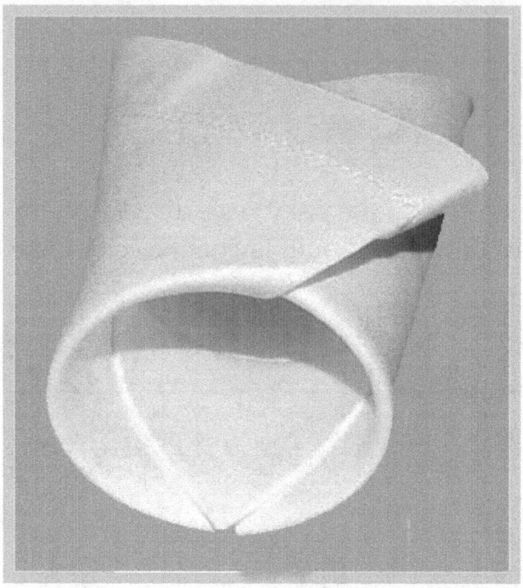

curl the left and right sides of the napkin up so they meet in the middle and tuck one into the other.

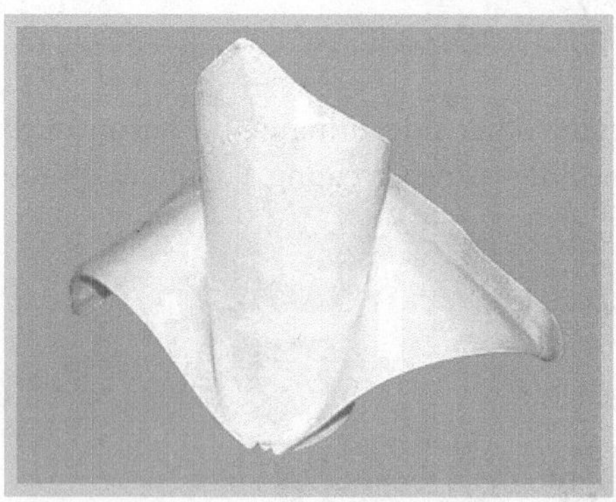

Stand it up and tug at it where needed to even it up and round it out.
If your napkins are too limp then think of starch as napkin viagra
and make them good and stiff.

THE STANDING FAN NAPKIN FOLD

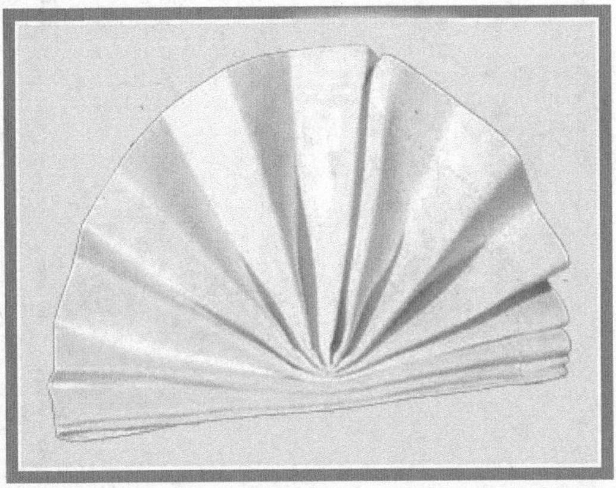

Elegant and decorative, this is a classic napkin folding technique. As usual, and iron helps but is not necessary.

Lay the Napkin Face-down in Front of You.

Fold the Napkin in Half and Orient the Open end Towards You.

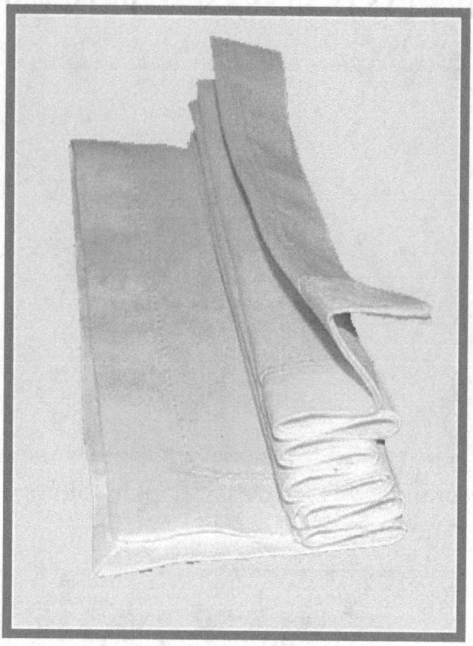

Fold the Napkin Like an Aaccordion Starting at Either Narrow end. Leave one End with 2-3 Inches of Unfolded Napkin to Support the Standing Fan.

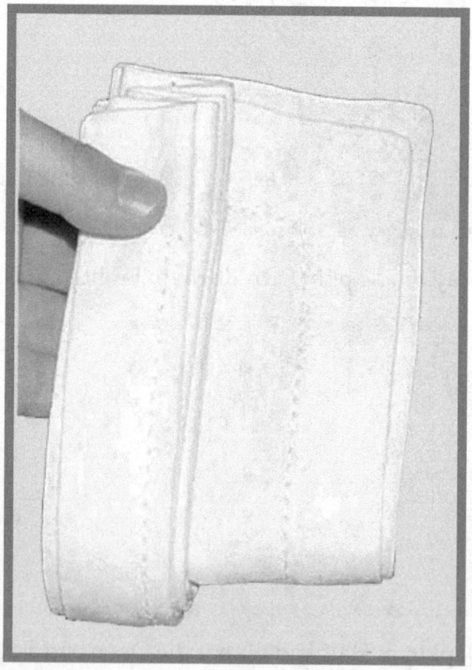

Fold the Napkin in Half with the Accordion Folds on the Outside.

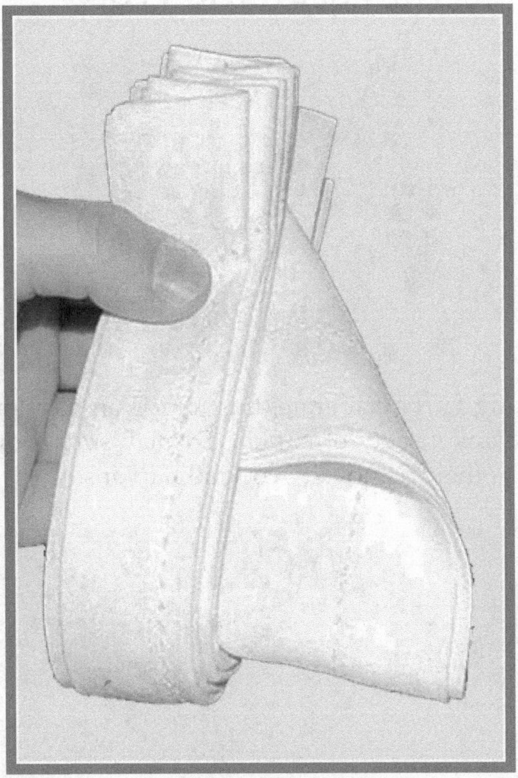

Grasp the Unfolded Corners where they Meet on the Open End and Fold them in Diagonally, Tucking them under the Accordion Folds.

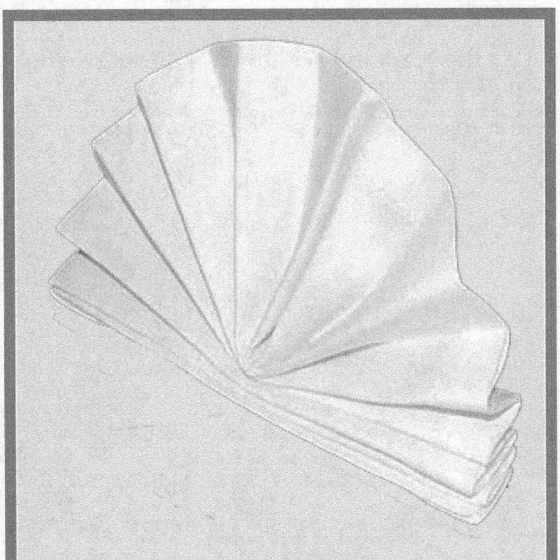

Open it and Stand it Up. A Beautiful Fan for a Beautiful Dinner.

THE ROSE NAPKIN FOLD

Despite looking fairly elaborate, this fold is an easy one, and it can be done with almost any variety of napkin. Display small bowls or glasses on top of these, or use them as novelty cocktail napkins.

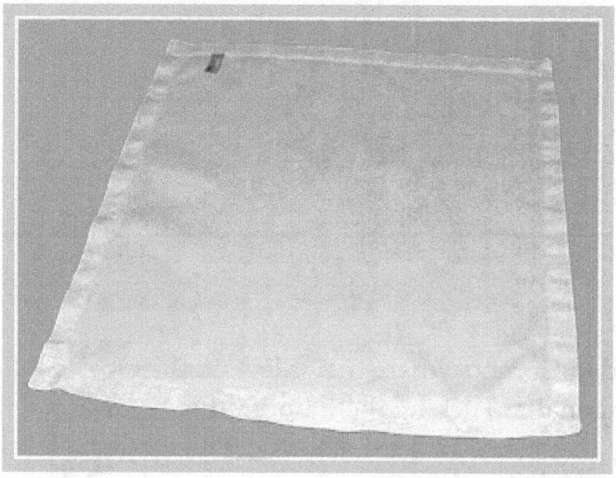

Lay the Napkin Face-down in Front of You.

Fold the Two Right Corners of the Napkin in so the Tips Rest at the Center.

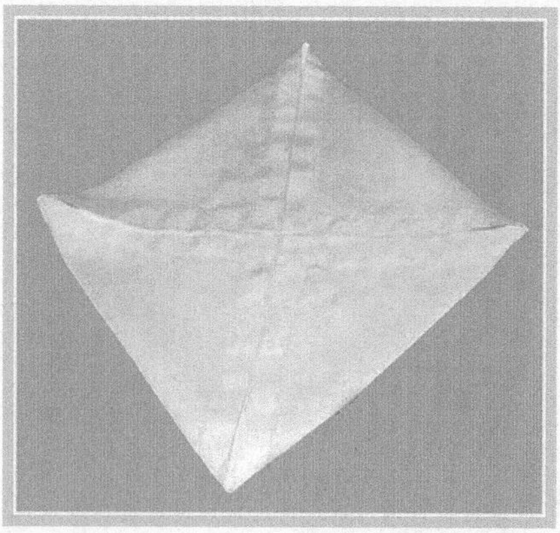

Fold the Remaining Two Corners of the Napkin in so the Tips Meet with the Last Two in the Center.

Once again, begin Folding the Outer Corners in so they Meet at the Center.

Once all of the Tips are Folded you are Left with a Square about 1/4 the Size of the Unfolded Napkin.

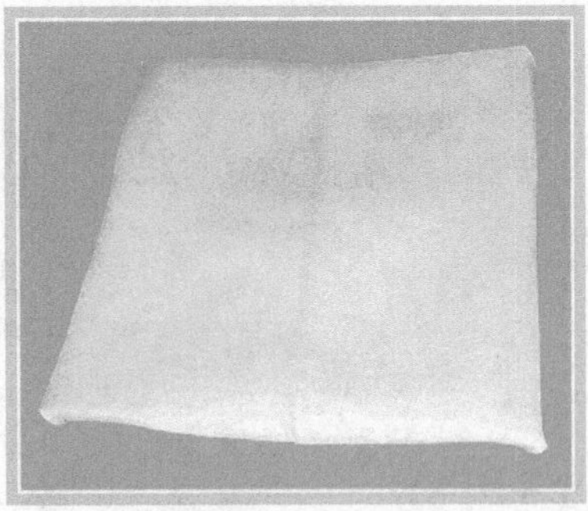

Flip it Over.

Fold the Corners in so they Meet in the Center and then Place Something Sturdy in the Center, or Hold it with your Fingers.

While maintaining Downward Pressure in the Center of the Napkin, reach Underneath each Corner and Pull out the Flaps to create Petals.

Remove the Center Weight and your Rose Should Look as Pictured Here.

If you Like you can reach Underneath the Center of each Side and Pull out a Second set of Petals to Fancy it up some more. Place Something in the Center and you're done, have a rosy meal!

THE NECKTIE NAPKIN FOLD

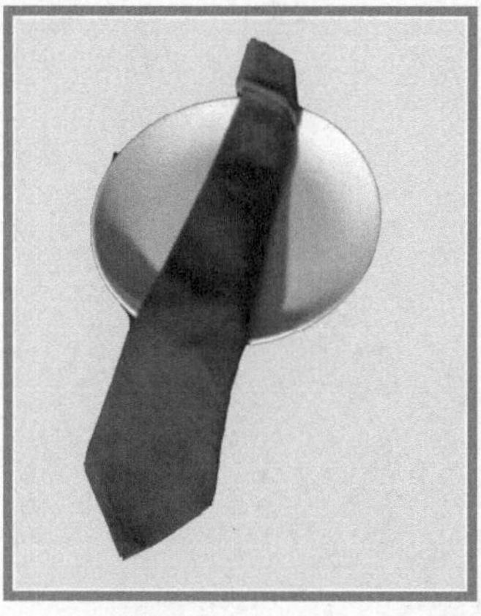

Now your guests can wipe food off of their expensive ties with... inexpensive ties! Isn't that special? This one's easier with limp napkins, but if you only have stiffies then an iron will make this simple to do. Remember that the larger the napkin is, the longer the tie will be.

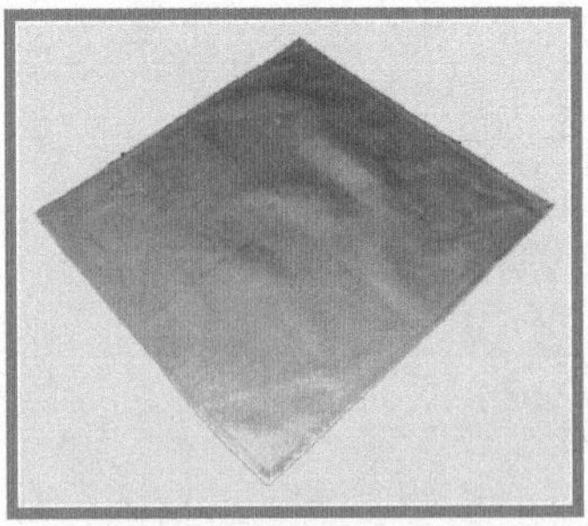

Lay the Napkin Face-down and Orient it so that one of the Corners Points to You.

Starting at the upper Tip, fold the Right Side about 1/3
of the way Diagonally to the Left. Don't Press the Fold down Yet.

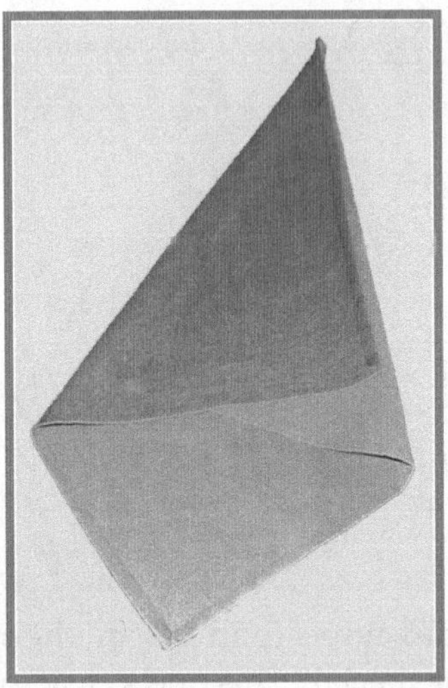

Repeat the Last Step with the Left Side and then Adjust them both if Needed so that both sides are Symmetrical. Now Press Down the Folds.

Fold the Right Side in about 1/3 of the way Starting from the Upper Tip, Similar to what we did in the Last Two Steps. Don't Press it Down Yet.

Repeat the Last Fold Along the Left Side and adjust for Symmetry. When you're Happy with the Shape of Your Tie, Press the Folds Down.

Fold the Upper 1/3 of the Tie Diagonally to the Right so the Tip of the Tie is Perpendicular to he Lower Part.

Turn the Tie Over so the Tip is now Pointing Left.

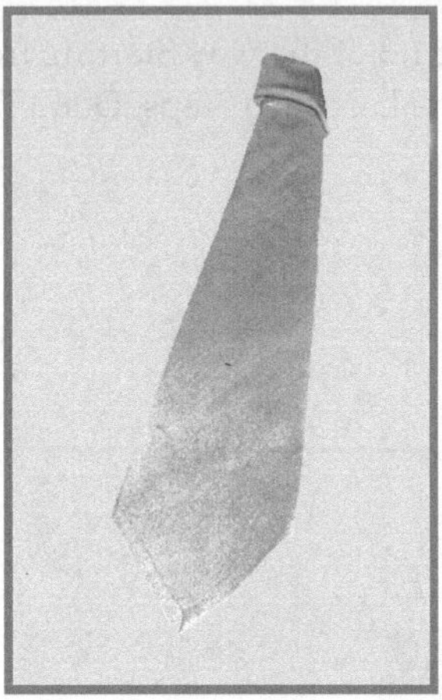

Wrap the Tip Around the Top of the Tie and Tuck it in Underneath to Create the Knot. There you are, your very Own Clever Necktie Napkin!

THE SHIRT NAPKIN FOLD

This is a neat fold to have sitting on your guests dinner plates, and it's pretty easy assuming that you have an iron. I repeat, break out the iron! Iron, iron ironironironiron.

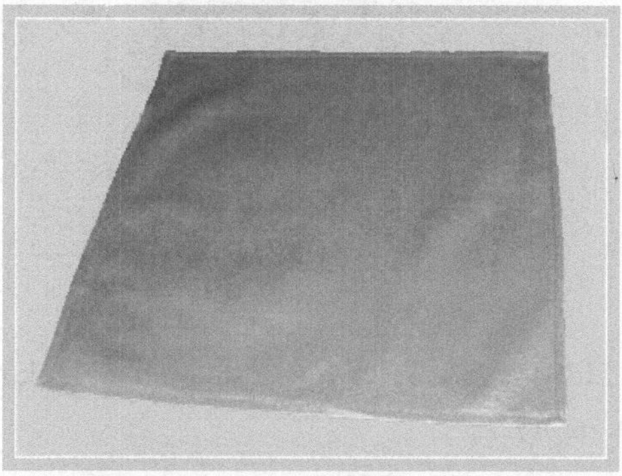

Lay the Napkin Face-down in Front of You.

Fold the Two Right Corners of the Napkin Diagonally so the Tips Rest at the Center.

Fold the Two Left Corners of the Napkin Diagonally so the Tips Meet the other Two in the Center.

Fold the Right Side Over so it's Edge Rests on the Napkins Center-line.

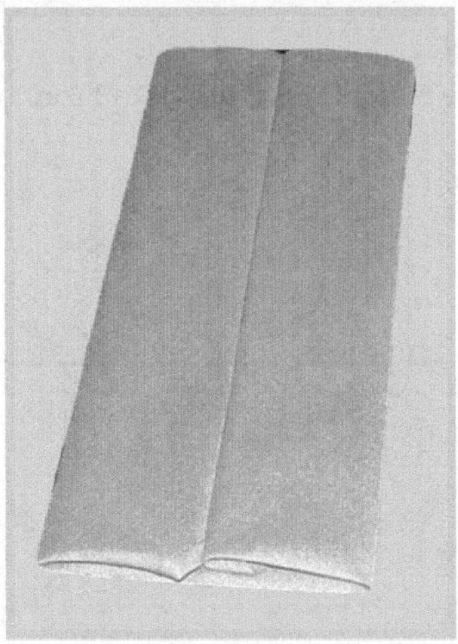

Fold the Left Side Over to Meet the Last Fold at the Center-line of the Napkin.

Turn the Napkin Over.

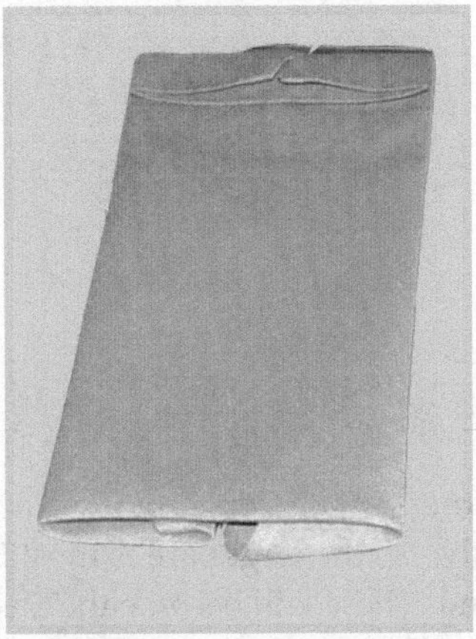

Fold the Top 1/4" – 1" Down and Press it with your Iron. This Will be the Collar of the Shirt.

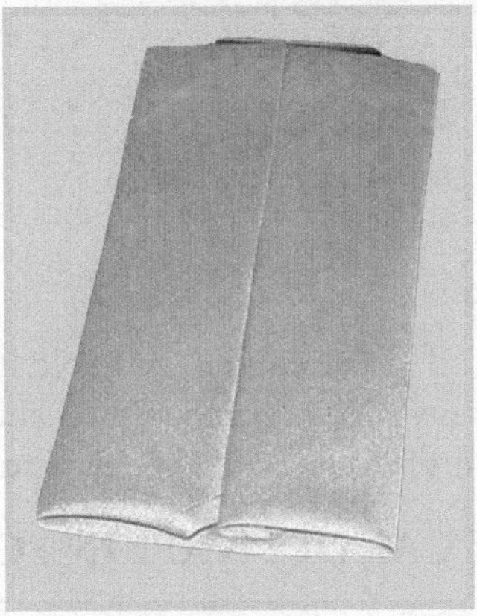

Flip the Napkin Over Again.

Fold Both Upper Corners in Diagonally, so the Points Meet in the Center at an Angle to form the Front Collar of the Shirt.

Take Hold of the Two Corners in the Center of the Napkin's Near Side and Fold them up and out Diagonally - so the Edges are Almost Parallel to the Folds at the Far End. These will become the Sleeves.

Take Hold of the Near End of the Napkin, and Fold it up Towards the Collar, Tucking it Underneath the Lower Points of the Collar and Pressing it Down. A Tiny Shirt to Stain with Dinner, Yum!

THE CANDLE NAPKIN FOLD

So you want something easy and elegant? Something that looks nice and fancy but doesn't take a boat-load of time? Try this one on for size.

Lay the Napkin Face Down in Front of You.

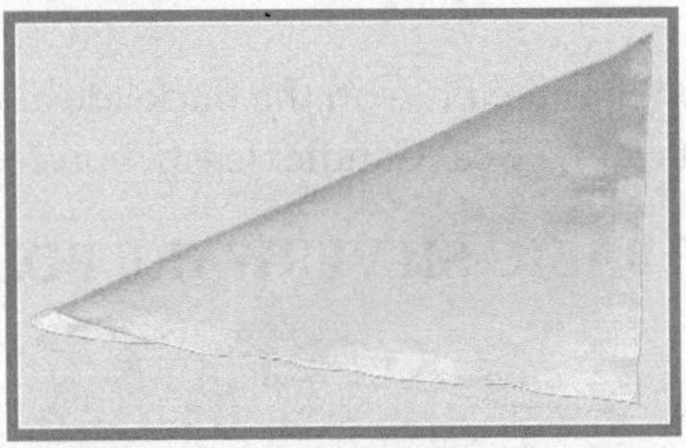

Fold the Napkin in Half Diagonally.

Orient the Napkin so the Open Ends Point Away from You.

Fold the Long Side up just about an Inch. Press this Fold Down Well or it will Interfere with the Next Step.

Starting at Either End, Tightly Roll the Napkin into a Cylinder. Take Care to Roll it Straight so it will Stand Solidly.

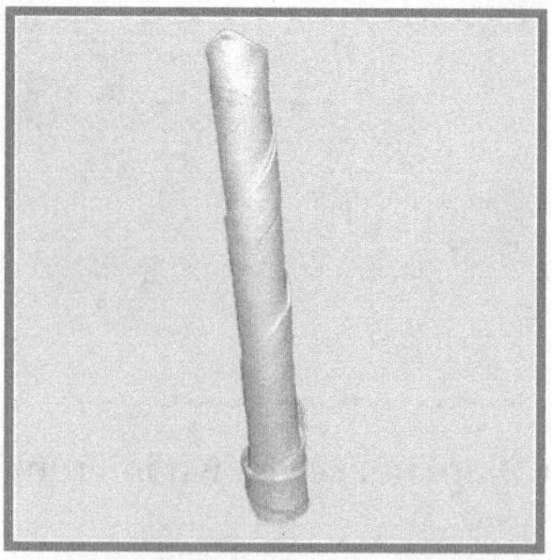

Tuck the End of the Roll into the Base on the Backside and Stand it up. Put those Matches Down, it's not a Real Candle. Jeesh, you're just Like a Child.

THE BASIC SILVERWARE POUCH

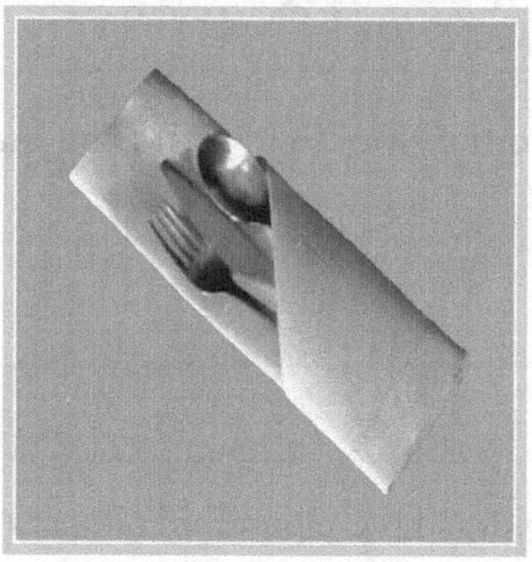

Setting the table for lunch? Want simple and functional? Then go with a classic. These also work well with chopsticks.

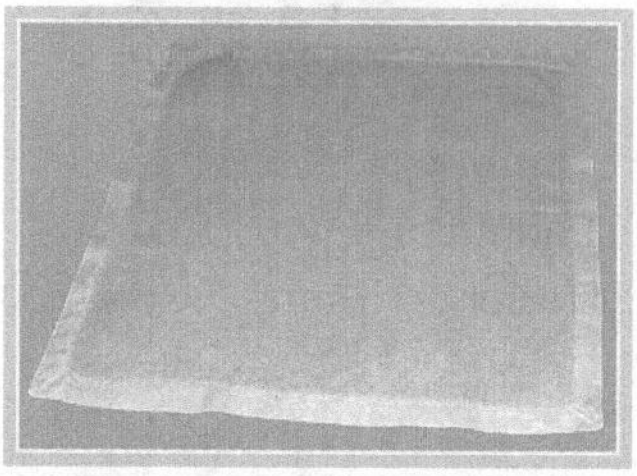

Lay the Napkin Face-down in Front of You.

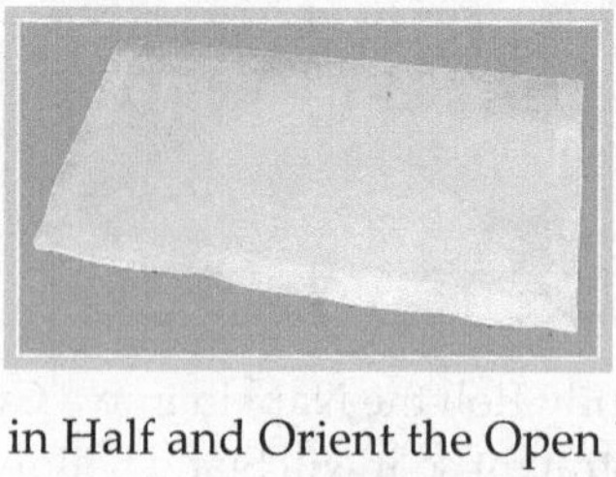

Fold the Napkin in Half and Orient the Open End toward You.

Fold the Napkin into Quarters.

Orient the Napkin so the Open Corner is Facing Away and to the Left.

Fold the Top-most Layer of Napkin in Half Diagonally and Press it Down.

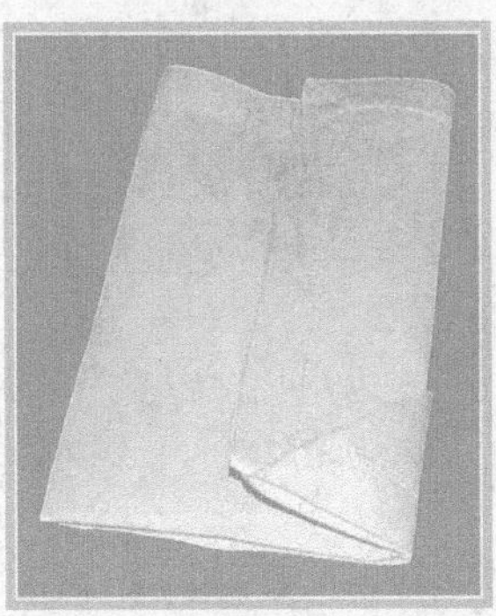

Turn the Napkin Over so that the Open
Corner is now Facing Away and to the Right.

Fold the Right-side Back about 1/3 of the Way and Press it Down.

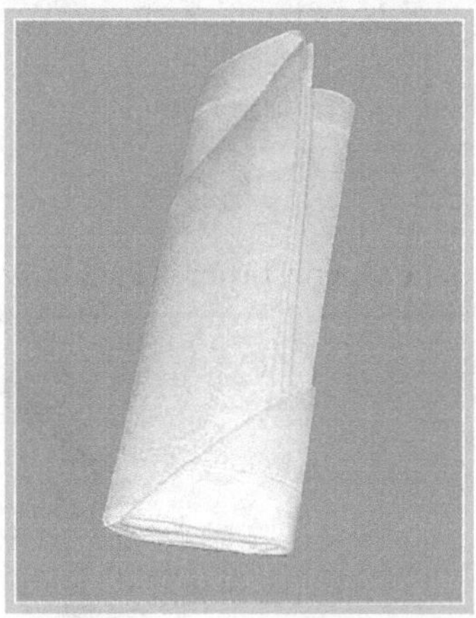

Fold the Left-side Back also about 1/3 of the Way and Press.

Flip it Over, Straighten it up and Insert those Shiny Eating Instruments. Perfecto!

THE FANCY SILVERWARE POUCH

This is similar to the basic silverware pouch, except for two more folds near the end. It is good for a more decorative touch than the basic pouch.

Lay the Napkin Face-down in Front of You.

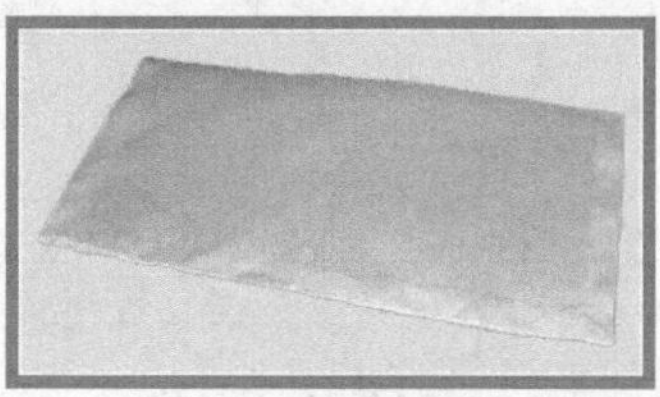

Fold the Napkin in Half and Orient the Open End toward You.

Fold the Napkin into Quarters.

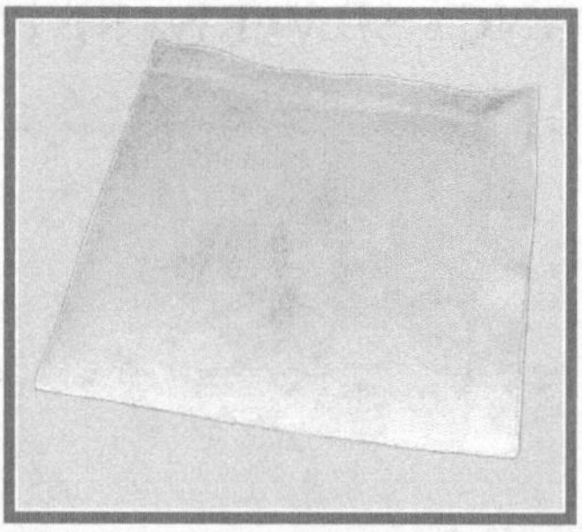

Orient the Napkin so the Open Corner is Facing Away and to the Right.

Roll the Top-most Layer of Napkin Diagonally
Down to the Center and Press it Flat.

Roll the Next Layer Down Until it Meets the First and Press that One as Well.

Repeat the Last Step Once More.

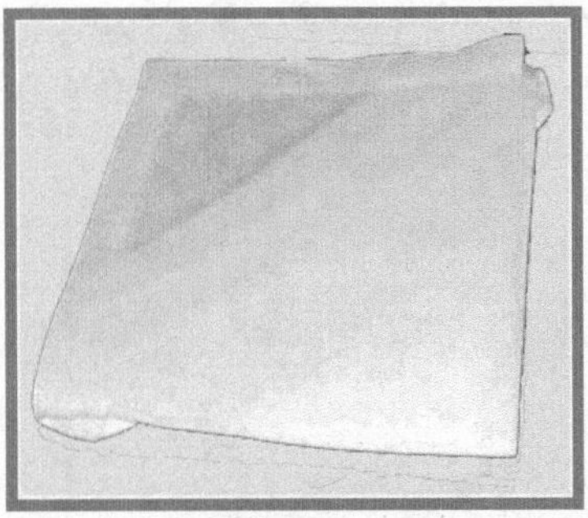

Turn the Napkin Over.

Fold the Right Side back About 1/3 of the Way and Press it Down.

Fold the Left Side back also About 1/2 of the Way and Press.

Flip it Over and Insert the Food Poker, Slicer, and Scooper. So what's for Dinner?

THE SILVERWARE NAPKIN ROLL

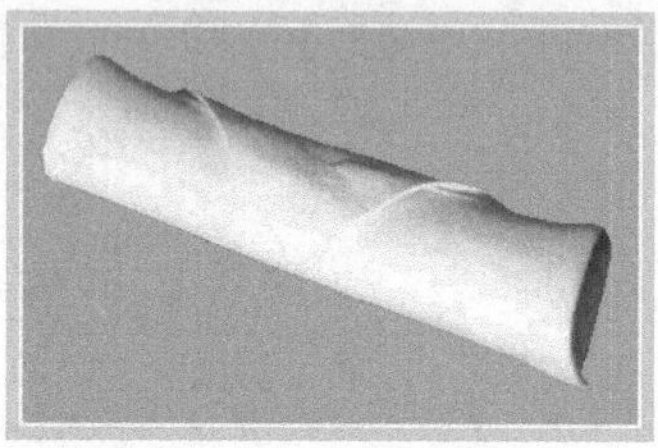

If you're going on a picnic or need your silverware to be portable, then a silverware roll is the way to go. You can load them up and pack them away for later and they keep your silverware nice and clean. This is as simple as it gets, folks.

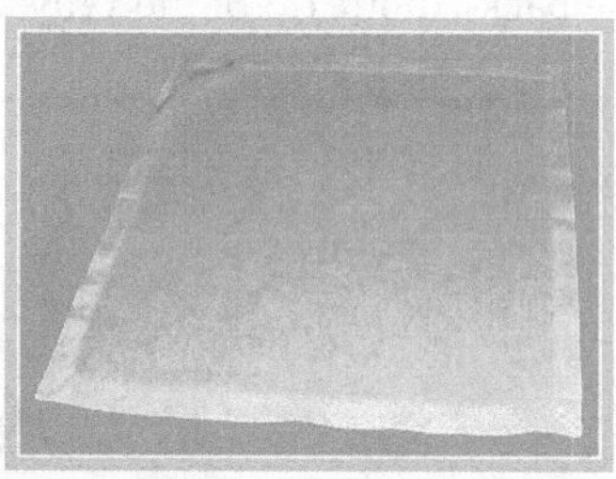

Lay the Napkin Face-down in Front of You.

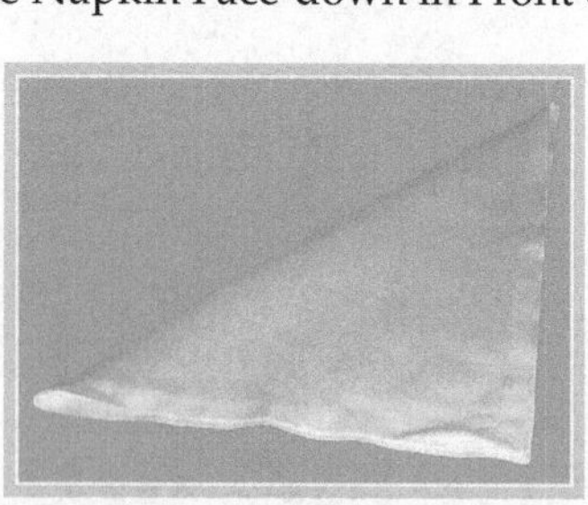

Fold the Napkin in Half Diagonally.

Orient the Napkin so the Longest Side is Toward you, and
then Place the Silverware on the Inner-edge of the Long Side.

Fold both Sides in and Over the Silverware. Do not Crease.

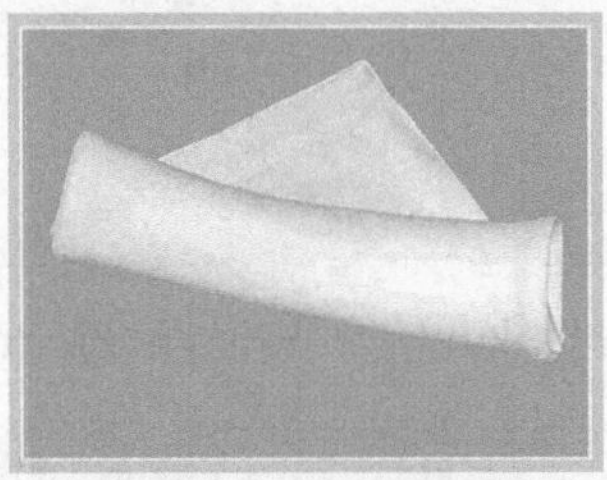

Tightly Roll the Silverware into the Napkin.

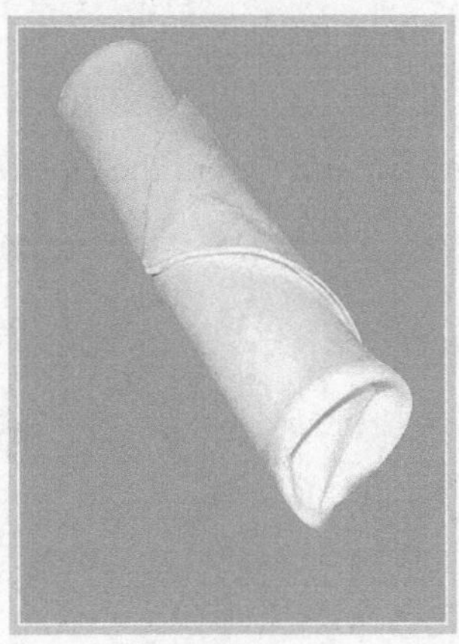

There you are, Easy Peazy Mac and Cheezy!

THE DIAMOND POUCH

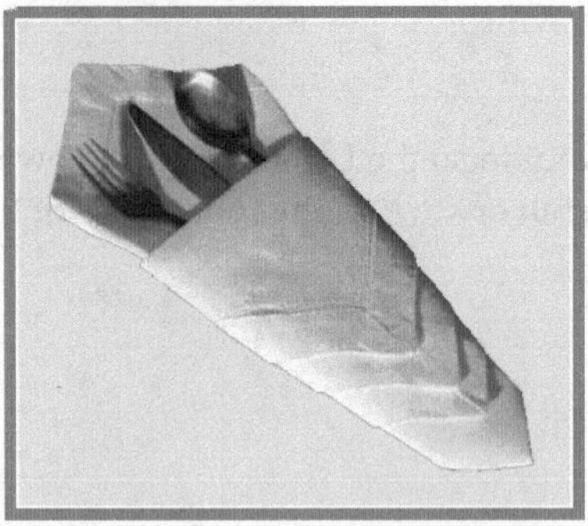

Here we have another variation of the silverware pouch. Also simple to make, this design tends to look nicer when it is pressed down almost flat. You wouldn't want your silverware getting cold, would you?

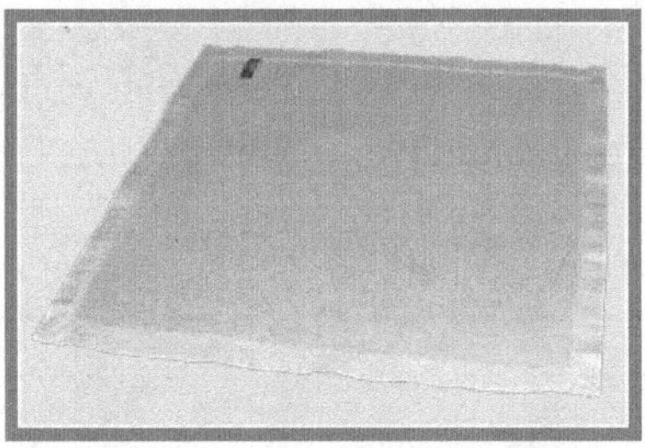

Lay the Napkin Face-down in Front of You.

Fold the Napkin in Half and Orient the Open End Toward You.

Fold the Napkin into Quarters.

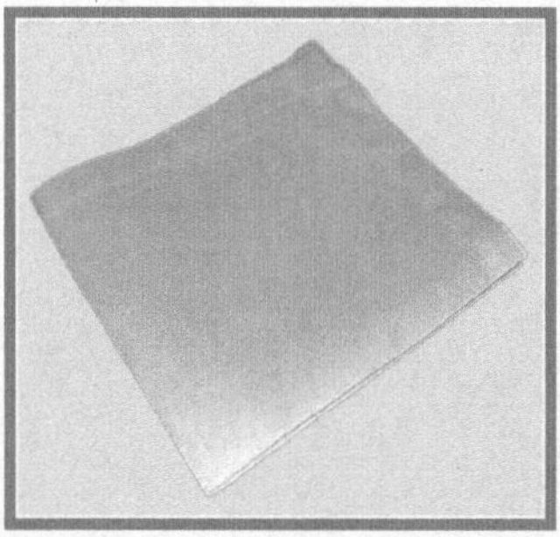

Orient the Napkin so the Open end Faces Away from You.

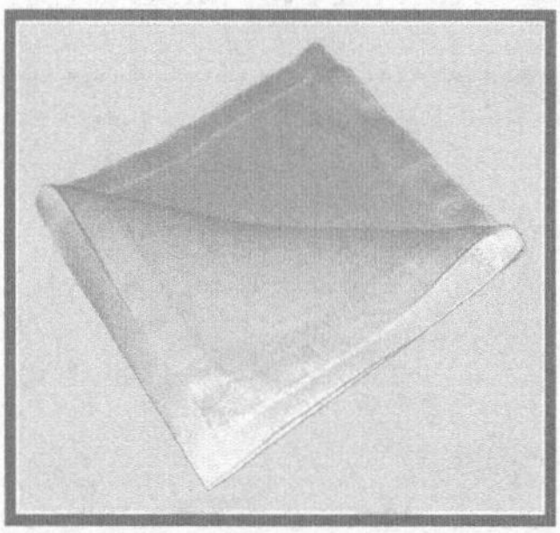

Fold the Top-most Layer Almost all the Way Forward and Press it Down Flat.

Fold the Next Top-most Layer of Napkin Forward Almost as Far as the Previous one and Press it Down as Well. Make Sure the Edges are even with the Previous Fold.

Fold the Next Layer Back as you did the Two before It.

Turn the Napkin Over.

Fold Both Sides back and Over one Another (about 1/3 of the way), Check for Symmetry and Press the Fold Down Well.

Flip it Over and Insert your Favorite Silverware.

THE CANDLE FAN FOLD

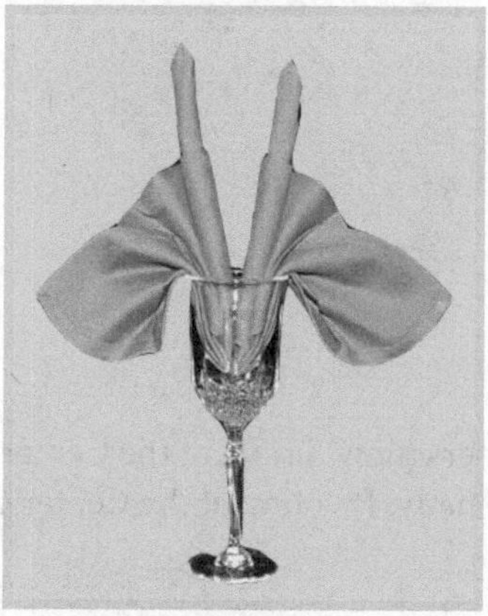

Sometimes you just need something a little different. The candle fan stuffed into a goblet or mug is very different. The larger the napkin that you use is, the longer the 'candles' will be.

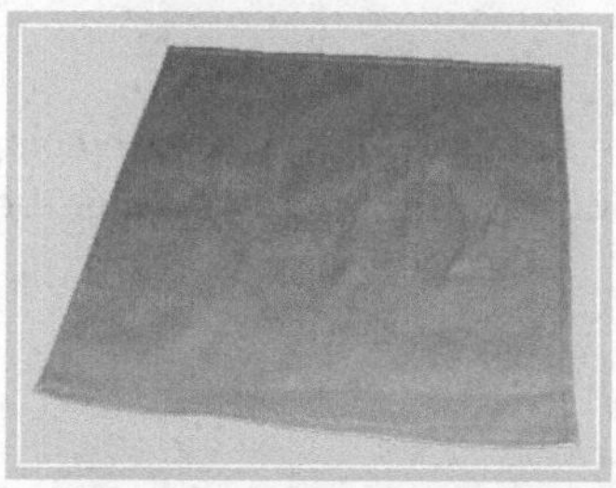

Lay the Napkin Face-down in Front of You.

Fold Both Sides in so they Meet at the Center. Press the Folds Down Well.

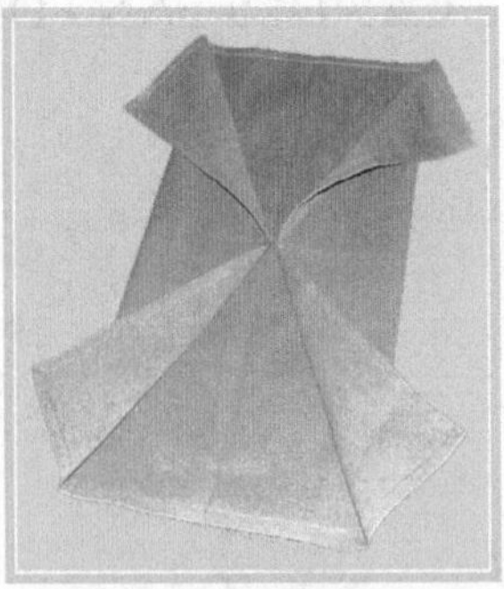

Take Each of the Four Corners (now Sitting at the Center of the Far and Near Sides) and Fold them out Diagonally, Pivoting at the Center of the Napkin as Shown.

Starting at one End, Tightly Roll the Napkin Half way Along it's Length. The Tighter the Better.

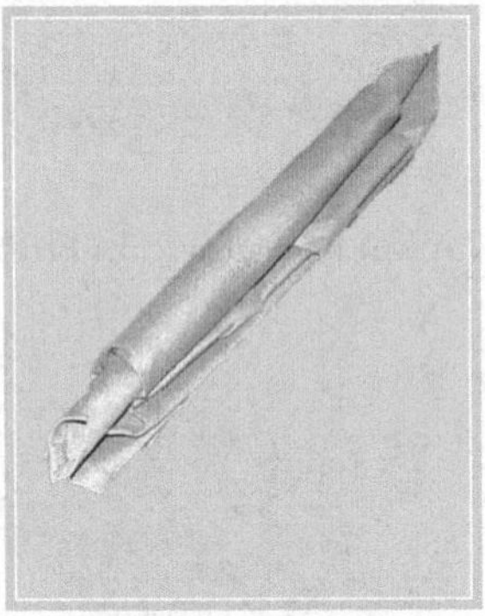

Accordion-fold the other Side of the Napkin and Gather it Together.

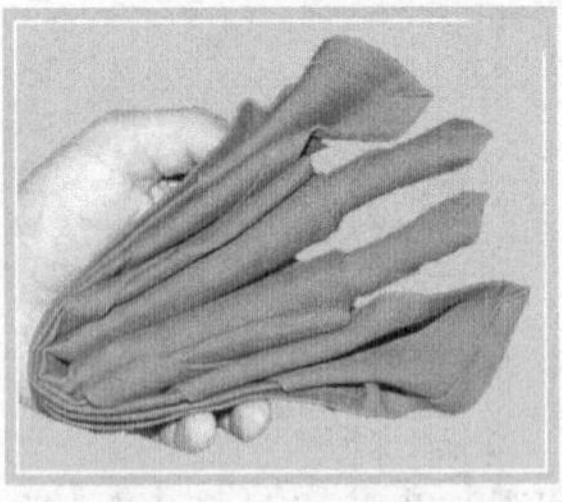

Fold the Napkin in Half with the Roll in the Middle.

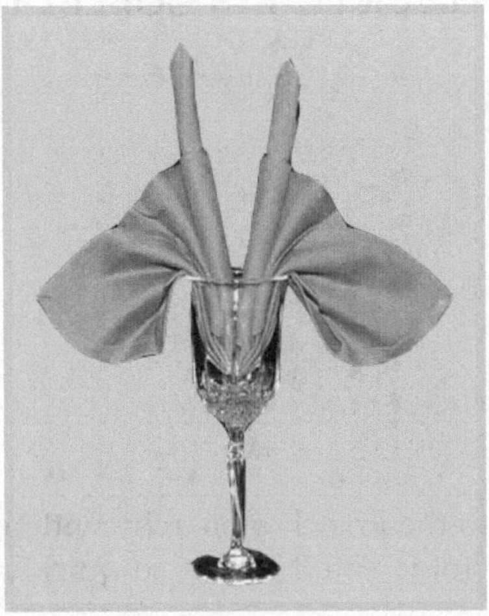

Place it into your Goblet of Choice and you're Done! Mmmmmm, nothing Like a Crappy Blue Napkin to Demonstrate with, eh? Larger ones Look much Nicer.

THE GOBLET FAN FOLD

The goblet fan is one of the easiest goblet folds to accomplish. There is no ironing needed and almost any napkin will do.

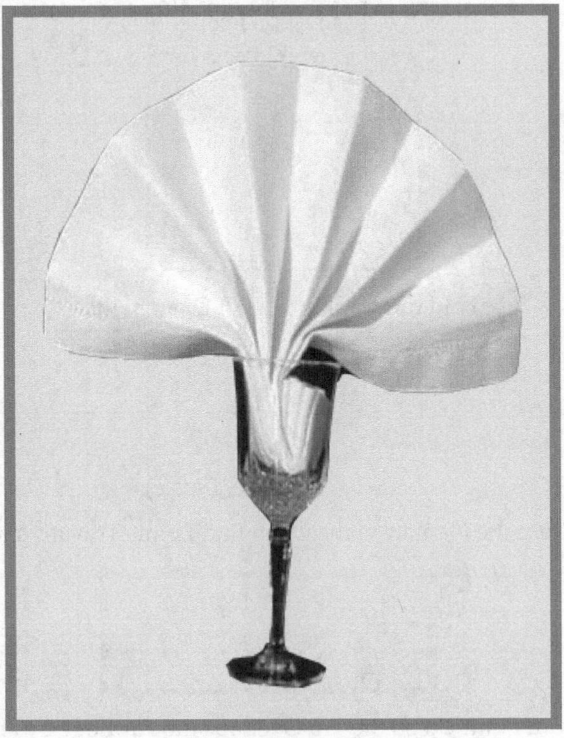

THE FLEUR DE LYS GOBLET FOLD

Pay your respects to the French monarchy with a Fleur de Lys in a cup. This is a fast and easy fold. You'll fold it so quickly you won't remember doing it!

Lay the Napkin Face-down in Front of You.

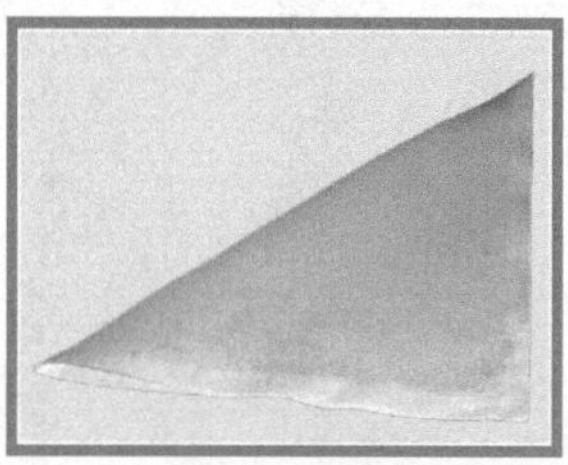

Fold the Napkin in Half Diagonally.

Orient the Napkin so the Open End Points Toward You.

Fold the Bottom Point Up so the Tip Overlaps the Far Edge by about an Inch.

Accordion Fold the Entire Napkin from Left to Right.

Firmly Grasp the Base and Insert it into a Glass or a Napkin Ring and you're Proudly Displaying a Fleur de Lys for each of your Dinner Guests.

THE LILY GOBLET FOLD

Here is an elegant goblet fold similar to the bird of paradise. A slightly starched or stiff napkin works best for this one and an iron can make the work much easier to do.

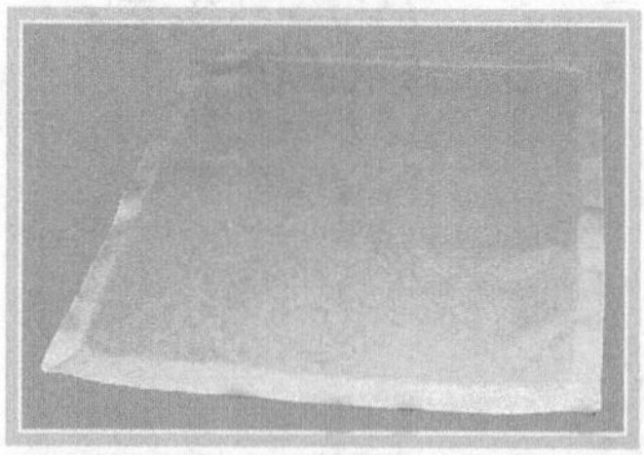

Lay the Napkin Face-down in Front of You.

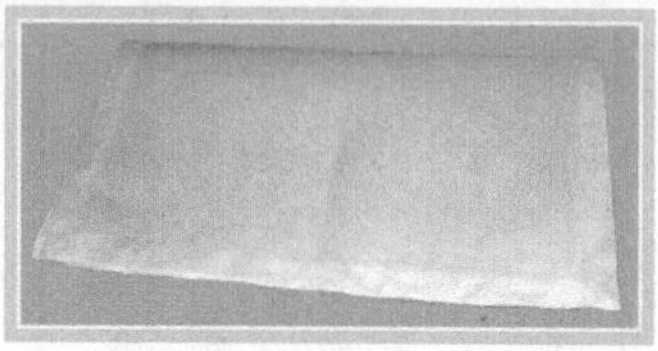

Fold the Napkin in Half and Orient the Open End Toward You.

Fold the Napkin into Quarters.

Accordion-fold the Entire Napkin from Corner to Corner, Keeping the Open Ends at the Top.

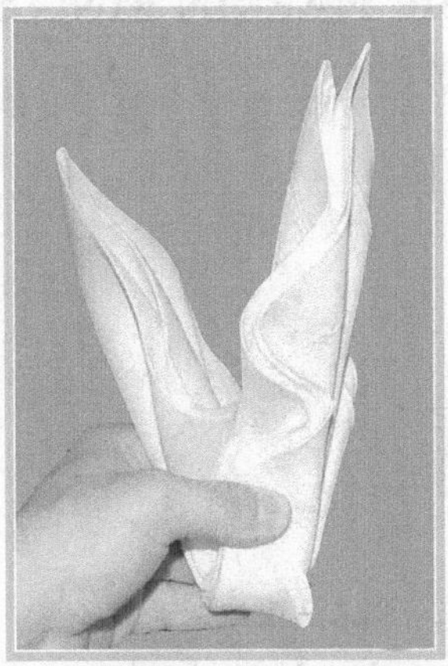

Fold the Napkin in Half as Shown.

Tuck the Napkin into the Glass of Your Choice.

Using your Fingers, gently Pull Apart the Loose Corners Sticking up so they are Evenly Distributed. If you're Flaps don't want to Stay where You put them, then Ironing a Little Starch into the Napkin will Help.

THE BASIC NAPKIN RING STUFFER

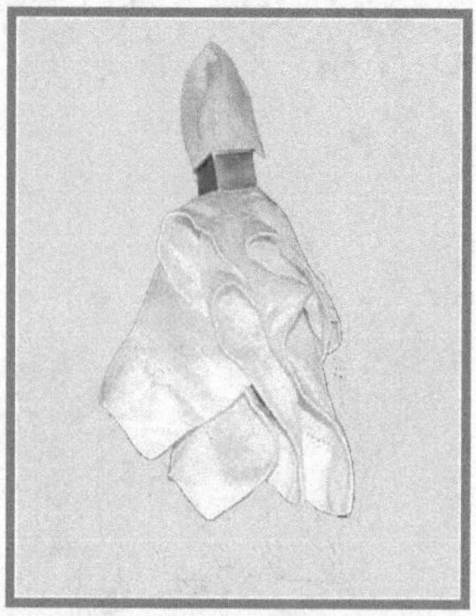

It's fast, easy, and looks nice. You don't need a wrinkle free napkin and there is no pressing or ironing involved. If you want easy then nothing beats this one - the only catch is that you need napkin rings.

Lay the Napkin Face-up in Front of You.

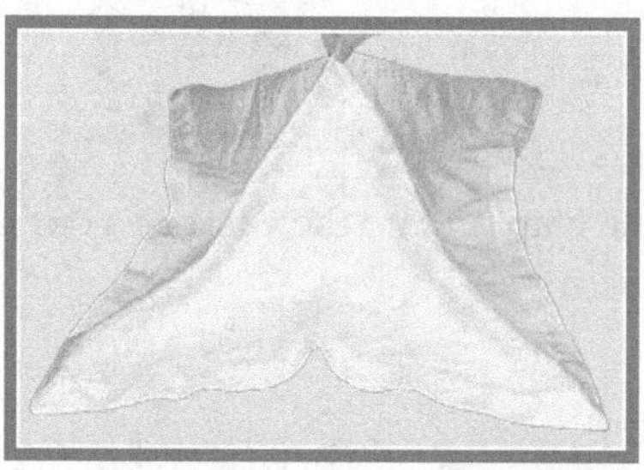

Pick it Up from the very Center.

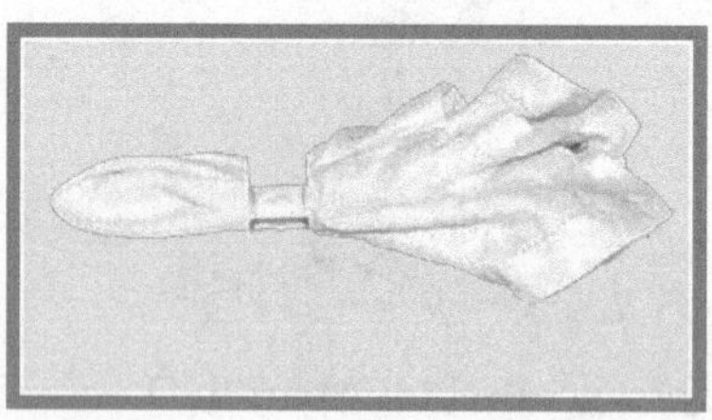

Stuff it Through a Napkin Ring Center-first.
Careful now, you don't want to Strain Yourself.

THE NAPKIN RING FAN FOLD

Fan folds are always a simple way of nicely presenting your napkins. This one uses a napkin ring to hold the base.

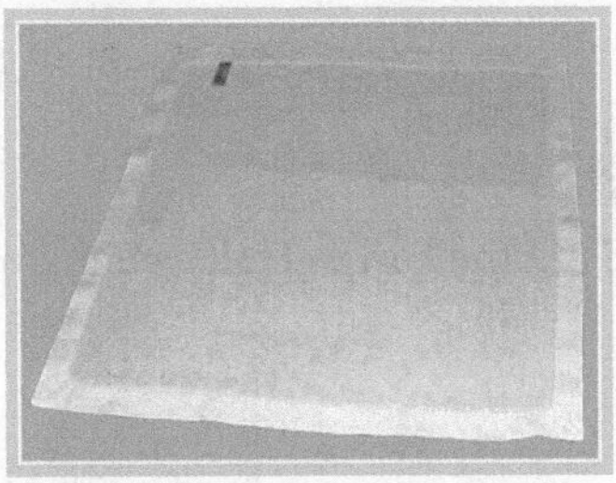

Lay the Napkin Face-down in Front of You.

Fold the Napkin in Half and the Re-open it, Leaving a Crease in the Center.

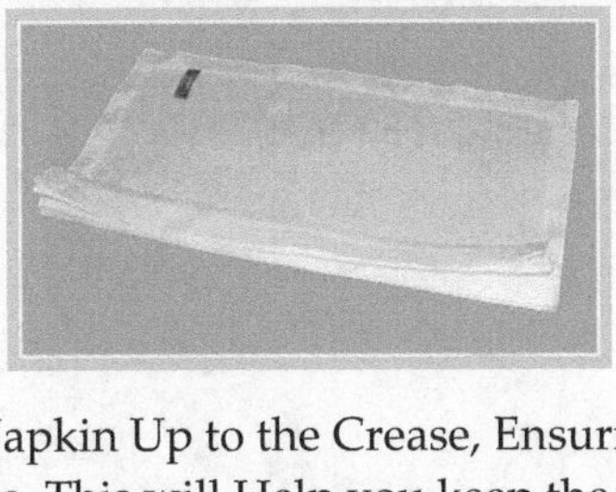

Accordion-fold the Napkin Up to the Crease, Ensuring that the Final Fold Rests Nicely on the Crease. This will Help you keep the Ends of the Fan Uniform.

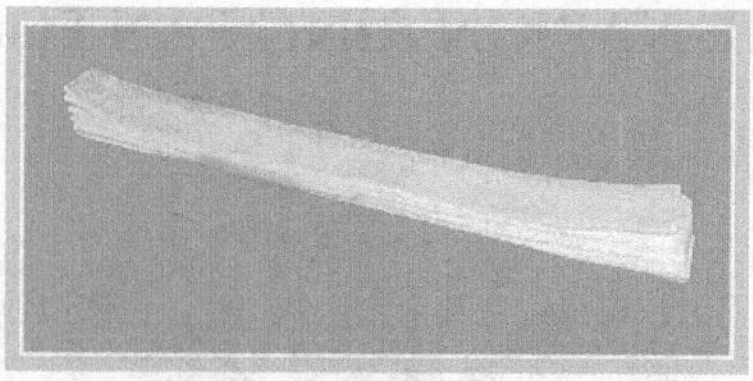

Finish Accordion-folding the Napkin.

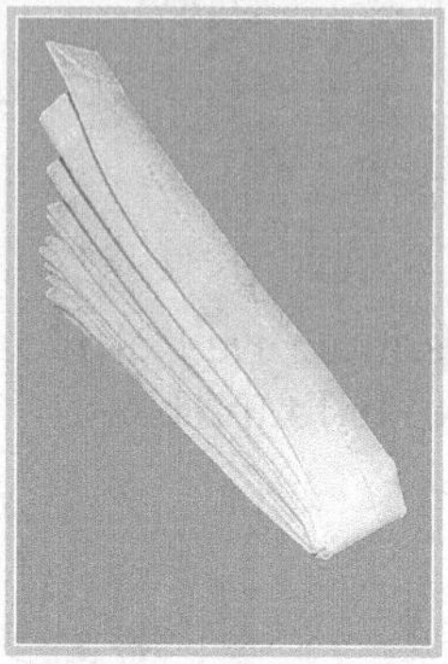

Fold the Fan in Half as Shown.

Insert the Folded End into a Napkin Ring. It's a Fan Suitable for a Samurai. A Hungry Samura

THE TWIN CANDLE NAPKIN ROLL

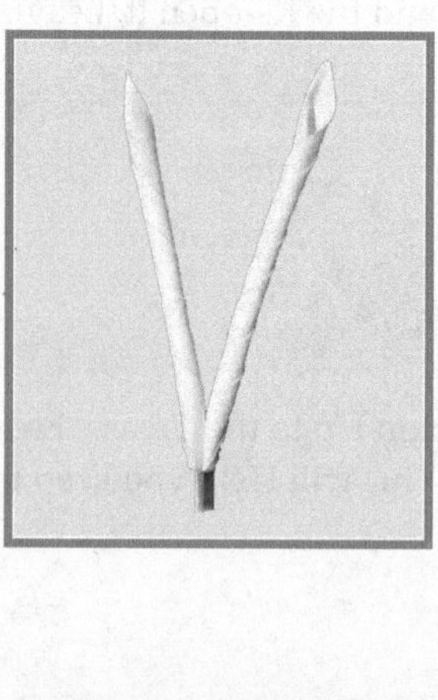

This napkin roll is easy and elegant. Use it to spruce up a table with a flat landscape. This fold requires no ironing, starching, or pressing. Stiff material will help larger napkins stand up without sagging.

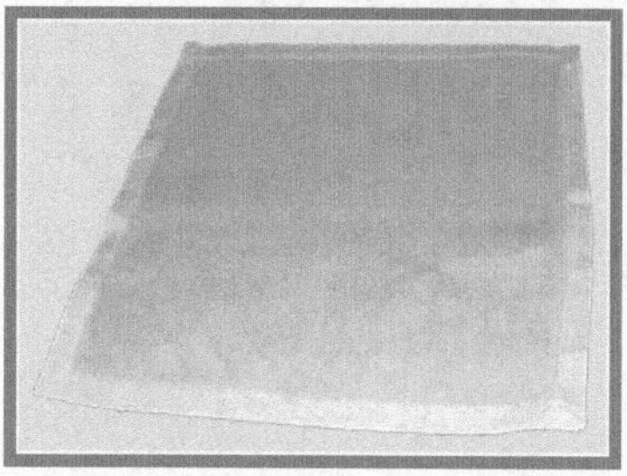

Lay the Napkin Face-down in Front of You.

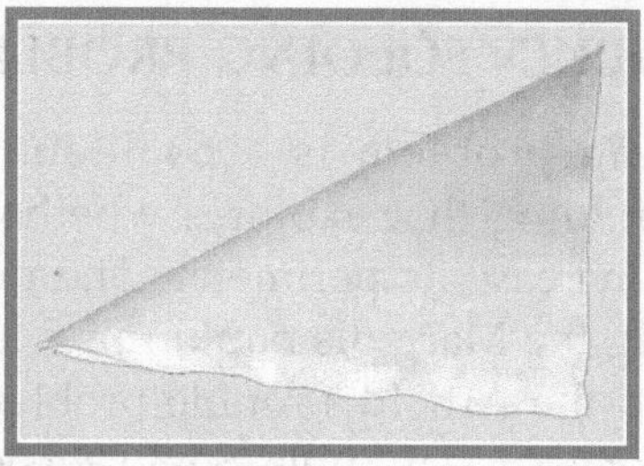

Fold the Napkin in Half Diagonally.

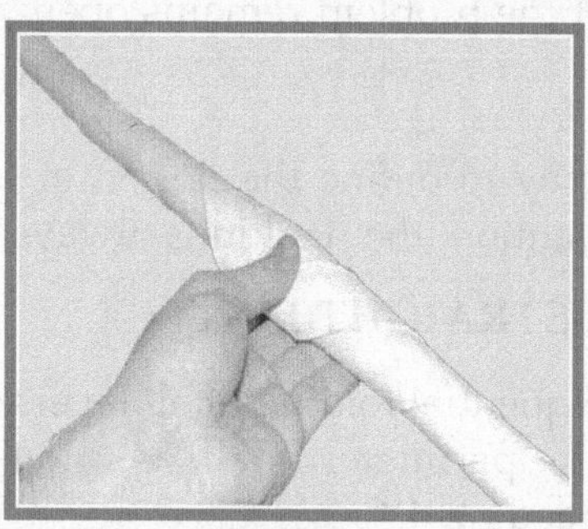

Roll the Napkin from the Long Side to the Point as Tightly as You can. A Tighter Roll will Create a Stiffer Candle in the End Product.

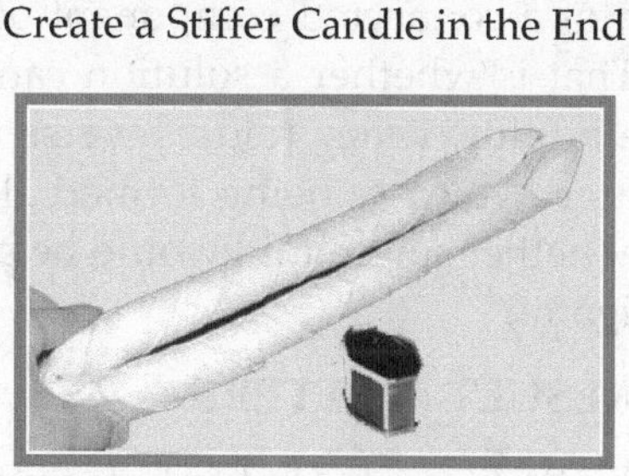

Fold the Candle Roll in Half.

Stick it in Your Napkin Ring and Stand it up on the Table.
Now Sit back and Laugh as Everyone Knocks them Over!

NAPKIN FOLDING PROBLEM

The napkin folding problem is a problem in geometry and the mathematics of paper folding that explores whether folding a square or a rectangularnapkin can increase its perimeter. The problem is known under several names, including the Margulis napkin problem, suggesting it is due to GrigoryMargulis, and the Arnold's rouble problem referring to Vladimir Arnold and the folding of a Russian ruble. Some versions of the problem were solved by Robert J. Lang, Svetlana Krat, Alexey S. Tarasov, and Ivan Yaschenko. One form of the problem remains open.

FORMULATIONS

There are several way to define the notion of folding, giving different interpretations. By convention, the napkin is always a unit square.

FOLDING ALONG A STRAIGHT LINE

One can consider sequential folding of all layers along a line. In this case it can be shown that the perimeter is always non-increasing under such foldings, thus never exceeding 4.

It is still unknown if there is a solution using a sequence of foldings, such that each is a reflection of a connected component of folded napkin on one side of a straight line.That is whether a solution can be folded using some combination of mountain folds, valley folds, reverse folds, and/or sink folds (with all folds in the latter two cases being formed along a single line). Also unknown, of course, is whether such a fold would be possible using the more-restrictive pureland origami.

WHERE ONLY THE RESULT MATTERS

One can ask whether there exists a folded planar napkin (without regard as to how it was folded into that shape). Robert J. Lang showed in 1997 that several classical origami constructions give rise to an easy solution. In fact, Lang showed that the perimeter can be made as large as desired by making the construction more complicated. However his constructions are not rigid origami because of their use of sink folds and related forms; although no stretching is needed in sink and unsink folds, it is necessary to curve facets and/or sweep one or more creases continuously through the paper in intermediate steps before obtaining a flat result.

In 1998, I. Yaschenko constructed a 3D folding with projection onto a plane which has a bigger perimeter. This indicated to mathematicians that there was probably a flat folded solution to the problem. The same conclusion was made by Svetlana Krat. Her approach is different, she gives very simple construction of a "rumpling" which increase perimeter and then proves that any "rumpling" can be arbitrary well approximated by a "folding". In essence she shows that the precise details of the how to do the folds don't matter much if stretching is allowed in intermediate steps.

FOLDING WITHOUT STRETCHING

One can ask for a realizable construction within the constraints of rigid origami where the napkin is never stretched whilst being folded. In 2004 A. Tarasov showed that that such constructions can indeed be obtained. This can be considered a complete solution to the original problem.

SOLUTIONS

LANG'S SOLUTIONS

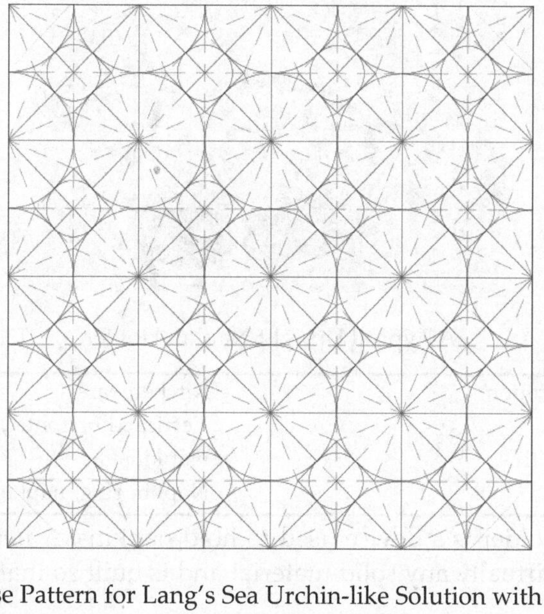

Crease Pattern for Lang's Sea Urchin-like Solution with $N = 5$

Lang devised two different solutions. Both involved sinking flaps and so were not rigid origami. The simplest was based on the origami bird base and gave a solution with a perimeter of about 4.12 compared to the original perimeter of 4.

The second solution can be used to make a figure with a perimeter as large as desired. He divides the square into a large number of smaller squares and employs the 'sea urchin' type origami construction described in his 1990 book, *Origami Sea Life*. The crease pattern shown is the $n = 5$ case and can be used to produce a flat figure with 25 flaps, one for each of the large circles, and sinking is used to thin them. When very thin the 25 arms will give a 25 pointed star with a small center and a perimeter approaching $N/(N-1)$. In the case of $N = 5$ this is about 6.25, and the total length goes up approximately as N.

HISTORY

Arnold states in his book that he formulated the problem in 1956, but the formulation was left intentionally vague. He called it 'the rumpled rouble problem', and it was the first of many interesting problems he set at seminars in Moscow over 40 years. In the West, it became known as Margulis napkin problem after Jim Propp'snewsgroup posting in 1996. Despite attention, it received folklore status and its origin is often referred as "unknown".

NAPKIN HOLDER

A Typical Upright Napkin Holder

Classification	Kitchenware
Types	Vertical, horizontal. Plastic, metal.
Used with	Napkins
Related	Napkin ring, napkin dispenser

A napkin holder is a device used to hold napkins. A napkin holder can be made from virtually any solid material and is built so that the napkins do not slip from its hold, either by way of sandwiching them between two surfaces, or simply enclosing them on their sides in a horizontal design. Napkin holders range in price and styles from wooden designs to wrought iron or ceramic styles and many others. One iteration of the napkin holder, better known as a napkin dispenser, offers additional functionality with its design: folded napkins are enclosed in a snug metal casing, allowing users to retrieve a single napkin each time they reach into the container; this particular device is usually found in restaurants, diners, and other public eateries, while its simpler—often more aesthetically pleasing—counterpart, the holder, is common to households and classrooms.

FUNCTION

The Outward Pressure from a Full Load of Napkins helps keep them between the Two Outer Walls of the Holder

Napkin holders, as their name implies, are tools in which napkins are held and stored, most often sandwiched between two surfaces. Among basic holders, there are several kinds, those principally belonging in two categories; vertical and horizontal. While their main function is to hold napkins, napkin holders can also serve to complement decorations, either internally or externally. In addition, the creation of napkin holders by amateur woodsmiths and metalworkers serves as a fairly easy project, and has been touted by do it yourself magazines such as *Popular Mechanics* and *Popular Science*. Even simpler designs have been sold as projects that children can do, the napkin holders in these being made of paper plates and yarn. Napkin holders are used in many locations, ranging from classrooms to eateries.

HISTORY

The popularity of napkin holders corresponded with the invention (and popularization) of the paper napkin by the Scott Paper Company in 1930, although cloth napkins had existed–often as handkerchiefs–since Greek and

Roman times. Wrought iron napkin holders and rings were a common part of a blacksmith's repertoire during the 19th century as well as other holders and household items. Mechanically made napkin holders have replaced many of those made by hand, as blacksmithing is now primarily an art form, as opposed to a means of creation of household utility items.

VINTAGE NAPKIN HOLDERS

A Non-plastic Vintage Napkin Holder, with the Design of an Owl

Vintage napkin holders were an integral part of kitchens during the 1950s, 60s, and 70s. Made in large quantities, these napkin holders were often made of brightly colored plastic, either transparent or solid. Other non-plastic napkin holders were also produced, but in smaller quantities.

DESIGN

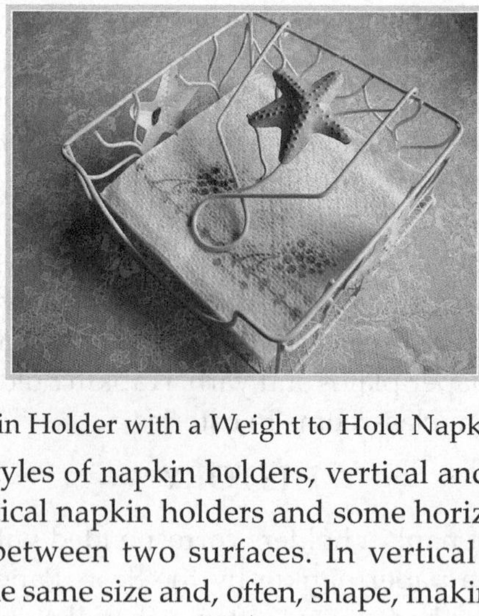

A Horizontal Napkin Holder with a Weight to Hold Napkins Down and Edges

The two main styles of napkin holders, vertical and horizontal, function in similar ways. Vertical napkin holders and some horizontal napkin holders sandwich napkins between two surfaces. In vertical napkin holders, the surfaces tend to be the same size and, often, shape, making the napkin holders symmetrical.

In vertical holders that sandwich, however, the bottom is usually around the size of a conventional paper napkin, about 7.25 inches (184 mm) by 7.75 inches (197 mm) while the top side can be any virtually any shape, as it acts as a paperweight. Within this style, there is variation. Some napkin holders have edges as the weight alone could not keep the napkins down, while others rely entirely on their weight to secure the napkins. Another type of horizontal holder lacks a weight altogether, and is simply a base and four edges. The design of napkin holders is largely based upon preconditions of the space or spaces that the napkin holder will occupy. For example, if limited table space is available, a vertical design may be more practical. However, if conserving space is not an issue, a horizontal napkin holder is advantageous, as well as slightly easier for the subject to access. Color, style, and durability are also based on the environment and the architectural styles of the selected room or rooms. Lastly, price and budget are determining factors of a napkin holder's design, which usually range between 10 and 50 US dollars.

CONSTRUCTION

Metal and Combination Metal/wood Napkin Holders

While the basic design of napkin holders is consistent, the tools and construction materials will vary based on what material the maker is using.

WOOD

While less common than metal or wrought iron napkin holders, wooden napkin holders are often made as art projects, due to the relative ease of making them, and easy access to the materials needed.

Common materials used in wooden napkin holder construction include:

- Hardwood or plywood for extra strength and durability.
- Brad nails.
- Wood glue.

METAL

Metal napkin holders may be made from wrought iron, wire, or sheet metal.

NAPKIN DISPENSERS

A Wide Napkin Dispenser

The variant of the napkin holder, the napkin dispenser, is most often seen as a part of restaurant equipment. Napkin dispensers serve in restaurants not only because they are easy to access, but more importantly because they provide diners with autonomy from the restaurant staff, so if a spill or other accident occurs, the diners can clean it up on their own, which frees the burden from waiters and other busy members of the staff.

FLOWER BUQUET

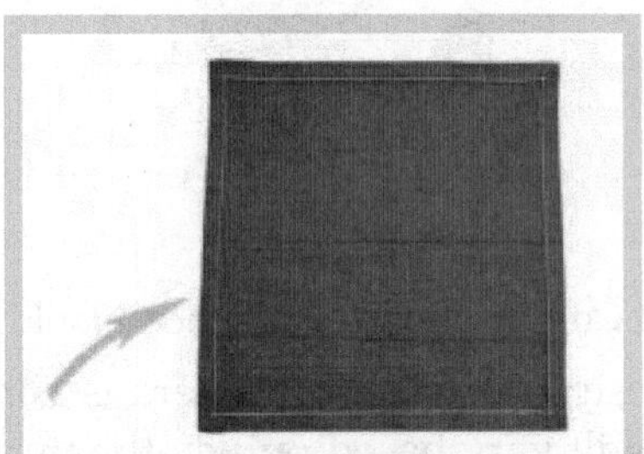

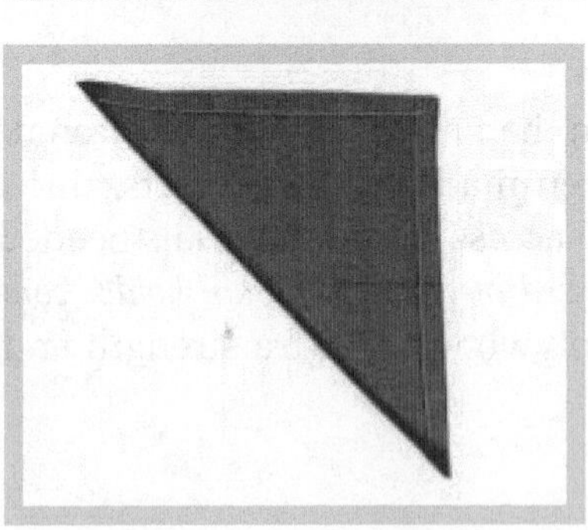

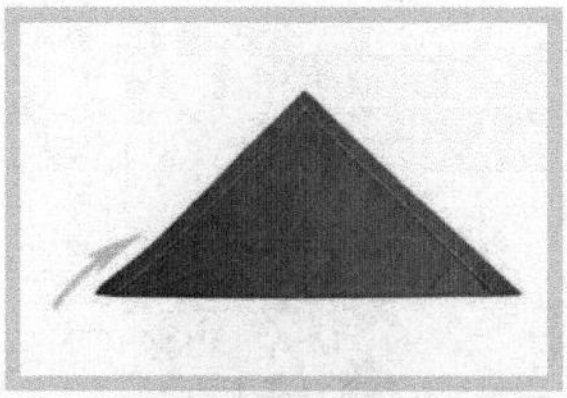

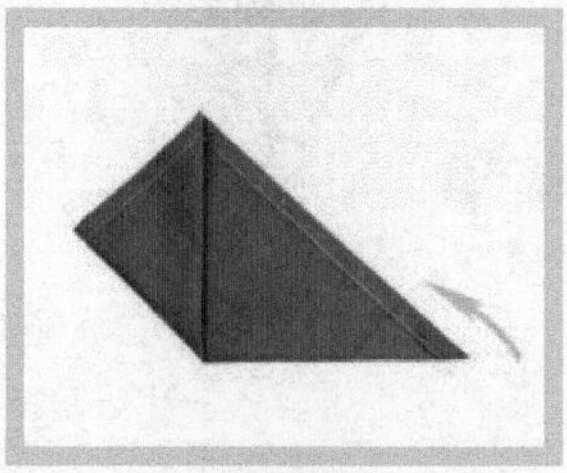

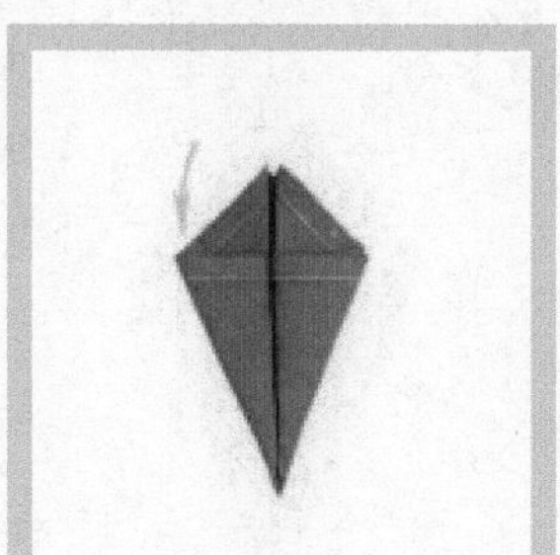

NAPKIN FOLDING: FLOWER BUQUET - FOLDING INSTRUCTIONS

- Place the open napkin in front of you
- Fold the bottom left corner of the napkin to the top right corner
- Place the napkin in front of you so that you have the closed side of the napkin on the bottom side.
- Fold the right corner up to the edge of the top.
- Now fold the left corner up to the top.
- Fold the left corner to the middle. You have a triangle in front of you which is upside down.
- Fold the right corner to the middle.
- Swing open the left and the right (only the upper part of the napkin) down.
- Ready is your flower buquet napkin fold.

WATER LILY

How to fold a napkin into a water lily?

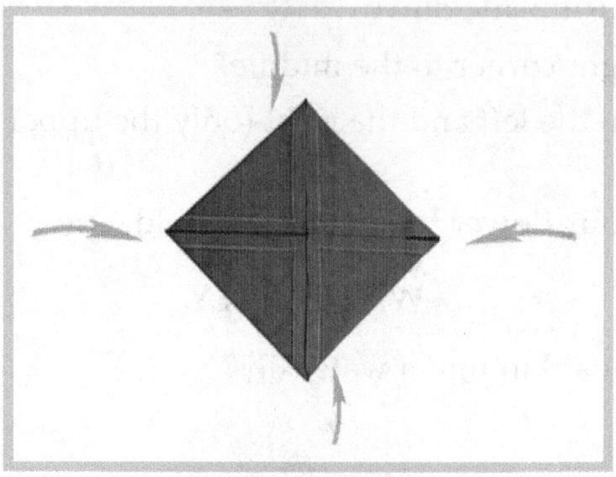

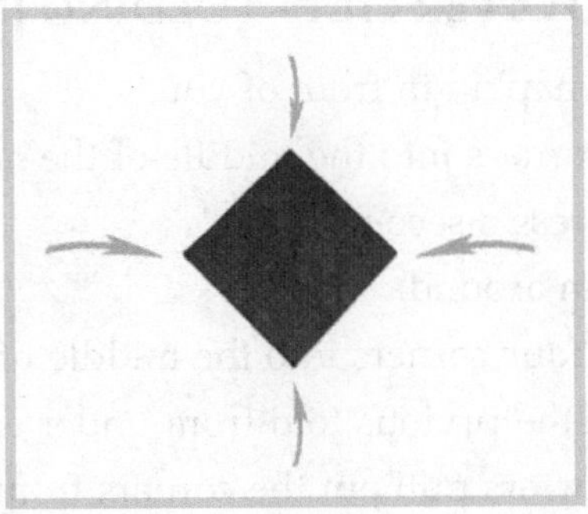

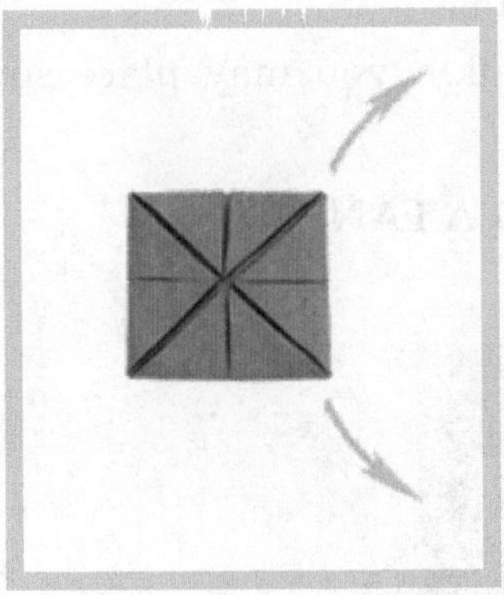

NAPKIN FOLDING: WATER LILY - FOLDING INSTRUCTIONS

- Place the open napkin in front of you
- Fold the four corners into the middle of the napkin
- Repeat the process a second time.
- Turn the napkin around.
- Fold again the four corners into the middle of the napkin.
- Pull gently out the prvious fold from under each corner..
- Between the flowers pull out the corners from underneath.
- The stronger you fold the edges the better.
- In the middle of the water lily napkin you may place some decoration.

FOLD A NAPKIN INTO A FAN

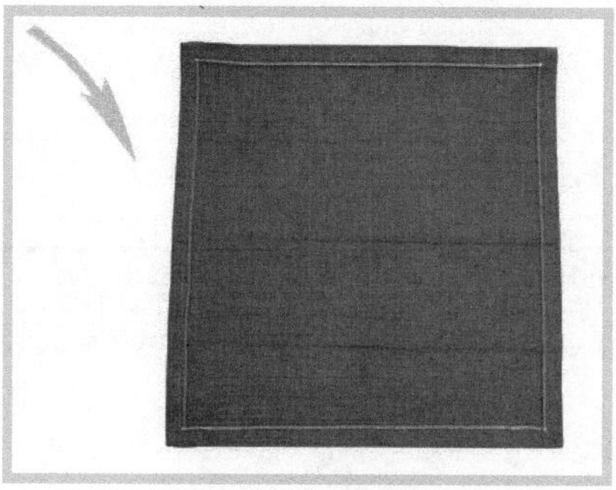

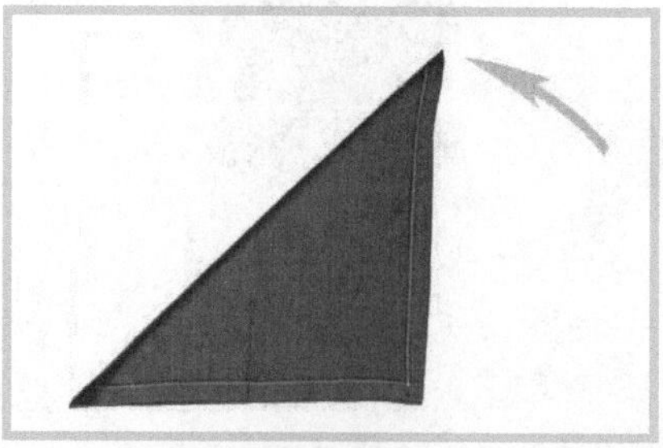

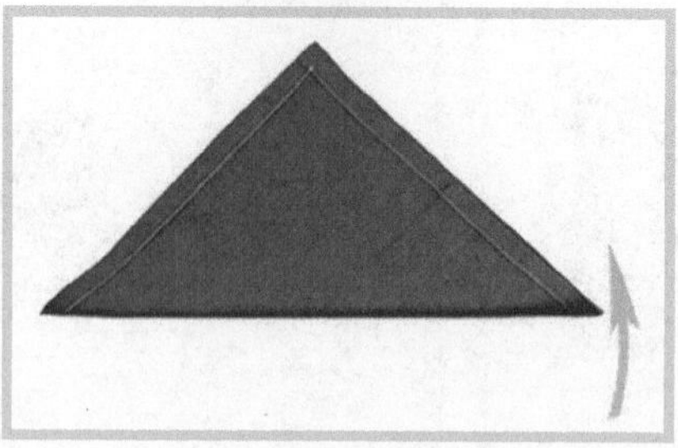

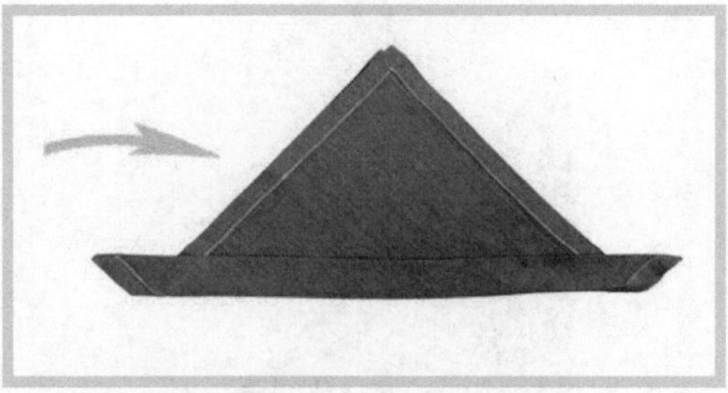

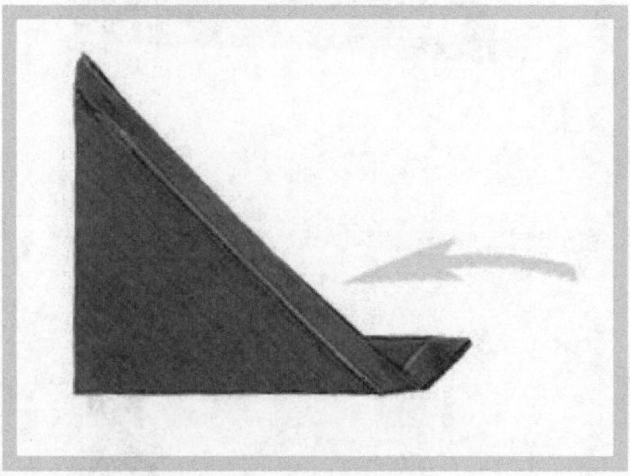

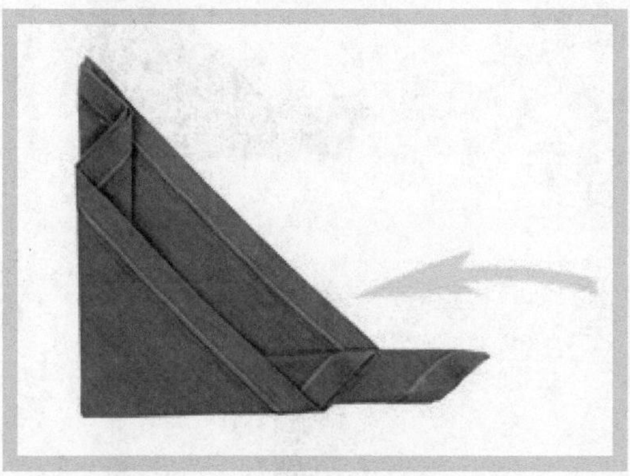

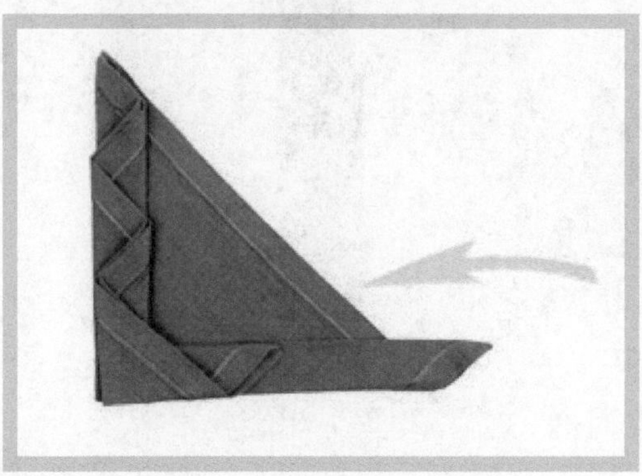

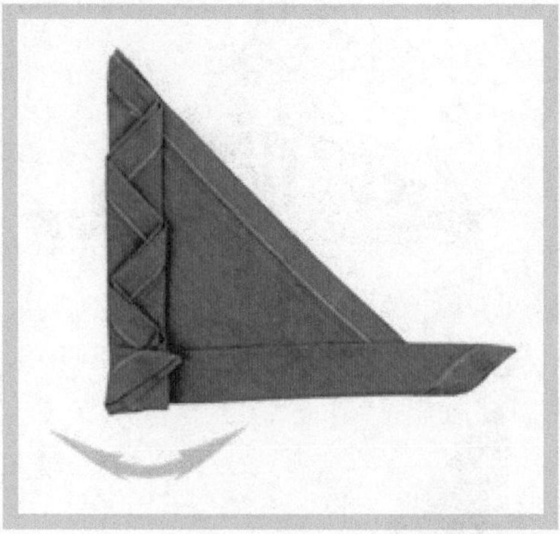

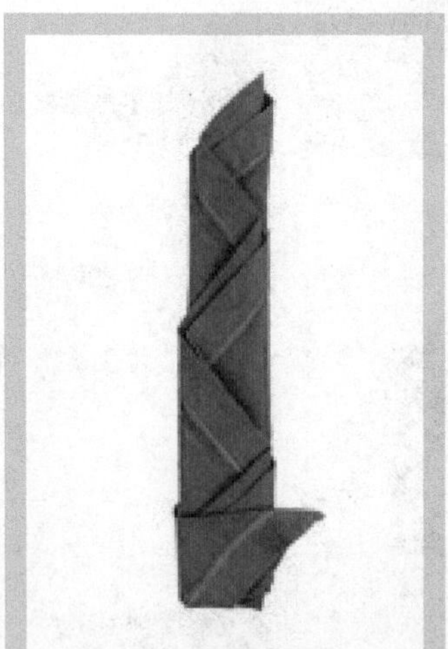

NAPKIN FOLDING: FAN – FOLDING INSTRUCTIONS

- Place the open napkin in front of you
- Fold the bottom left corner of the napkin to the top right corner
- Place the napkin in front of you so that you have the closed side of the napkin on the bottom side.
- Fold the bottom side of the napkin about 4 cm up.
- Start with one side to fold a fan vertical in 3 cm wide stripes. Turn around and fold again until the fan is ready.
- Fix the base with a napkin ring or a fork.

FOLDING A NAPKIN WITH A CLASSIC 3 POINT FOLD

The three point napkin fold is very classic yet extremely quick to fold. Because the three point fold leaves the napkin mostly open, this fold is ideal for showing off any delicate embroidery that may be stitched on your napkin. This fold works well with all of our cotton and linen dinner napkins. For best folding results, it may help to first iron the napkins thoroughly with starch to ensure a more rigid napkin.

Iron the Napkin Flat.

Fold the Napkin in Half Diagonally.

Fold the Right Corner of the Napkin Over to the Left as Shown in the Picture

Fold the Right Side of the Napkin Towards the Left Until the Desired Necktie sh

FOLDING A NAPKIN INTO A BISHOPS HAT

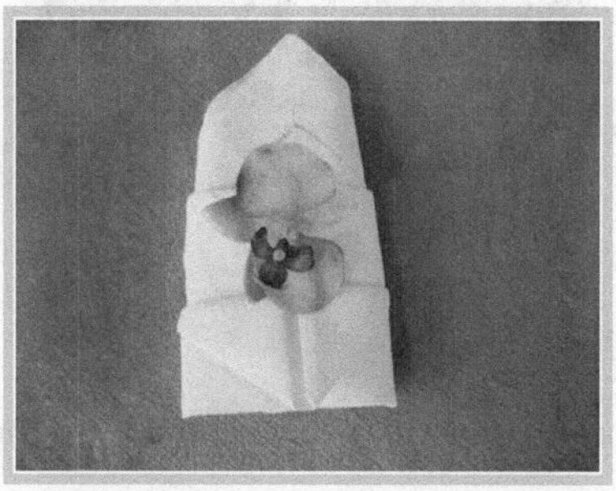

The Bishops Hat napkin fold is a very classic fold used in many restaurants. This fold looks great lying down or standing up on the place setting and works well with most of our cotton and linen dinner napkins. For best folding results, it may help to first iron the napkins thoroughly with starch to ensure a more rigid napkin.

Iron the Napkin Flat.

Fold the Napkin in Half Diagonally.

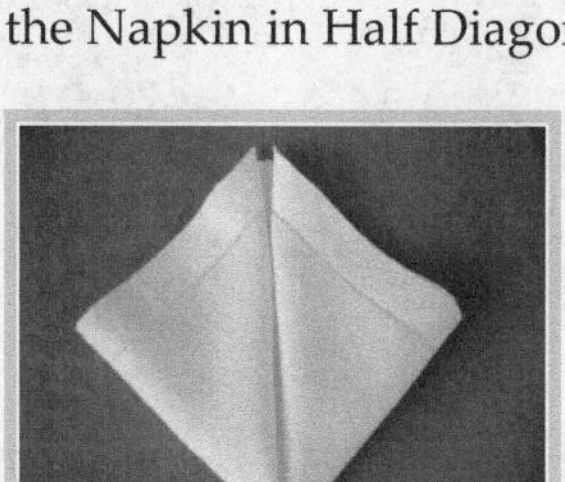

Fold the Bottom Right and Left Corners Up to the Top Corner.

Fold the Bottom Corner 3/4 of the Way Up to the Top Corner.

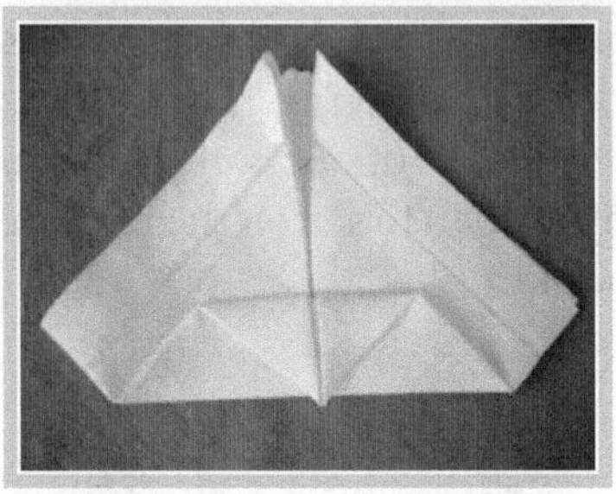

Fold the Front Top Corner Down Flush with the Bottom as Shown.

Fold the Two Top Flaps Down and Tuck the
Edges Under the Front Fold as Shown.

Turn the Napkin Over and Fold the Left Hand Side Over One-third of the Way.

Fold the Right Hand Side Over and Tuck the Napkin Underneath the Left Hand Fold

Flip the Napkin Over and You are Done. Looks Great Standing Up or Lying on the Table!

FOLDING A NAPKIN FOR A BUFFET

If you are looking for a fold that is both simple and functional, the buffet style napkin fold will work for you. Usually used with more casual dining occasions, the buffet napkin fold will frame your silverware nicely into an elegant and compact place setting. This fold works well with most of our cotton and linen dinner napkins. For best folding results, it may help to first iron the napkins thoroughly with starch to ensure a more rigid napkin.

Iron the Napkin Flat.

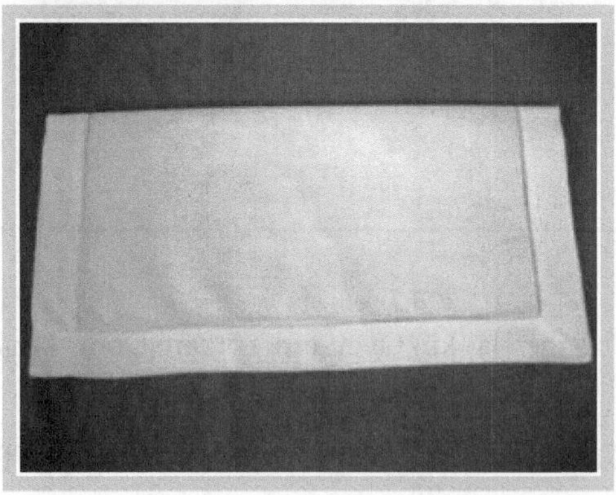

Fold the Napkin in Half and Orient the Open End toward You.

Fold the Napkin into Quarters.

Orient the Napkin so the Open Corner is Facing Away and to the Right. Fold the Top-most Layer of Napkin Diagonally Down to the Center and Press it flat.

Roll the Same Layer Down as Shown in the Picture.

Take the Next Layer Corner and Fold it to Meet the First Fold

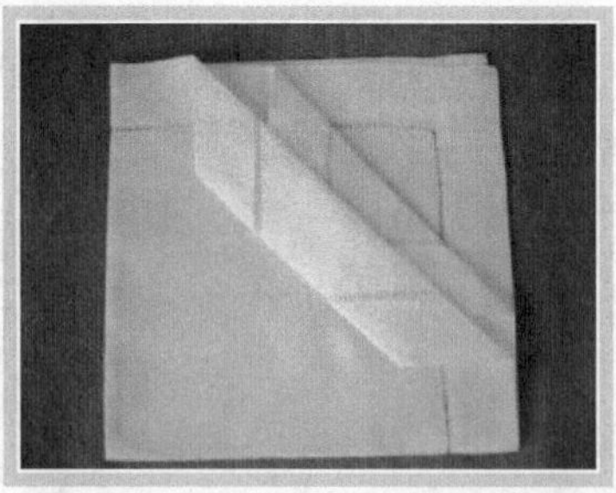

Roll the Same Layer Down and Tuck Underneath the First Layer

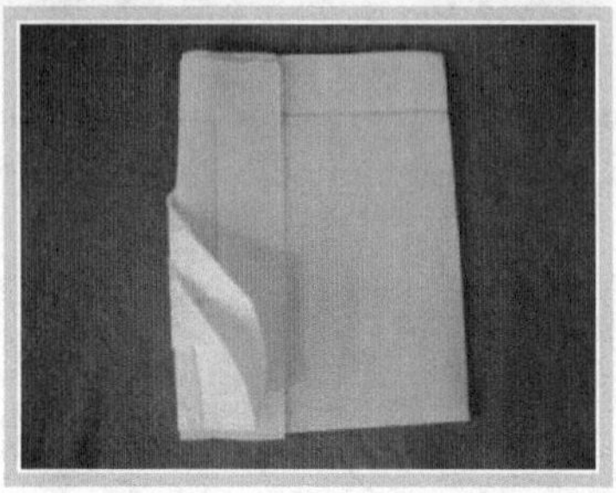

Turn the Napkin Over. Fold the Left Side back about
1/3 of the Way and Press it Down

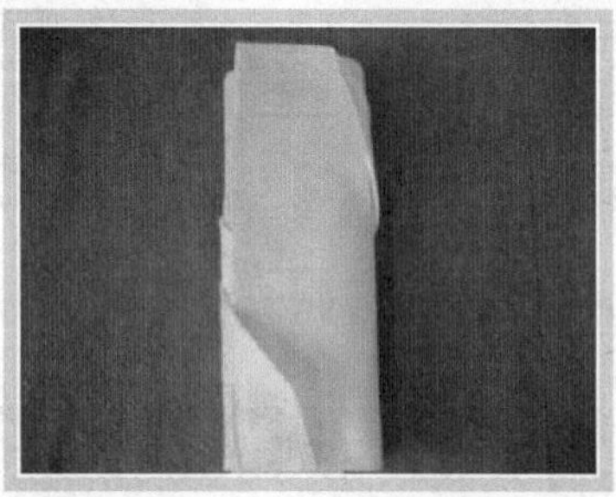

Fold the Right Side Cack to Meet the Left hand Fold
and Tuck Underneath the Flap. Press with an Iron.

Flip it Over and Insert the Silverware

FOLDING A NAPKIN INTO A CROWN

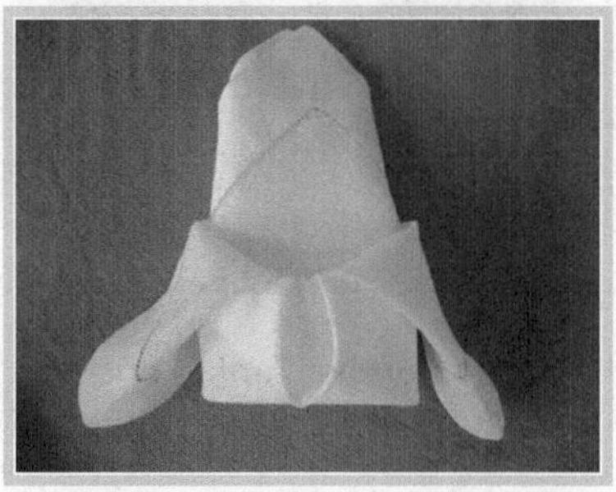

The crown fold is very similar to the bishops hat fold in that it looks great lying down or standing up. For this fold in particular, it is especially important to make sure the napkin is rigid prior to folding the napkin. We suggest ironing the napkin with starch before you begin. This fold works well with several of our cotton and linen dinner napkins.

Iron the Napkin Flat.

Fold the Napkin in Half Diagonally.

Orient the Napkin so the Open Ends are Pointing Away from You. Bring the Left and Right Corners of the Napkin to the Point of the Triangle (Center of the Napkin)

Fold the Bottom of the Napkin one Half of the Way up and Press this Fold Down as Well.

Flip the Napkin Over and Fold the Left Hand Side Over one Third of the way. Fold the Right Side Over and Tuck the Napkin Underneath the Left Fold

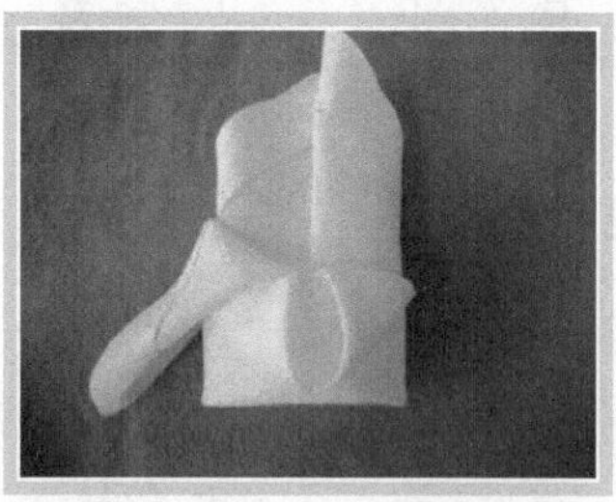

Flip the Napkin Over Again and Pull the Two Tips of the Napkins Down to form Petals

FOLDING A NAPKIN INTO A DIAMOND ARROW

The diamond arrow is one of the faster folds to make and does not require a rigid napkin. If you are in a crunch for time or are using old soft napkins, the diamond arrow fold is the one you want. This fold works well with several of our cotton and linen dinner napkins.

Iron the Napkin Flat.

Fold the Napkin in Half and Orient the Open End Toward You.

Fold the Napkin into Quarters.

Orient the Napkin so that the Open End is Facing Away from You.

Fold the Top-most Layer Almost all the Way Forward and Press it Down Flat.

Step6 Fold the next top-most layer of napkin forward almost as far as the previous one and press it down as well. Make sure the edges are even with the previous fold.

Fold the Next Layer Forward as You did the Two before It.

Finally, Fold the Last Layer Forward Similar to the Three before It.

Turn the Napkin Over

Now Fold Both Sides of the Napkin Under and in to
Create an even, Staggered Diamond Effect on the Napkin.

You now have a Beautiful Diamond Arrow Napkin Fold!

FOLDING A NAPKIN INTO A DIAMOND ENVELOPE

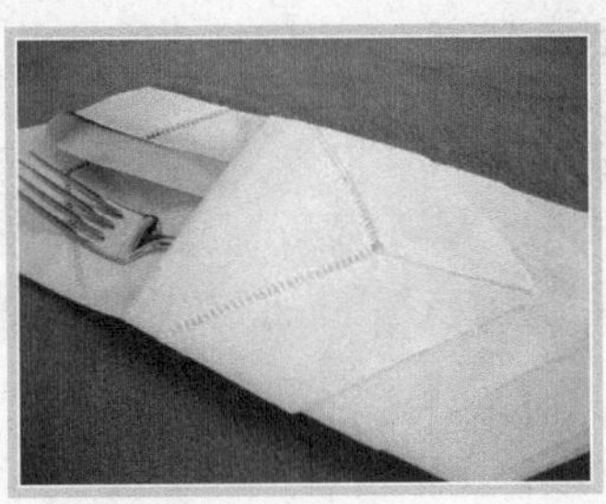

The diamond envelope fold is a more elegant variation of the simple napkin pocket but requires a bit more effort to fold. If are looking to use your dinner napkin to frame your silverware in a more formal setting, this fold is the one you want. This fold works well with several of our cotton and linen dinner napkins. For best folding results, it may help to first iron the napkins thoroughly with starch to ensure a more rigid napkin.

Iron the Napkin Flat.

Fold the Napkin in Half and Orient the Open End Toward You.

Fold the Napkin into Quarters.

Orient the Napkin so that the Open End is Facing Away from You.

Fold the Top-most Layer Almost all the Way Forward and Press it Down Flat.

Fold the Next Top-most Layer of Napkin Forward Almost as Far as the Previous One and Press it Down as Well. Make Sure the Edges are even with the Previous Fold.

Fold the Next Layer Forward as You did the Two before It.

Turn the Napkin Over and Fold the Right Side Back about 1/3 of the Way.

Fold the Left Side Back and Over the Right Side (about 1/3 of the way), Check for Symmetry and Press the Fold Down Well.

Flip the Napkin Over.

Insert Your Favorite Silverware into this Lovely Diamond Envelope Napkin!

HOW TO USE A NAPKIN RING

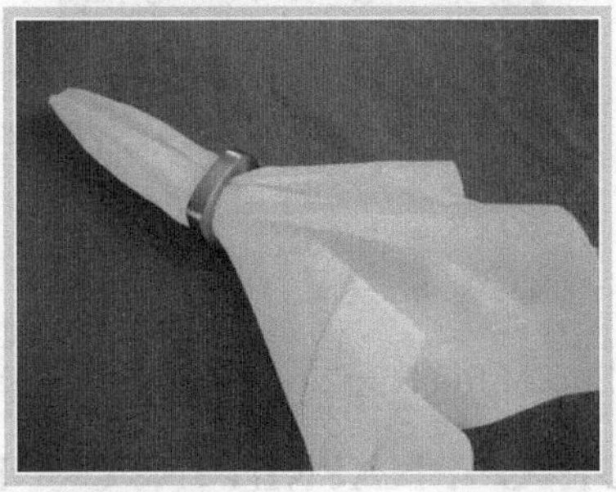

There is no quicker and easier way to present your napkin than with a traditional napkin ring. Accessorizing your napkin takes just seconds and makes for an elegant dining experience. Many of our cotton and linen dinner napkins will benefit from the use of a napkin ring.

Iron the Napkin Flat.

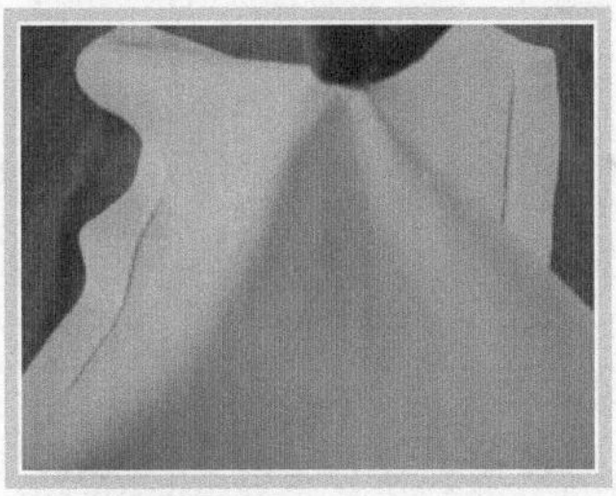

Pick the Napkin Up from the Very Center.

Spread Out the Napkin as Shown in the Picture

Insert the End of the Napkin Through the Napkin Ring.

FOLDING A NAPKIN INTO A ROSE

The rose napkin fold is one of our favorite folds. Despite coming across as intricate and fancy, the rose fold is not that difficult to do. This fold is perfect if you are looking to impress your guests or if you are looking for a fancy, ornate table setting. This fold works well with most of our cotton and linen dinner napkins. For best folding results, it may help to first iron the napkins thoroughly with starch to ensure a more rigid napkin.

Iron the Napkin Flat.

Fold all the Tips of the Napkins into the Center

Turn the Napkin Over

Fold the Outer Corners in so they Meet at the Center Once Again.

Once all of the Tips are Folded you are Left with a
Square About 1/4 the Size of the Unfolded Napkin.

Place Something Sturdy in the Center (A Drinking Glass Works Great!)

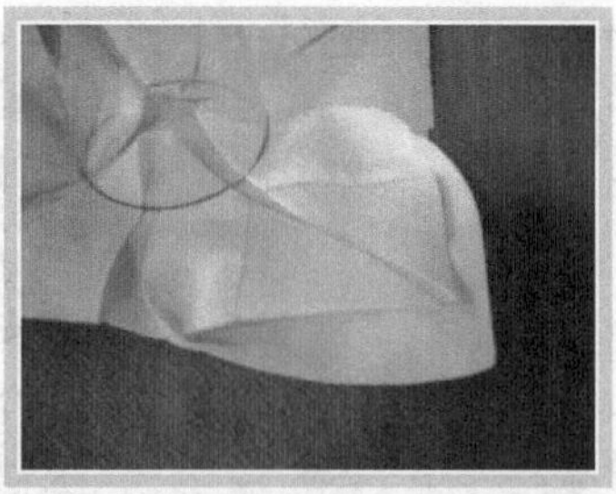

While Maintaining Downward Pressure in the Center of the Napkin, Reach Underneath each Corner and Pull out the Flaps to Create Petals.

Pull Out the Flaps on all Four Corners of the Napkin

Remove the Center Weight and Your Rose is Finished.

FOLDING A NAPKIN INTO A ROSEBUD

The rosebud is a simple yet elegant napkin fold. It works well standing up or lying down on the place setting and provides a sophisticated dining experience. This fold works well with many of our cotton and linen dinner napkins. For best folding results, you should first iron the napkins thoroughly with starch to ensure a more rigid napkin.

Iron the Napkin Flat.

Fold the Napkin in Half Diagonally.

Orient the Napkin so the Open End Points Away from You. Fold the Far-right Corner up Diagonally so that the Point Rests on Top of the Far Corner. The Edge of this New Flap should Lay Right on the Center Line.

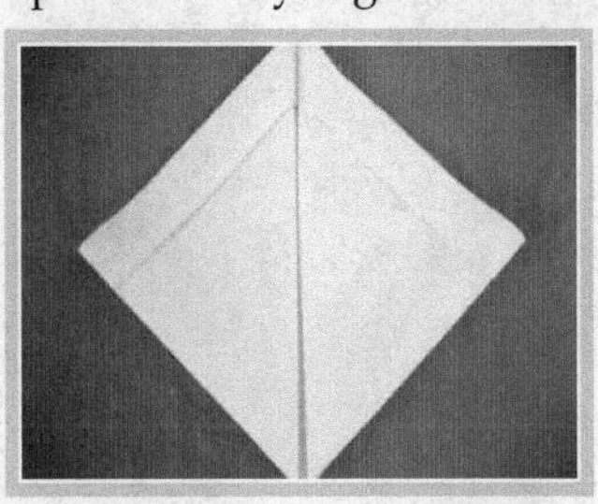

Repeat Step three on the other Side, Bringing the Left-most Corner up to Meet the Far Corner, Creating a Diamond Shape.

Flip the Napkin Over While Keeping the Open End Pointing Away from You.

Fold the Bottom of the Napkin up About 3/4's of the
Way as Shown and Press the Fold Down Well.

Flip the Napkin Over.

Curl the Left Side up Towards the Middle of the Napkin.

Curl the Right Side up so both the Left and Right Folds
Meet in the Middle and Tuck One into the other.

Flip the Napkin Over and You are Done. Looks
Great Standing Up or on the Table!

FOLDING A NAPKIN INTO A SILVERWARE ROLL

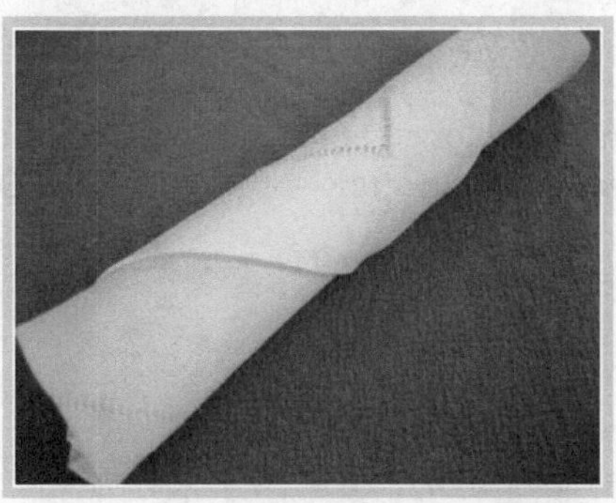

If you are holding a buffet line for a large group of people and you need your napkins and silverware to be as compact as possible, the silverware roll is the perfect solution. It takes seconds to fold, is extremely portable and keeps your silverware nice and clean. Any of our cotton and linen dinner napkins will work.

Iron the Napkin Flat.

Fold the Napkin in Half Diagonally.

Orient the Napkin so the Longest Side is Toward You, and then Place the Silverware on the Inner-edge of the Long Side.

Fold Both Sides in and Over the Silverware. Do not Crease.

The Napkin Should now Look Like the Picture on the Left.

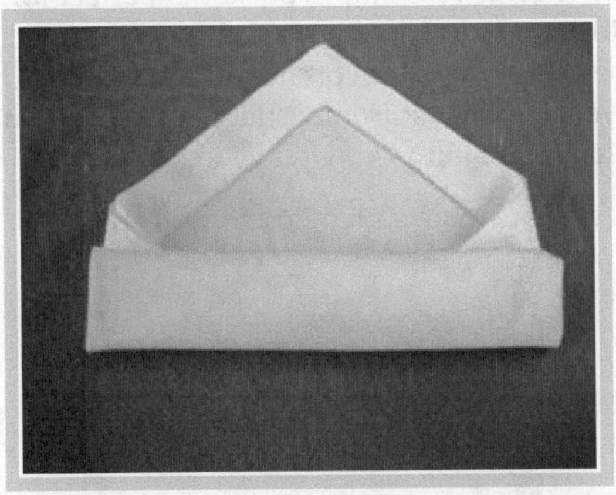

Tightly Roll the Silverware into the Napkin.

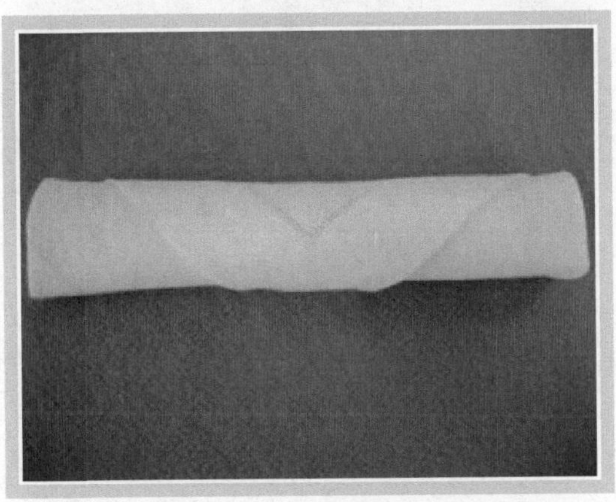

You have Created a Silverware Roll!

FOLDING A NAPKIN INTO A SIMPLE POCKET

Of all of our envelope style napkin folds, the simple pocket is by far the easiest and fastest to fold. The simple pocket is perfect for hosting a casual lunch or dinner for family or friends and is both functional and classic. This fold works well with many of our cotton and linen dinner napkins. For best folding results, we suggest first ironing the napkins thoroughly with starch to ensure a more rigid napkin.

Iron the Napkin Flat.

Fold the Napkin in Half and Orient the Open End toward You.

Fold the Napkin into Quarters.

Orient the Napkin so the Open Corner is Facing Away and to the Left. Fold the Top-most Layer of Napkin in Half Diagonally and Press it Down.

Turn the Napkin Over so that the Open Corner is now Facing Away and to the Right. Fold the Right-side Back About 1/3 of the Way and Press it Down.

Fold the Left-side Back also About 1/3 of the Way and Press

Flip the Napkin Over and Insert Your Silverware.

FOLDING A NAPKIN INTO A HEART

Planning a romantic dinner for a loved one? The heart napkin fold will show how much you care. This fold works extremely well with our hemstitched linen napkins.

Iron the Napkin Flat.

Fold the Napkin in Half

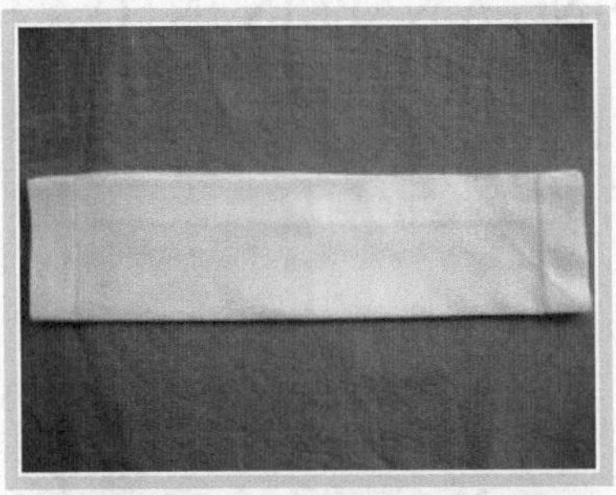

Fold the Napkin in Half Again

Fold the Right Hand Side Up Vertically. Repeat with the Left Side.

You will Now Shape the Heart by Tucking the Center Flaps Under

Finish by Tucking the Corner Flaps Underneath.

FOLDING A NAPKIN INTO A KNOT

Whoever thought that tying a napkin into a knot could be so elegant? The knotted napkin fold is easy to do but takes a bit of practice to get it right. This fold works extremely well with all lace edged and hemstitched napkins.

Iron the Napkin Flat.

Fold the Napkin in Half Diagonally.

Starting from the Long Edge, Fold the Napkin Edge Up one Inch

Continue Folding the Napkin Over Until it makes One Long Strip

Finish by Folding the Right Edge Over the Left and Loop to Create a Knot.

FOLDING A NAPKIN INTO A CAP

Throwing a party for the kids? These little hats made out of napkins are really popular with children. Ideal for birthday parties or informal dining occasions.

Iron the Napkin Flat

Fold the Napkin in Half

Fold the Left and Right Edges of the Rectangle to the Center

Take Hold of the Inner Left Edge of the Napkin and
Pull it Out to form a Tent Like Shape

Repeat with the Right Hand Side

Turn the Napkin Over and Fold Both Outer Edges to the Center

With One Layer, Fold Up the Bottom Edge Up Twice. Repeat with the Second Layer

Open Out the Napkin and have it Stand Up. Use Your
Finger and Dimple the Top of the Napkin Cap

FOLDING A NAPKIN INTO A TULIP

The tulip fold is an elegant napkin fold that works well with our hemstitched linen napkins. Ideal for fun and informal dining occasions!

Iron the Napkin Flat.

Fold the Napkin in Half Diagonally.

Fold Both Layers of the Top of the Triangle Down to the Bottom Edge

Take the Right Edge of the Triangle and Fold up at an Angle. Repeat on the Left Side.

Turn the Napkin Over and Finish by Taking the Lower Flaps and Folding them Up and at an Angle

FOLDING A NAPKIN INTO A SPEAR

If you want to show off your hemstitched linen napkins, the spear napkin fold makes a simple yet elegant statement to your guests. The sharp angles of the folds will bring out the texture and crispness of your linen napkins.

Iron the Napkin Flat.

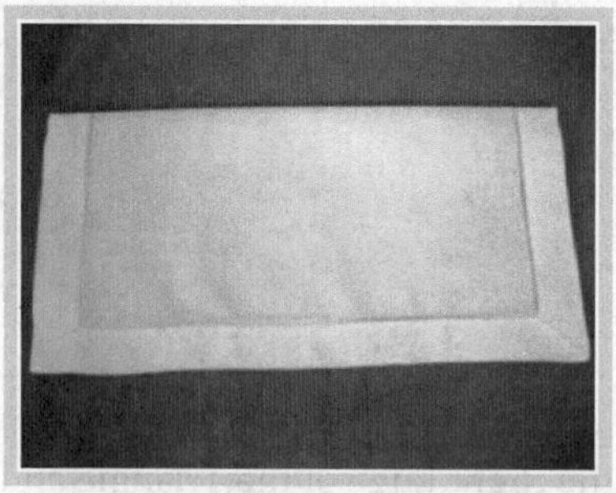

Fold the Napkin in Half and Orient the Open End toward You

Fold the Napkin into Quarters.

Orient the Napkin so that the Open End is Facing Away from You.

Fold the Top-most Layer Almost all the Way Forward and Press it Down Flat.

Fold the Next Top-most Layer of Napkin Forward Almost as Far as the Previous One and Press it Down as Well. Make Sure the Edges are Even with the Previous Fold.

Fold the Next Layer Forward as you did the Two before It.

Fold the Last Layer Forward Similar to the Three before It.

Finally Turn the Napkin Over and Fold the Both Sides of the Napkin to the Center.

FOLDING A NAPKIN INTO A FAN

The fan napkin fold works particularly well with starched cotton or linen napkins. The fan napkin fold can be used for practically any occasion.

Iron the Napkin Flat.

Fold the Bottom Edge of the Napkin up by
One Inch. You then Fold Back the Napkin One Inch.

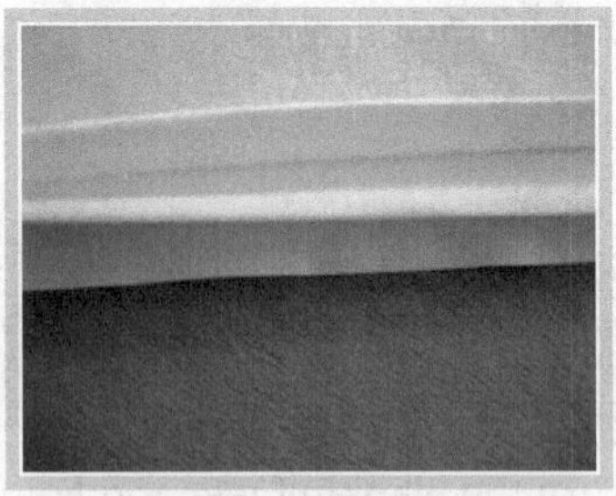

Continue this Back and Forth Folding

Motion Until the Entire Napkin is Complete.

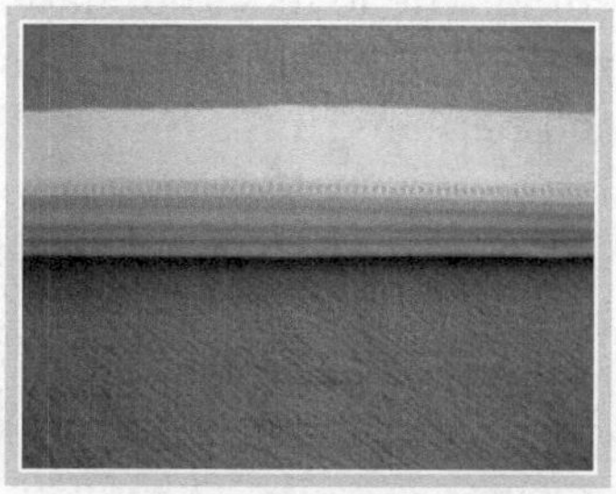

Holding a Finger in the Center, Fold the Pleated Napkin in Half.

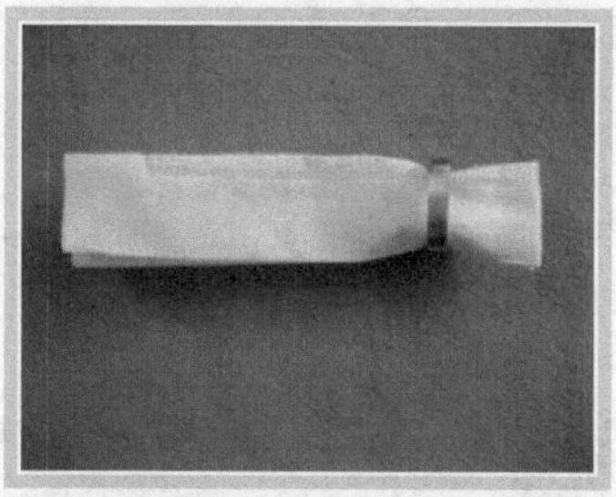

Slide a Napkin Ring Up the Pleats.

Fan Out the Top of the Napkin.

FOLDING A NAPKIN INTO A LOVERS KNOT

Planning a memorable engagement dinner? The lovers knot symbolizes the unity between two people. The lovers knot napkin fold is easy to do but takes a bit of practice to get it right. This fold works extremely well with all lace edged and hemstitched napkins.

Iron the Napkin Flat.

Fold the Napkin in Half

Fold it Again in Half Again.

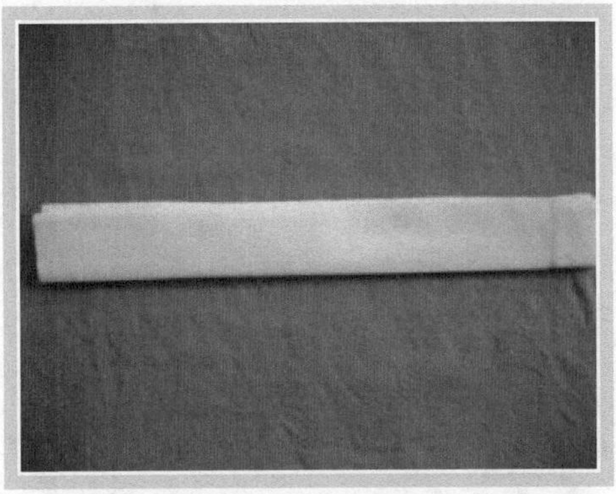

Continue to the Fold it in Half Twice More.

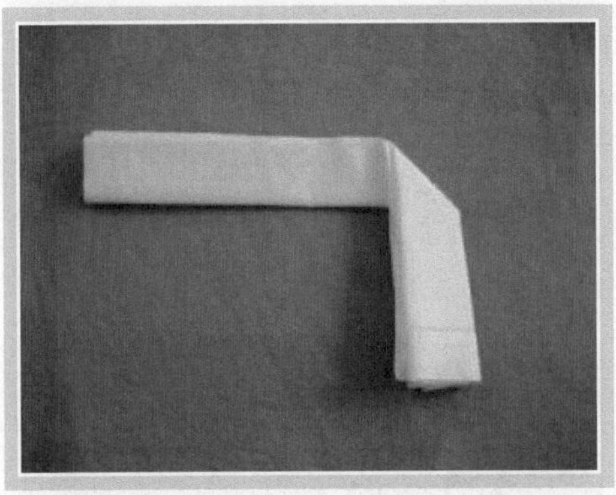

Approx One Third from the Right, Fold Down the
Edge of the Napkin so that the Folded Edge is Vertical

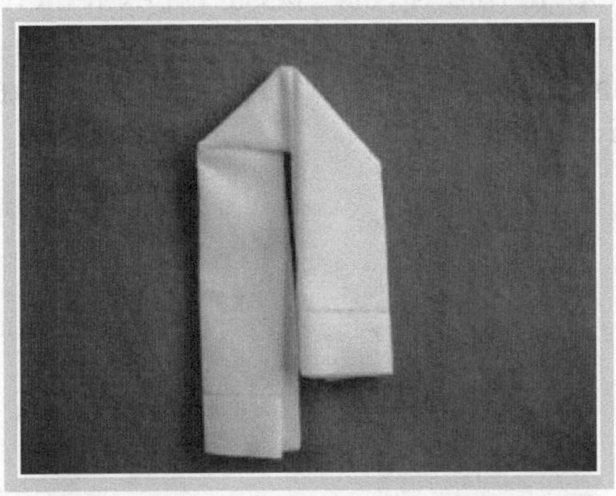

Fold the Left Half of the Strip Down from
the Same Point of the Top Edge, Folding it Back

Fold the Longer End of the Strip Back a Second Time, Swing it in Front of the Right Side

FOLDING A NAPKIN INTO AN ENVELOPE

The envelope napkin fold is very classic yet extremely quick to fold. This fold works well with all of our cotton and linen dinner napkins. For best folding results, it may help to first iron the napkins thoroughly with starch to ensure a more rigid napkin.

Iron the Napkin Flat.

Fold the Napkin in Half so that the Open End is Facing Away from You.

On the Right Hand Side of the Napkin, Fold Both
Corner Edges Towards the Center to form Two Triangles

Fold the Left Side of the Napkin Over in Half to Meet the Right

Take Both Triangle Layers and Fold both Over to Create the Napkin Envelop Fold

FOLDING A NAPKIN INTO A DOUBLE ROLL

If are looking for an asian feel to your dining experience, the double roll is the perfect fold. This fold works well with all of our cotton and linen dinner napkins. For best folding results, it may help to first iron the napkins thoroughly with starch to ensure a more rigid napkin.

Iron the Napkin Flat.

Fold the Top and Bottom of the Napkin to the Center

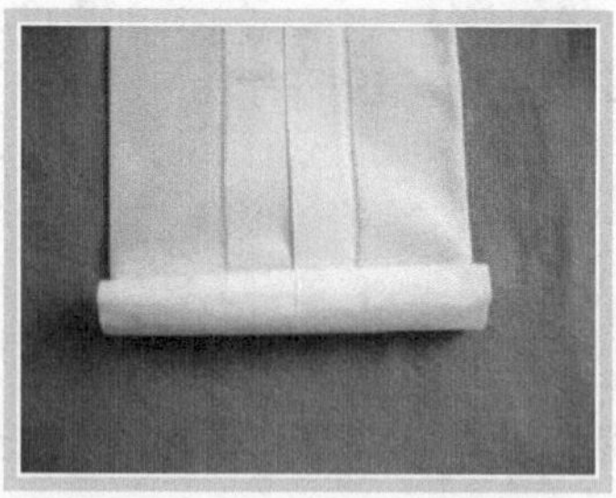

Orient the Napkin Vertically and Roll the Napkin
Up from the Short Edge to the Center

From the Top, Roll the Napkin Down to Meet the Bottom Roll.

FOLDING A NAPKIN INTO A CONE

The cone napkin fold is very classic and quick to fold. This fold works well with all of our cotton and linen dinner napkins. For best folding results, it may help to first iron the napkins thoroughly with starch to ensure a more rigid napkin.

Iron the Napkin Flat.

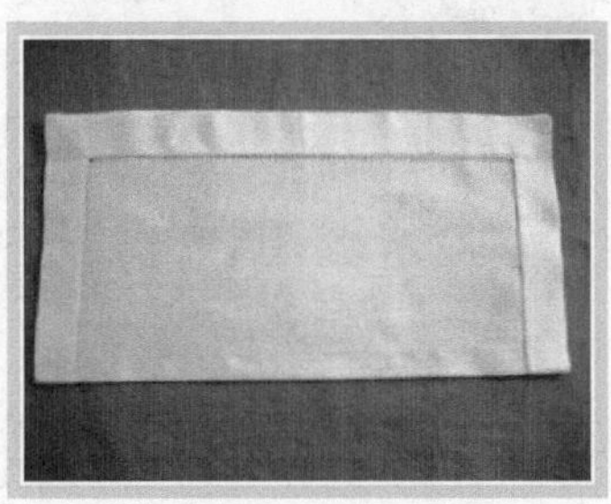

Fold the Napkin in Half and Orient the Open End Away from You.

Fold the Napkin into Quarters.

Orient the Napkin so that the Open End is Facing Away from You. Fold the Top-most Layer all the Way Forward and Press it Down Flat.

Turn the Napkin Over and Fold the Left Hand Side of the Napkin Over Two Thirds of the Way

Fold the Right Hand Side of the Napkin Over to Match the Left Hand Side

Tuck the Corners of the Napkin into the Left Hand Side Flap

FOLDING A NAPKIN INTO A PINWHEEL

The pinwheel is a fun fold that looks fantastic on a table. Especially popular for kids, the napkin fold works particularly well with slightly starched cotton or linen napkins.

Iron the Napkin Flat.

Fold all the Tips of the Napkins into the Center

Fold Two Opposite Edges Towards the Center, Creating a Rectangle

Fold the Two Short Edges of the Rectangle towards the Center

Now Take One Flap and Pull Out One of the Edges to make a Point.

Repeat with the Second Flap

With the Right Flap, Pull it Down towards You

Turn the Napkin Around and Repeat
Steps 5-6 to Finish Up the Pinwheel Napkin Fold.

NAPKIN FOLDING: FOX

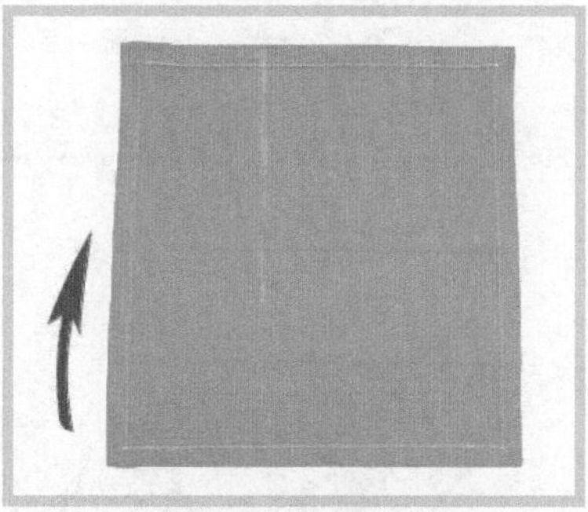

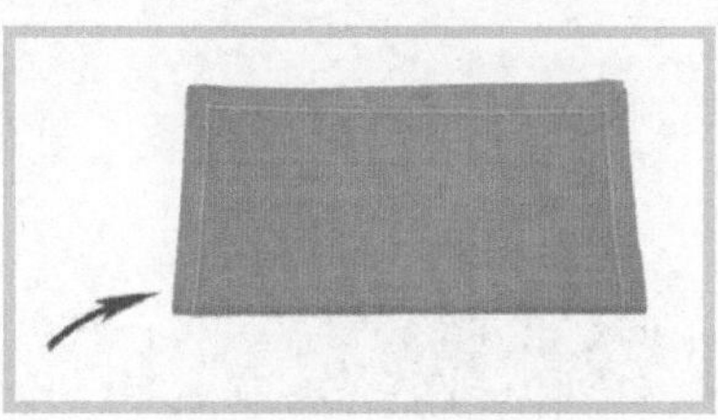

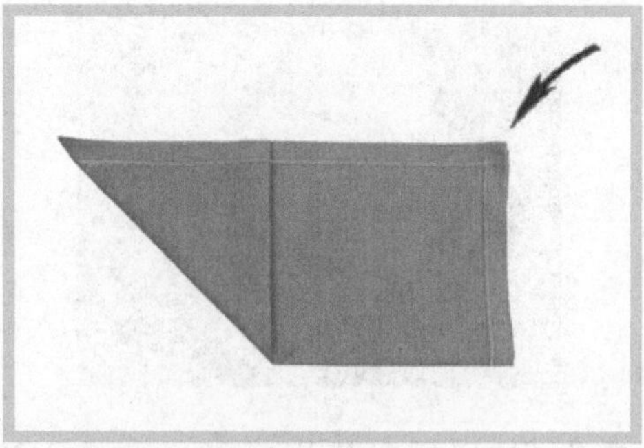

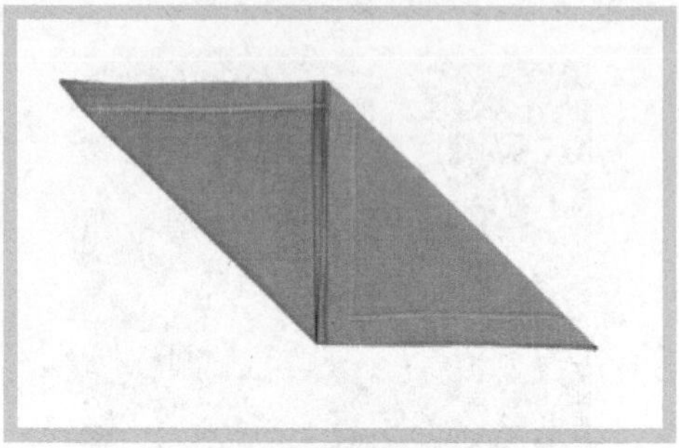

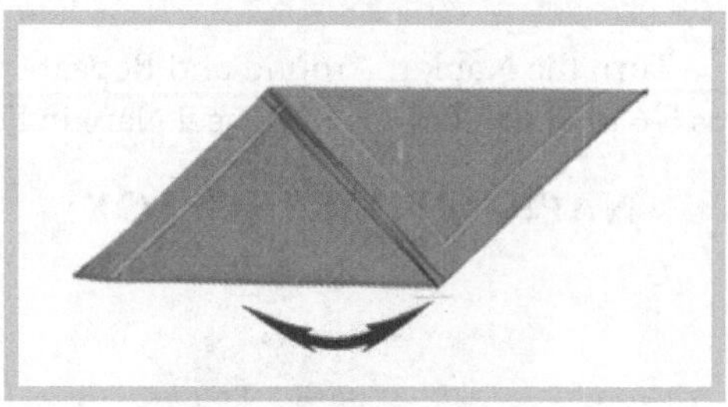

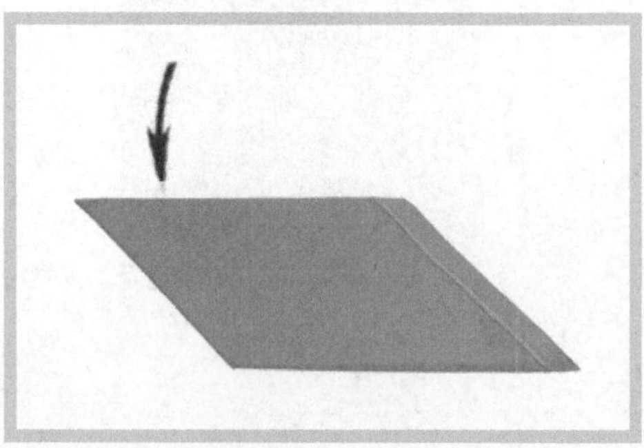

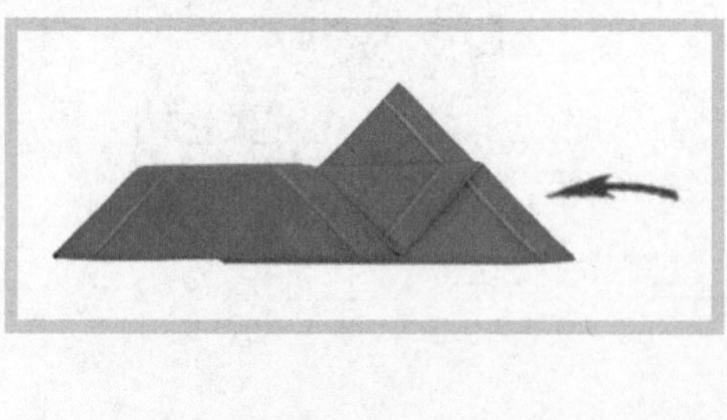

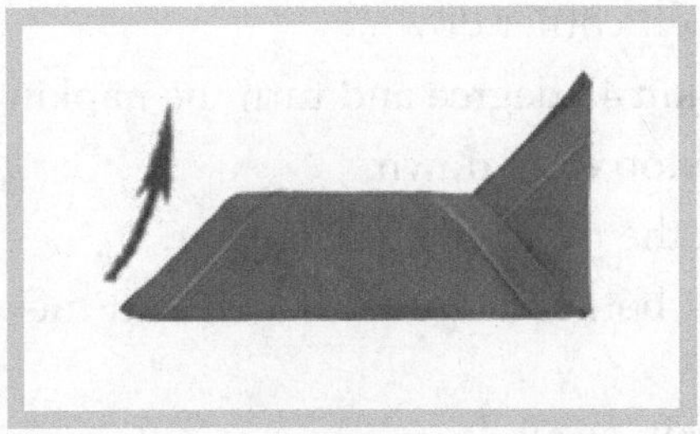

NAPKIN FOLDING: FOX – FOLDING INSTRUCTIONS

- Place the open napkin in front of you.
- Fold the edge nearest to you to meet the top edge. The closed side of the napkin is at the bottom..
- Fold the bottom right corner of the napkin up to the middle right.

- Fold the top left corner down.
- Turn the napkin 45 degree and turn the napkin around.
- Fold over the top edge down.
- A triangle on the right side will appear.
- Fold the right bottom edge to the left and tuck the point under the edge.
- Turn the napkin around.
- Fold the left bottom edge to the right and tuck the point under the edge.
- Gently open and stand up the napkin.

NAPKIN FOLDING: TABLE-PEAK

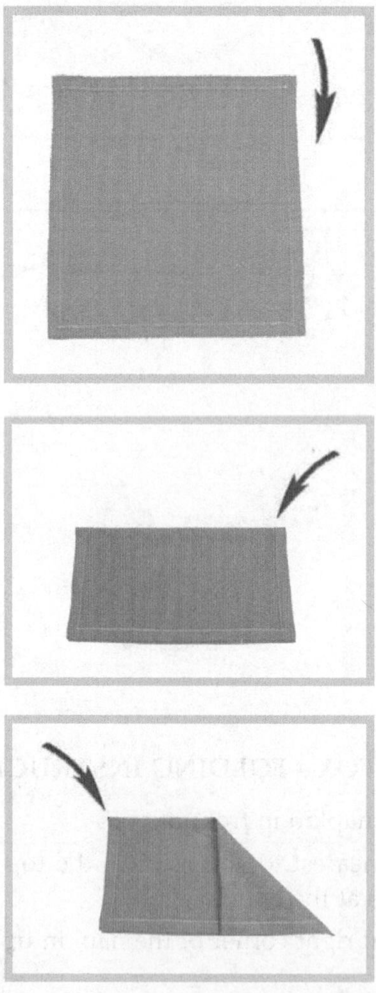

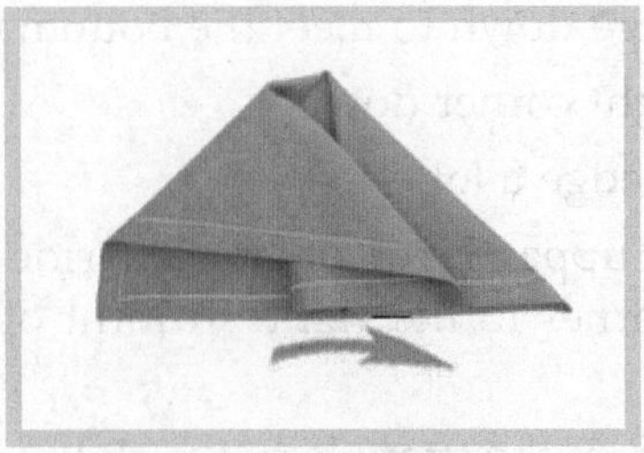

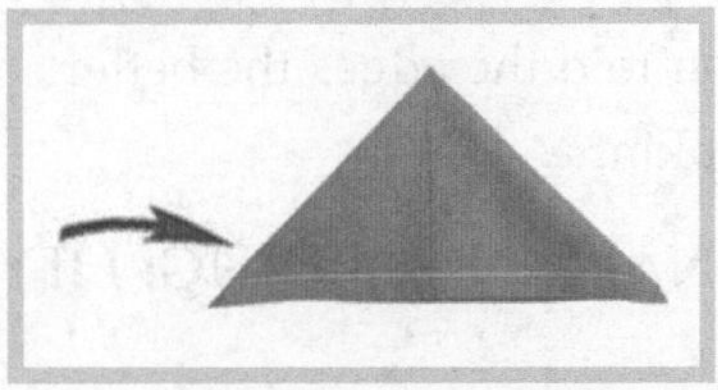

NAPKIN FOLDING: TABLE-PEAK- FOLDING INSTRUCTIONS

- Place the open napkin in front of you.

- Fold the top edge down to meet the bottom edge.
- Fold the top right corner down.
- Don't fold this edge a lot.
- Take from the upper layer of the left side the left bottom corner and pull the corner to the right. In fornt of you there should be a triangle.
- Fold the top left of the triangle to the right.
- The stronger you fold the edges the better.
- Arrange the napkin.

NAPKIN FOLDING: LILY

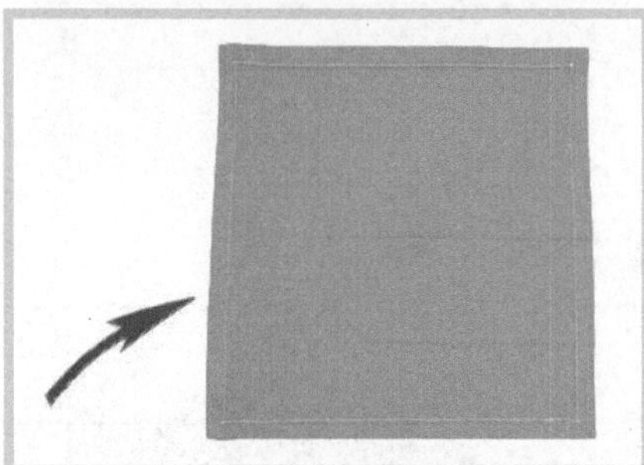

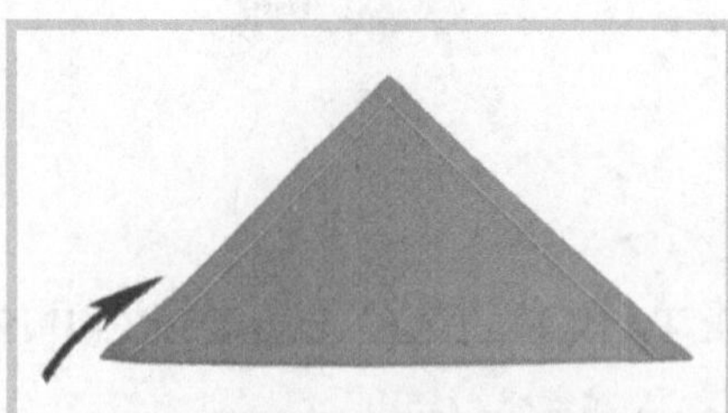

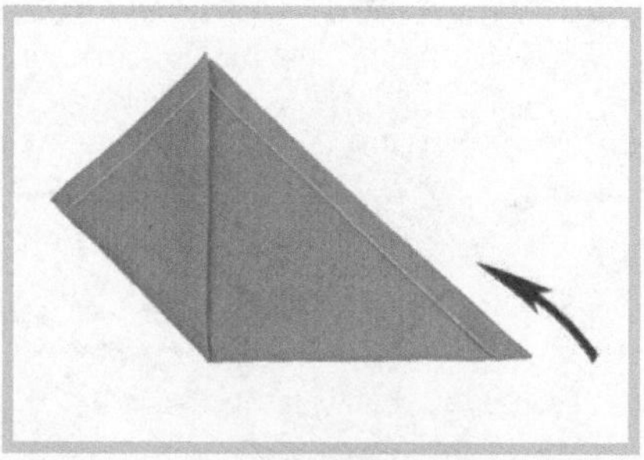

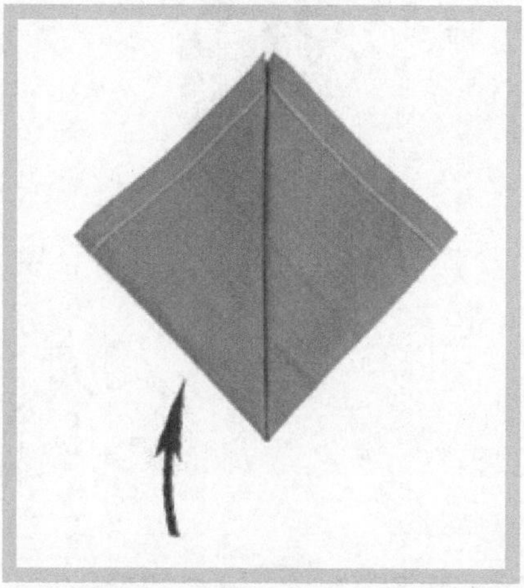

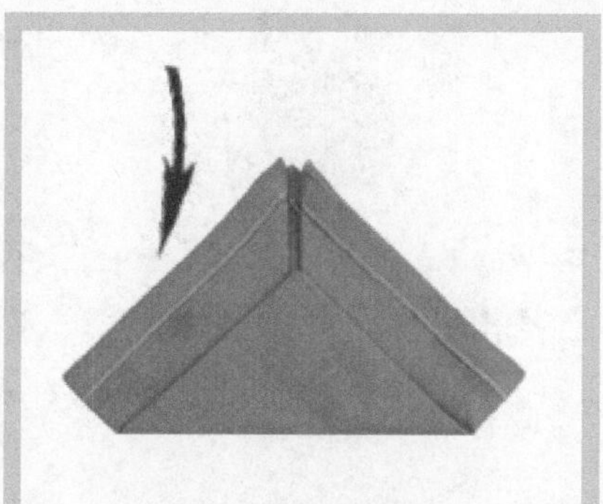

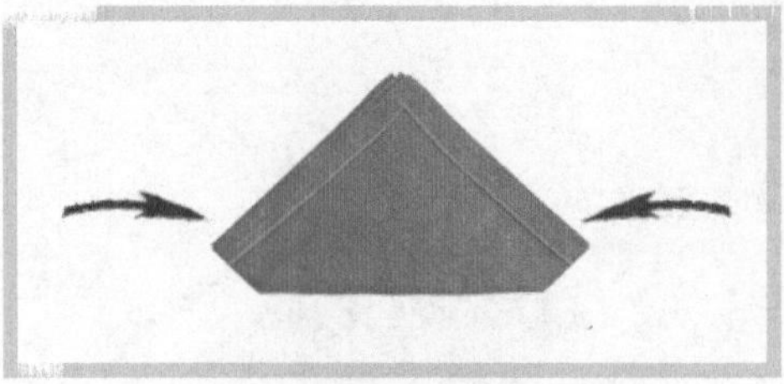

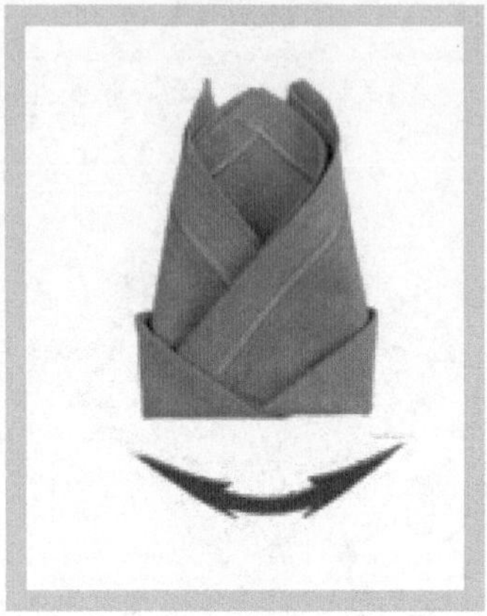

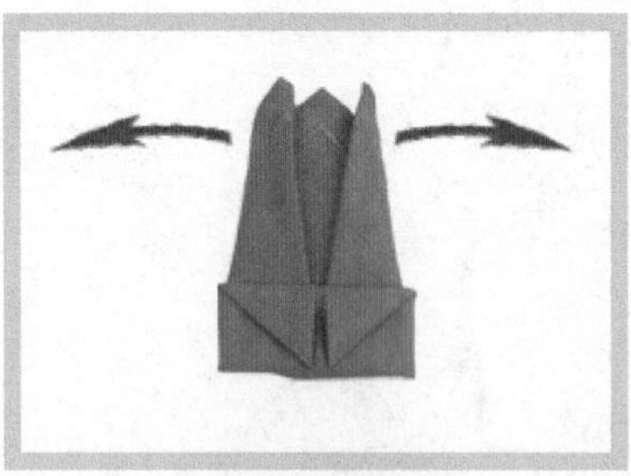

NAPKIN FOLDING: LILY – FOLDING INSTRUCTIONS

- Place the napkin in front of you
- Fold the four corners towards the middle, so a triangle forms.

- Repeat this process again.
- Turn around the napkin.
- Fold the four corners now once again to a square.
- Now get the corners underneath the peaks from back to front. results in beautiful flowers.
- Between the flower pull out the corners from underneath.
- At the bottom you can pull out now even the small leaves.
- The stronger you fold the edges the better.
- In the middle of the napkin you may place some decoration

NAPKIN FOLDING : PEAK

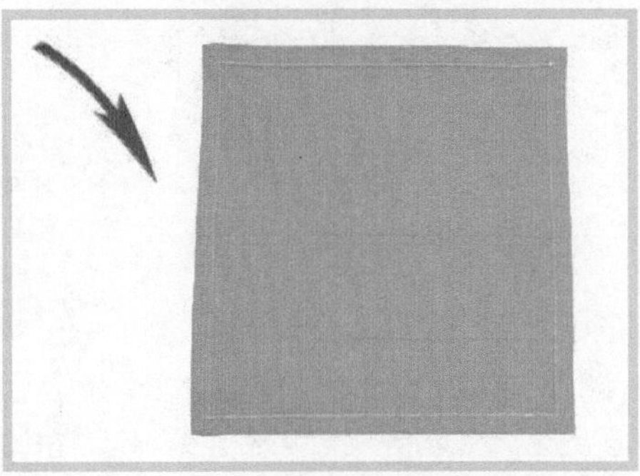

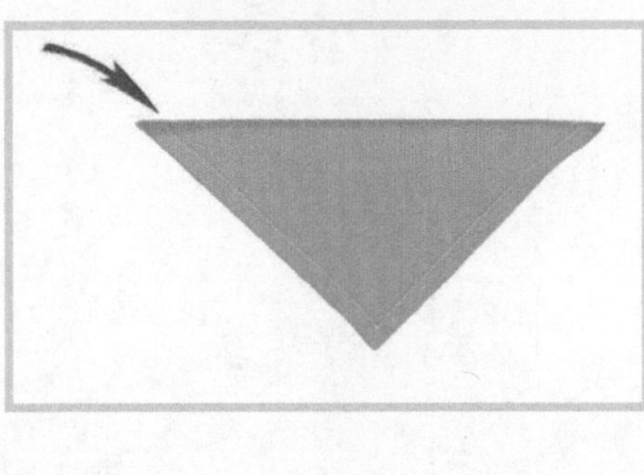

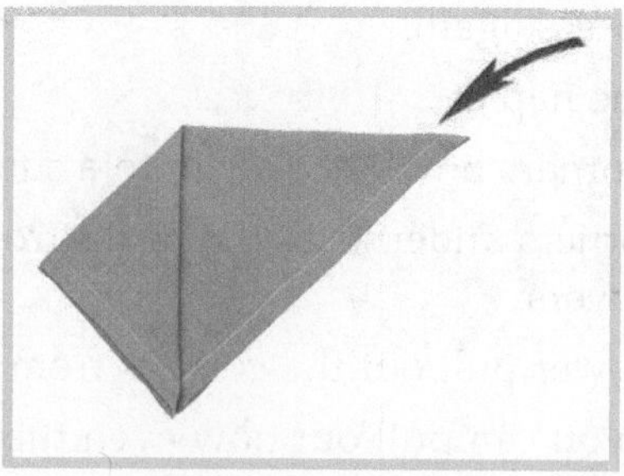

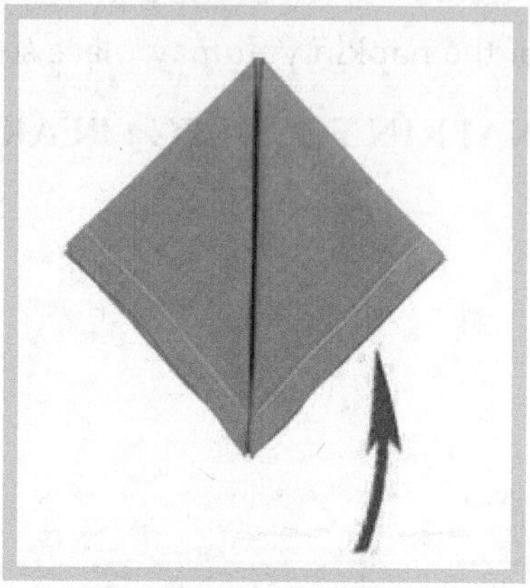

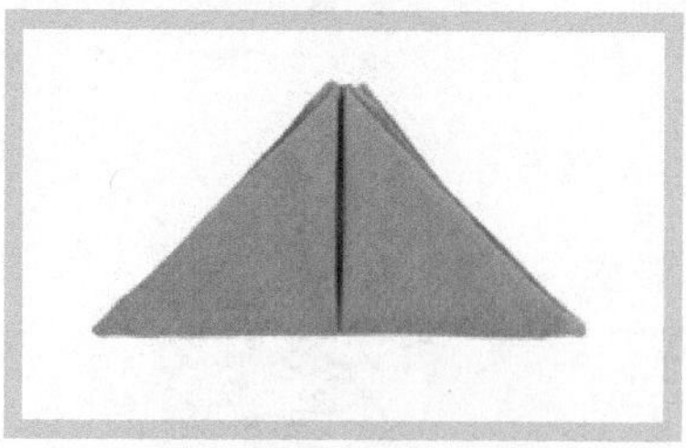

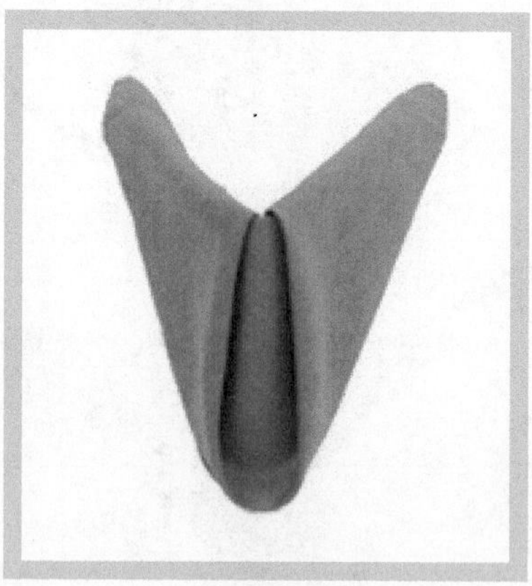

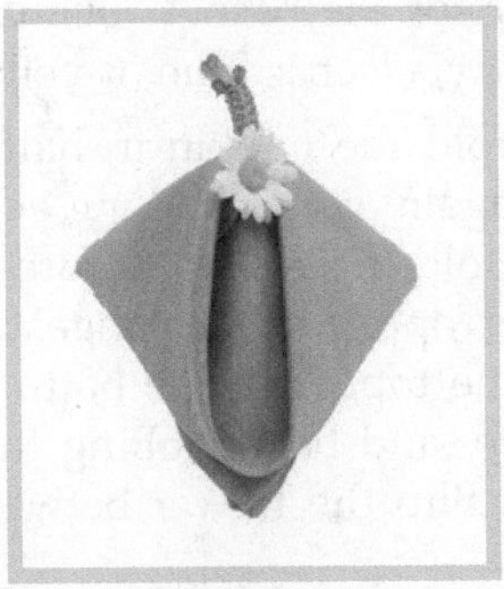

NAPKIN FOLDING: PEAK- FOLDING INSTRUCTIONS

- Place the open napkin in front of you
- Fold the napkin diagonally in the middle to a triangle
- Put the napkin in front of you, so that the closed side is above
- Fold the upper right corner down to the head of the triangle
- Fold the upper left corner down to the head of the triangle
- You now have a square standing on the top. The opened pages are below
- Fold the lower half of the square behind the upper, so a triangle forms.
- Turn the napkin around 180 degrees
- Place the napkin and fold the outer corners backwards.

EASY & IMPRESSIVE WAYS TO FOLD PAPER NAPKINS

Hold the expensive centerpieces and fine china. Add some playful touches to your tabletop with something you probably already have in the house – colorful paper napkins. Coordinate your napkin folding to reflect the theme of your summer fete: a rose for your garden lunch; a fan for your seaside dinner. And get the kids on board to help with the folding! It's an origami project with a practical twist.

- *A rose arrangement*: *Martha Stewart Living* has great directions for this. You can use two different color square napkins – one for the petals and another for the base – or make a monochromatic pop-art flower out of, say, electric blue or yellow.
  - For the base, fold the napkin in half along the diagonal. Then fold it in half again along the long edge. Repeat.
  - For the petals, fold the second square napkin along the diagonal, take the corner opposite the longest side, and fold it up so it extends over the top. Fold the bottom edge so that it falls just short of the top, and begin rolling the napkin from one end to make the bud. Slip the flower between the leaves and place it in a glass.
- *A fan fold*: Obviously appropriate for a hot summer's day and very easy to make. Use a large dinner napkin for the job. Make accordion-style pleats about half an inch wide. Bend the pleats in half to make a "handle" and insert the handle into the a shallow glass. Spread the fan out so it rests dramatically above the rim.
- *A lotus blossom bowl*: Set these on top of your dinner plate and fill them with snacks or battery-operated tea lights. The steps are a bit more challenging, but the result is worth it.

8

Fancy Folded Napkins

An inexpensive way to decorate your holiday table is to make fancy folded napkins. Crisply starched napkins or weighty paper dinner napkins that are folded in interesting shapes bring art to the table and can accentuate a decorated holiday table with style.

Try Your Hand with these Folded Napkin Designs

FAN FOLD

Using a simple accordion-style pleating technique, you can do a few napkin folds that work really well with napkin rings. Place these napkins in the center of your plate at each place setting.

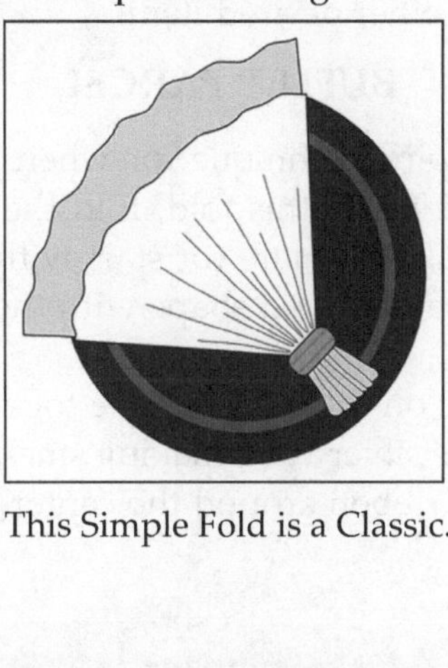

This Simple Fold is a Classic.

Fold your napkin in half. Beginning at one short end, start folding the napkin in an accordion style, making folds approximately every inch.

Insert one folded end into a napkin ring. Push the napkin ring up no further than 1/3 from the bottom. Fan out the top pleats.

DECORATIVE POCKET

Decorative pockets can hold silverware, a sprig of holly, place cards, or any other treat that you want to tuck in. You can place it in the center of each plate at each place setting, or if it'll be holding utensils, you can place it to the left of the plate.

A Decorative Pocket Fold is Pretty as Well as Functional.

To make a decorative pocket, fold the napkin in half and then fold it in half again to make a square (or start with a folded paper napkin). Turn the napkin to make a diamond shape with the folded point closest to you. Separate the free edges and begin folding each layer down to the point. Continue folding down layers, leaving last layer up. Tuck the sides of the napkin to the back. Insert your silverware or other desired item.

BUFFET PARCEL

Try this pretty wrapping technique for when you want to accent your table with special ribbon. To do this fold, fold the napkin in half and then fold it in half again to make a square (or start with a folded paper napkin). Turn the napkin to make a diamond shape with the folded point away from you.

Center the silverware on the napkin close together. Fold the side points in to touch the edges of the silverware, making small triangles. Overlap edges over the cutlery and tie a ribbon around the center of the parcel.

FLOWER

The center of this folded napkin lends itself to holding treasures such as chocolate gelt for Hanukkah, sprigs of evergreen at Christmas, or a small basket with a beautifully decorated egg nestled in it at Easter.

The Flower Fold is Deceptively Simple to do.

- To begin, fold each corner of the napkin into the center.
- Repeat again by folding the newly made corners into the center. Press or crease folds into place.

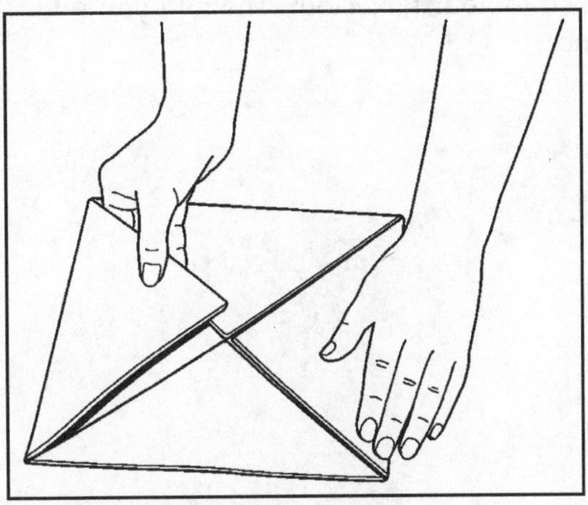

Fold Corners Twice into the Middle.

- Holding the folds together in the center, flip the napkin over Pressing a finger firmly in the middle of the napkin to hold folds in place, reach under the napkin and begin pulling all the points out until complete.

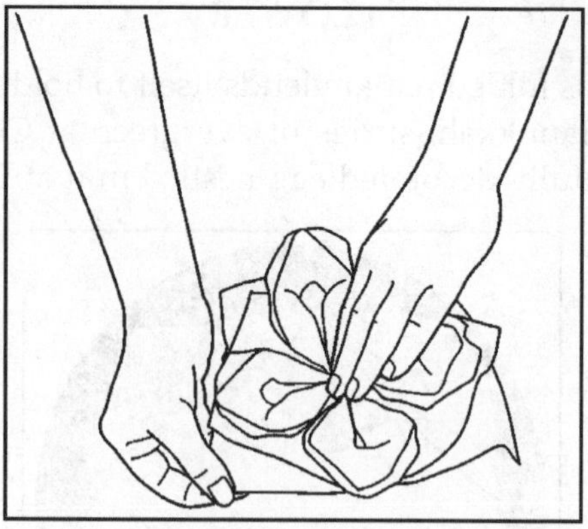

Pull out all the Points.

NAPKIN FOLDING TECHNIQUES

HOW TO BUILD THE PERFECT TABLE

- *Select Table Padding*: Add comfort and cushioning to your table with table padding. Italso helps muffle noise and reduces glassware breakage.
- *Select Tablecloth*: The color or design of the tablecloth sets the mood..
- *Select Napkins*: Napkins add a splash of color to the tableclothor can be matched to your tablecloth. The fold you select also setsthe level of elegance.

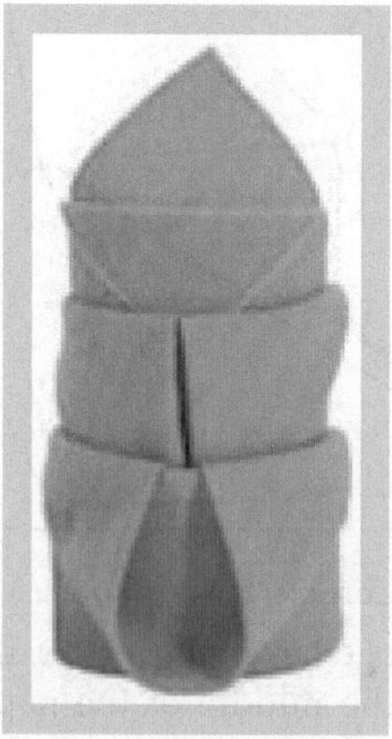

Atrium Lily

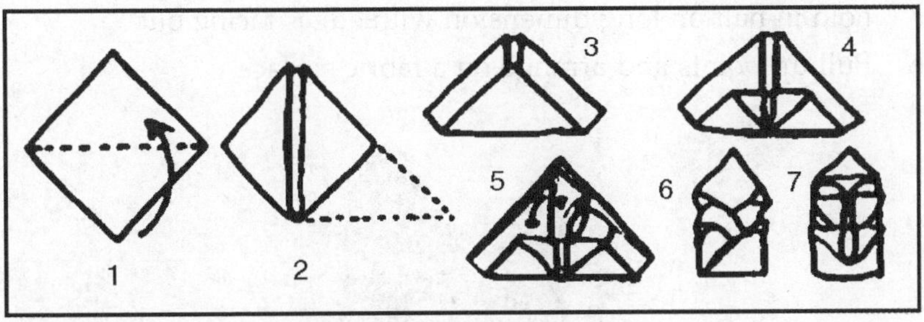

- Fold napkin bringing bottom up to top
- Fold corners to top
- Fold bottom point up to 1" below top
- Fold point back onto itself
- Fold each of points at top down and tuck under edge offolded up bottom. Fold down one layer of top point and tuckunder base fold.
- Turn napkin over and tuck left and right sides into eachother
- Open base and stand

Bird of Paradise

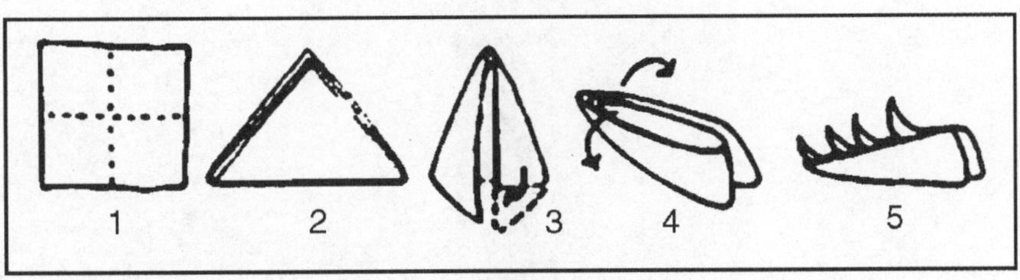

- Fold napkin in half and in half again
- Fold in half diagonally with points on the top and facingup
- Fold left and right sides down along center line, turningtheir extended points under

- Fold in half on long dimension with edges facing out
- Pull up points and arrange on a fabric surface

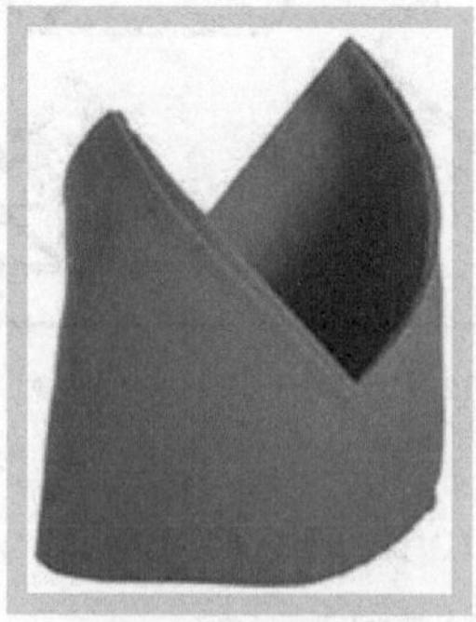

Bishop's Mitre

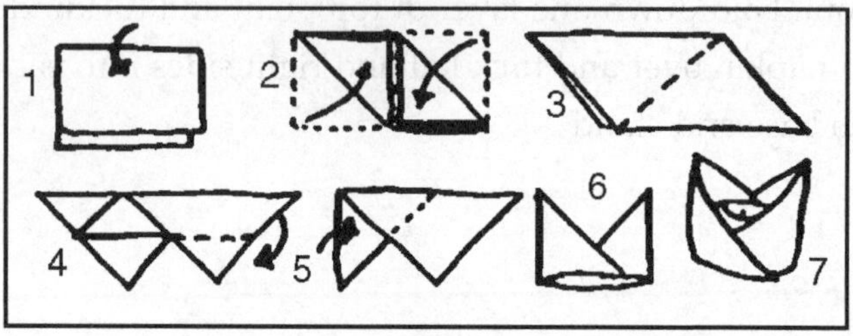

- Fold napkin in half diagonally
- Fold corners to meet at top point
- Turn napkin over with points to the top and fold lowercorner 2/3 of the way up
- Fold back onto itself
- Bring corners together, tucking one into the other
- Open base of fold
- Stand upright

Candle

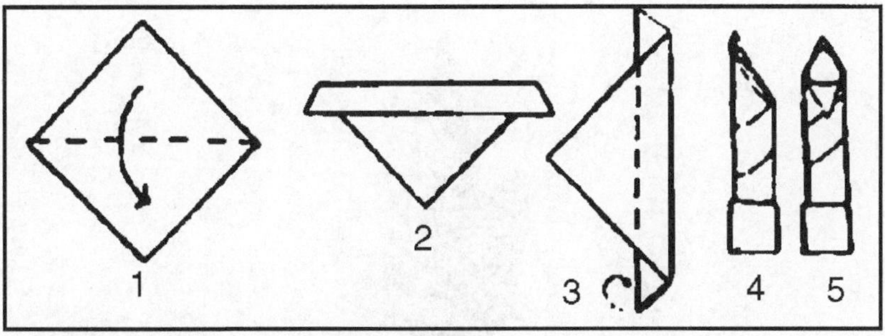

- Fold napkin in half diagonally
- Fold down base 1/3 of the way
- Turn napkin over and roll from bottom to top
- Tuck corners inside cuff at base of fold and stand
- Turn one layer of point down and set on base

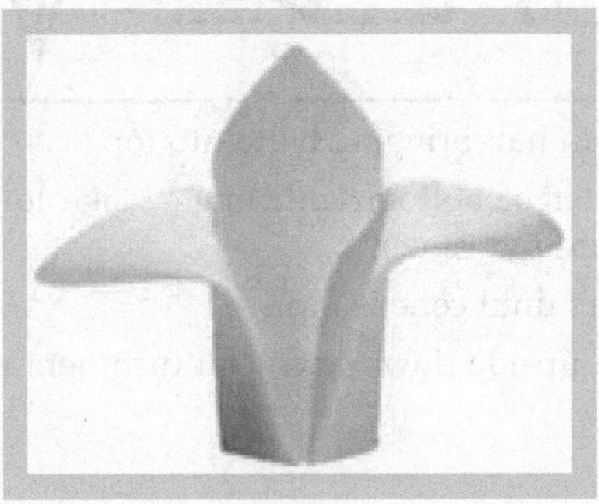

Cardinal's Hat

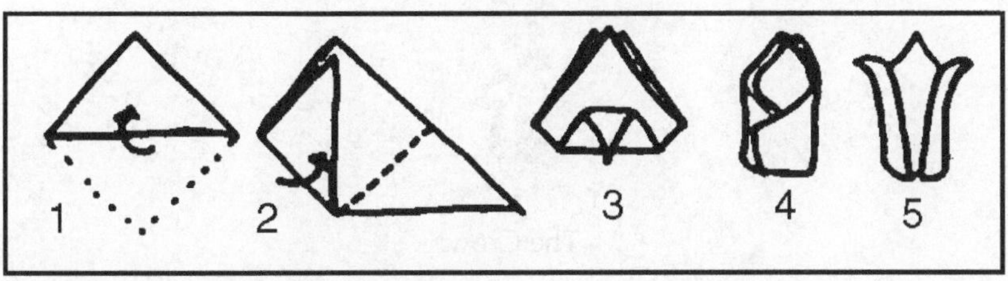

- Fold napkin in half diagonally
- Fold corners to meet at top point
- Turn napkin over with points to the top and fold lower corner 2/3 of the way up
- Fold Back onto itself
- Open base of fold and stand upright

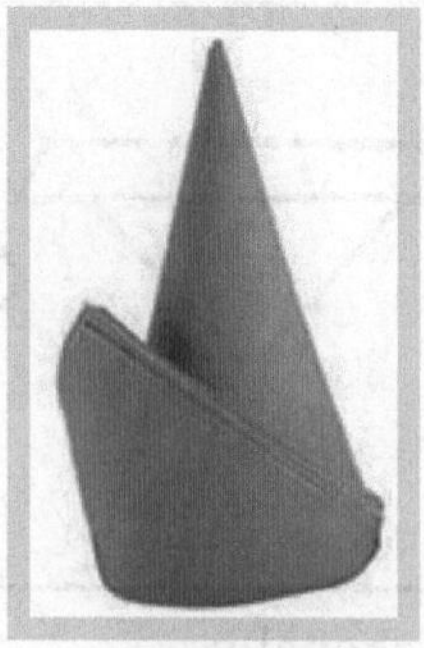

Clown's Hat

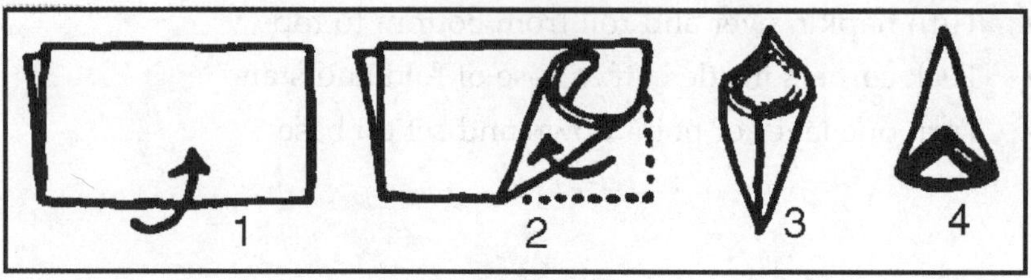

- Fold napkin in half bringing bottomto top
- Holding center of bottom with finger, take lower rightcorner and loosely roll around center.
- Match corners until cone is formed
- Turn napkin upside down and then turn hem all around. Turnand stand on base.

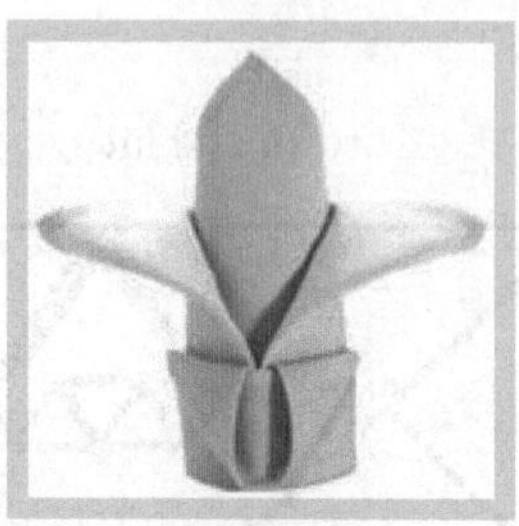

The Crown

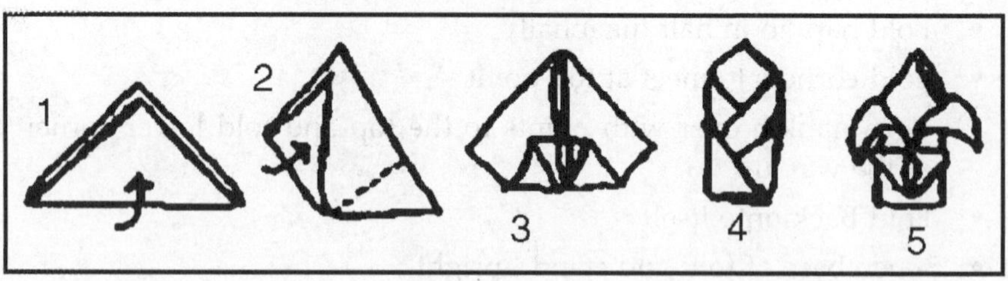

- Fold napkin in half diagonally
- Fold corners to meet at top point
- Fold bottom point 2/3 of the way to top and fold back ontoitself
- Turn napkin over, bringing corners together and tuckingone into the other
- Peel two top corners to make crown. Open base of fold andstand upright.

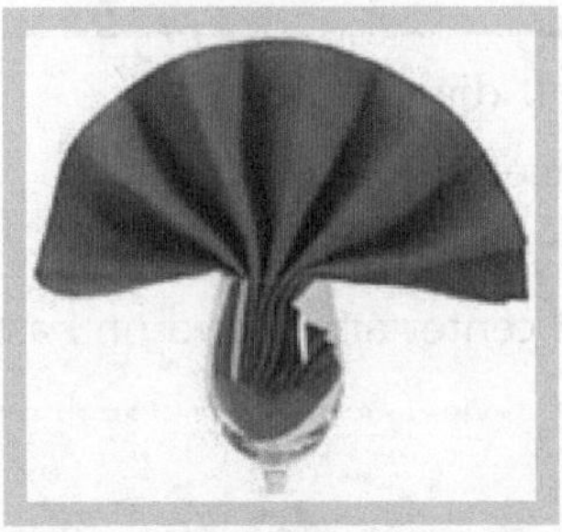

Goblet Fan

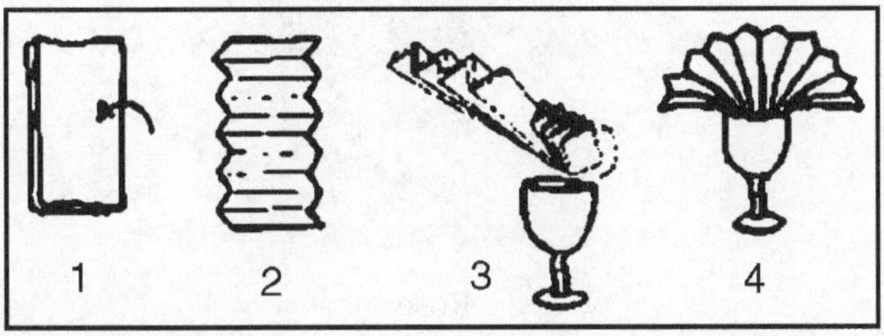

- Fold napkin in half
- Pleat from bottom to top
- Turn napkin back 1/3 of the way on right (folded) end andplace into goblet
- Spread out pleats at top

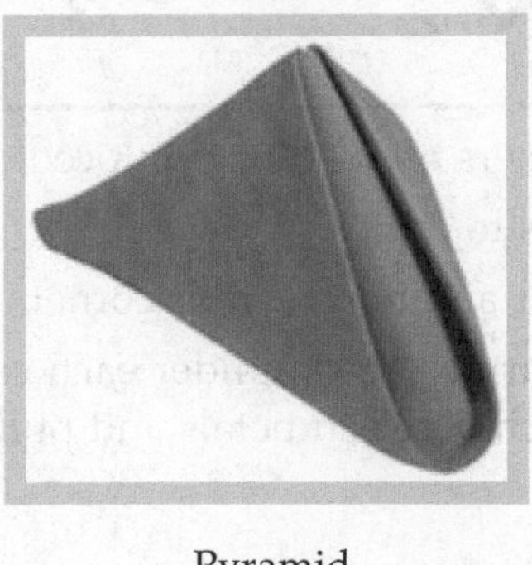

Pyramid

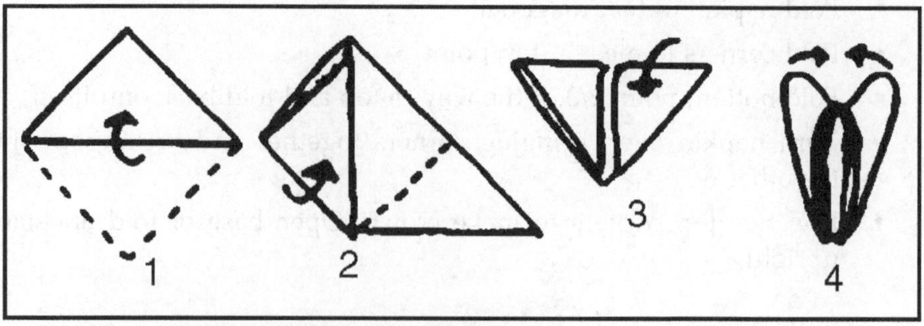

- Fold napkin in half diagonally
- Fold corners to meet at top point
- Turn napkin over and fold in half
- Pick napkin up at center and stand on base of triangle

Rose

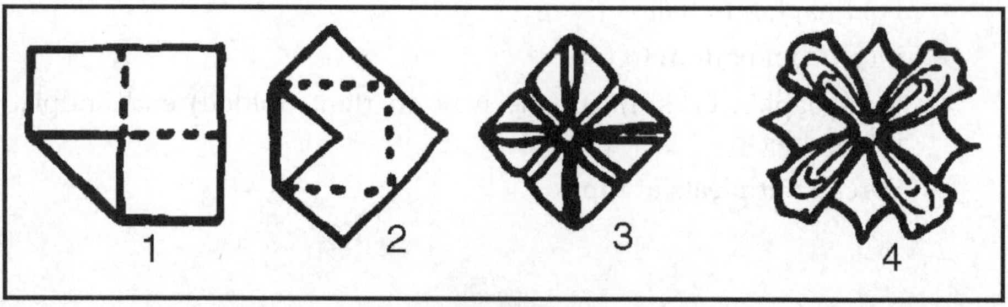

- Fold all four corners of open napkintocenter
- Fold new corners to center
- Turn napkin over and fold all four corners to center
- Holding center firmly, reach under each corner and pullup flaps to form petals. Reach between petals and pull flapsfrom underneath.

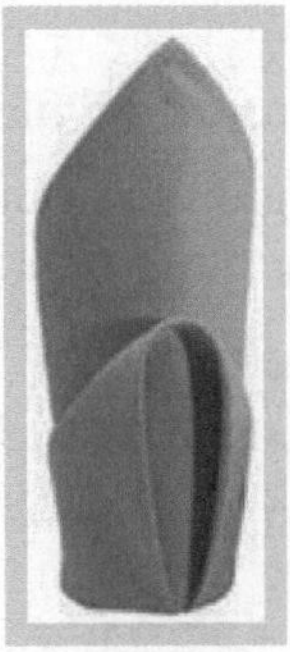

Rosebud

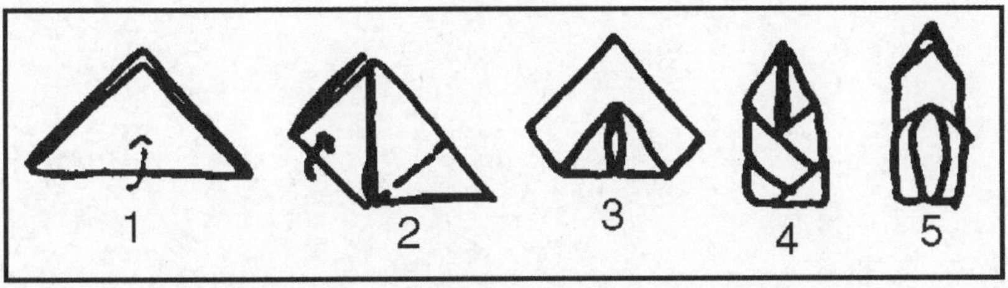

- Fold napkin in half diagonally
- Fold corners to meet at top point
- Turn napkin over and fold bottom 2/3 of the way up
- Turn napkin around and bring corners corners together,tucking one into the other
- Turn napkin around and stand on base

Lady Windermer's Fan

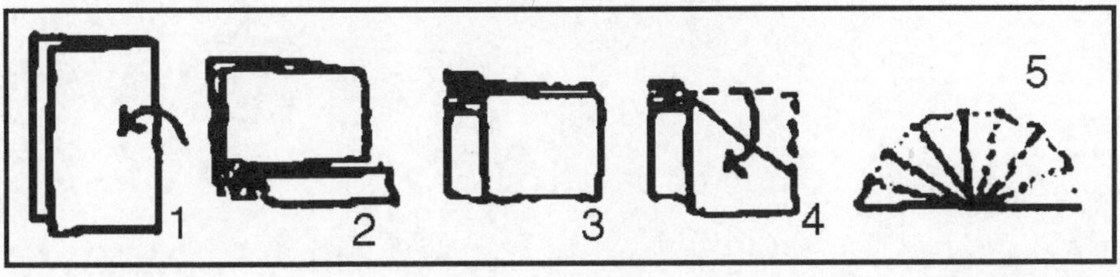

- Fold napkin in half
- Starting at the bottom, accordian pleat 2/3 of the wayup
- Fold in half with pleating on the outside
- Fold upper right corner diagonally down to folded baseof pleats and turn under edge
- Place on table and release pleats to form fan

9

Cloth Napkins for Beautiful Napkin Folding and Table Settings

Delight your guests with a special folded cloth napkin at their table place setting. See our easy napkin folding tutorials on how to create lots of different napkin folds.

A special table setting shows your guests how much you value them, since you take the extra effort to set the table beautifully. Show your family and friends what they mean to you by creating a special arrangement. Even if you have never folded a napkin in your life, the photo tutorials show you the simple processes to take.

These are not complicated or difficult. Each one will take only a few minutes, and you, and your guests will be pleased with the results. Start out with the easiest napkin folds to create the special look you want to achieve.

Additionally, the use of napkin rings or ties will enhance the look, from silver or brass napkin ring, to ribbons or herb or flower sprigs.

WHY USE CLOTH NAPKINS

- Cloth napkins are available in an almost infinite number of patterns and prints and sizes.
- Cloth napkins can be better for the environment and greener than paper napkins.
- There is a simple pleasure in a drawer or shelf filled with cloth napkins with the variety of colors, patterns and shapes.
- If you use cloth napkins you'll help to save trees.

CONTRIBUTE TO SAVING THE EARTH WITH CLOTH NAPKINS

- Wash your cloth napkins in a full load of clothes.
- Hang your napkins to dry or use an energy-efficient electric dryer.

- Because you'll reuse your cloth napkin time after time, it will not go into the landfill.
- Use napkins that are made from recycled hemp, linen, or organic cotton.
- Buy previously-used cloth napkins at flea markets, antique stores, and second hand stores.

Choose cloth napkins that have no added pigments, inks or dyes, or toxic metals.

MORE TIPS FOR USING CLOTH NAPKINS

- Most adults can reuse their cloth napkins. Wash them only when soiled.
- Designate a napkin ring for each family member to identify their napkin for the next meal.
- Wash dirty cloth napkins in with other laundry.
- Pre-spot stains on cloth napkins and then wash the napkins with cold water.

With little effort, you can save money, save paper, save landfills, enjoy beautiful fabrics and patterns, and set a beautiful table. And you'll feel good doing it! What more could you want?

SPECIAL NAPKIN FOLDING FOR YOUR TABLE

A beautifully set table is enhanced when you learn some simple napkin folding skills. See our easy tutorials on how to create 12 different napkin folds. You're sure to find one you love.

Haven't you gone to a party where the hostess has taken the time to make the table look really special? Didn't the napkins, folded to a pretty shape, add to the total feel of the setting? Some napkins are arranged so beautifully that you don't want to use them.

A special table says that you really value your guests when you make the extra effort to set the table beautifully. Even if you've never folded a napkin in your life, these photo tutorials will make it all simple. The napkin folds presented here are not complicated or difficult. Each one will take only a few minutes, and you'll be pleased with the results.

Start out with the easy ones and attempt something a bit more complicated when you've mastered one. Some are easy, and some more complicated, some use napkin rings, and all will look more presentable if you have the iron out when you're working.

Try all the folds to decide which one you prefer. You might feel that one style is more casual and another more formal. Choose your favorite for the occasion.

NAPKIN FOLDING - BIRD OF PARADISE

The bird of paradise is a stunning and easily recognizable tropical flower. Try this bit of napkin folding wizardry to impress your guests. Start by folding your napkin in half along the east-west line, folding the bottom edge up to meet the top.

NAPKIN FOLDING BIRD OF PARADISE

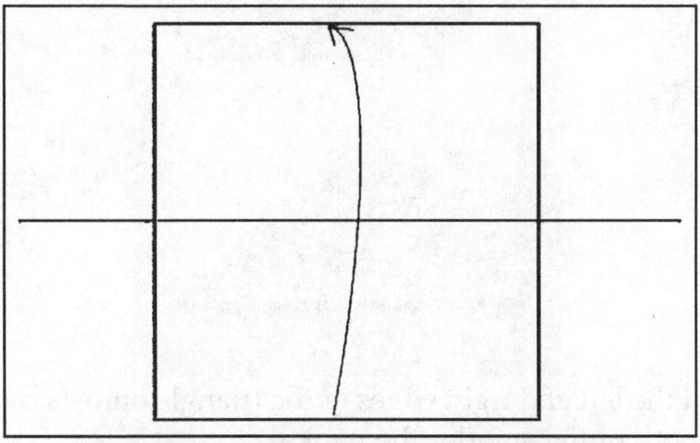

Then fold the napkin in half again, folding the left edge onto the right edge. Next you will make a triangle by folding the upper right corner to the lower left corner, as shown below.

Here is the Same Fold Shown from a Different Angle.

This photo was done just to show you that the open edges of the folded napkin are the ones being folded over.

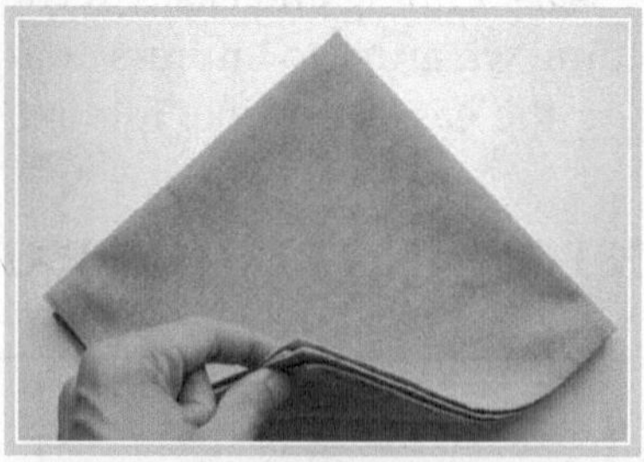

Next, fold the left and right edges of the triangle onto its centerline. Then tuck the two bottom flaps under the napkin.

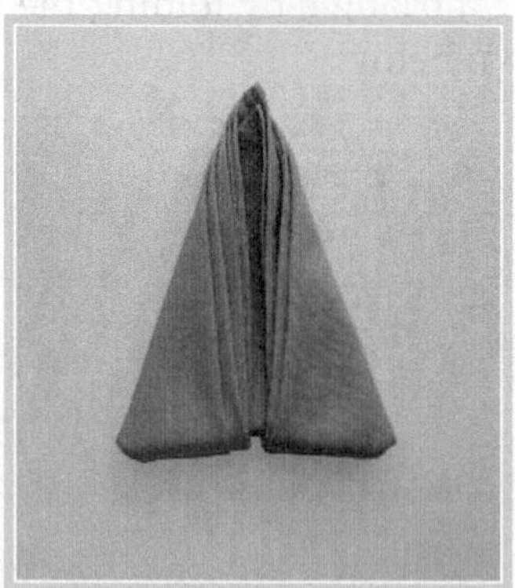

Now Fold in Half Along the Centerline.

Hold the napkin at the end shown and pull each individual napkin layer up and out...and voila! A napkin bird of paradise!

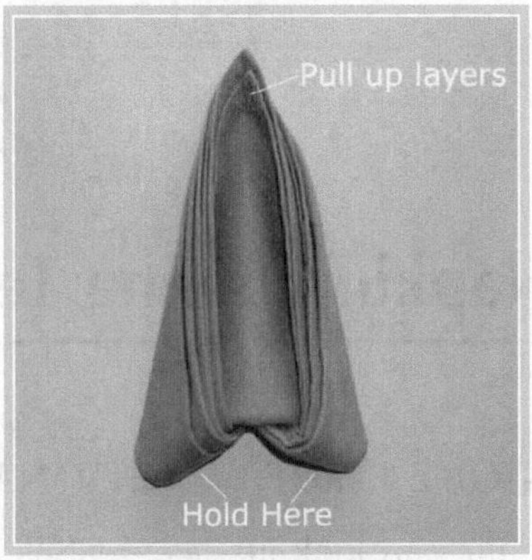

10

Decorative Napkin Folding Techniques

FOLDING TECHNIQUE 1: THE FUNCTIONAL CENTERPIECE

This folding technique can look just as great as a centerpiece for your table as it does resting next to silverware.

Try displaying candies, condiments or dips by placing a small dish in the center of your folded napkin:

1. Lay a large linen napkin flat on the table. Fold each corner diagonally into the center of the napkin, creating a square.
2. Turn the napkin over and fold each corner diagonally into the center of the napkin again.
3. Firmly hold down the center of the napkin or have a friend hold it down for you.
4. Carefully reach under the napkin and pull out the folded corners to form outer petals.
5. You should finish with a floral/rose shaped napkin. Place a small dish or candies in the center to hold it down.

FOLDING TECHNIQUE 2: THE POCKET

This technique works well with either paper or linen napkins, and the pocket doubles as a utensil holder and display for small decorations.

Place utensils in the large pocket and a sprig of flowers, herbs or holly in one of the smaller folds to add life to your table:

1. Start with a large square paper or linen napkin laid flat on a table.
2. Fold the napkin in half long-ways.
3. Fold the napkin in half top to bottom.
4. Fold in half again, left to right.
5. Rotate napkin to make sure the loose edges of the napkin are at the top right and carefully fold each layer diagonally and under each other, leaving one large pocket in the back. You can also fold the corner of the first layer under, to create a straight line or leave it open.
6. Place utensils in the back pocket and a sprig of decoration in the front pocket.

FOLDING TECHNIQUE 3: THE TREFOIL

This fold uses a large napkin ring to hold it together at the base. It can be placed on or next to plates for decoration—or inside stemware for added flair.

1. Place a large linen napkin flat on a table and fold the bottom corner to the top corner to form a triangle.
2. Fold the bottom part of the napkin up, about 2 inches from the top. You'll see a small triangle peeking out at the top and the bottom will be a straight line.
3. Fold the napkin accordion-style left to right (over, under, and repeat) until the end.
4. Stick the napkin into a wide napkin ring with about an inch left at the bottom. Carefully open with your hands.
5. Lay the folded napkin in the center of a plate or place inside stemware and fan out.

ARROWHEAD NAPKIN FOLD

When learning how to fold napkins the Arrowheads is not a bad place to start if you find the beginners section a little to easy. This fold does work best with a larger size napkin that is quite firm or has been starched.

Lay the Napkin Out in Front of You. If the Napkin has a Folded Over Seam or Tags on Make Sure these are Facing Upwards

Fold the Napkin in Half so the Opening is Facing towards Your Person.

Fold the Top Right Corner Down to Meet the Bottom Edge.

Repeat the Same Fold but this Time on the Left.

Start with the Right Hand Side. Take the Central Corner of the Fold you Made in Step Three. Now You want to Fold it Back on its self. This may Require You to use an Iron or Before you Start, Starch the Napkins.

Repeat the Same Fold Again but on the Opposite Side. This can be a Bit Tricky You may have to use Your Right Hand to keep the Right Side in Place. Now you're Learning how to Fold Napkins!

Now Slide both Thumbs Underneath the Napkin Fold and with Your Fingers Rested on the Top Bring the Middle Up.

It may Require a Little Re-jig of the Flaps but this Should only Take a Few Seconds. Finally Stand Back and be Impressed with Your New Napkin Folding Technique!

THE CROWN NAPKIN FOLD

Dinner napkin folds can some time require a fair amount of patience. The Crown fold is a good example of one. It is similar to the rosebud fold but with difficult twist. This fold is not for those amongst us with OCD.

Lay the Napkin Flat Out in Front of You.

A note on Tags and labels: Because this fold shows both sides of the napkin when completed, it may be best to give it a couple of try's to work out where the tags will be.

Fold the Napkin in Half Diagonally and then Place it Infront of You so the Longest Edge is Facing you and the Opening is Pointing Away.

Fold the Right Corner Up towards the Top of the Triangle.

Fold the Left Hand Side in the Same Way.

You Should Now have a Diamond in Front of You with the Openings at the Top. Take the Bottom and Fold it Back on its Self about an Inch Away form the Top.

Take the Tip of the Fold You just made and Fold that back on its Self so it Touches the Bottom Edge.

Flip the Napkin Over.

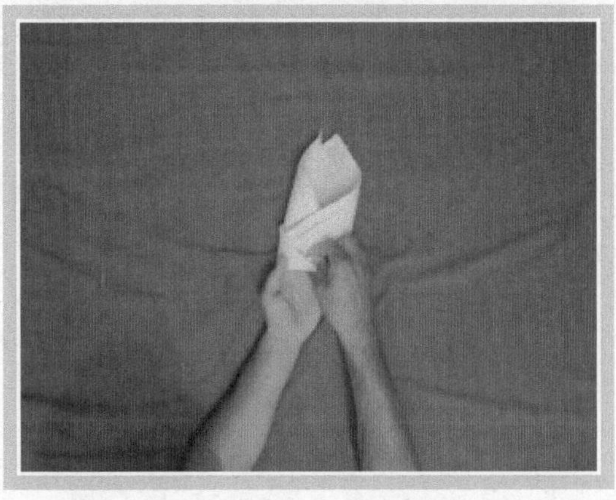

Wrap the Left and Right Side around Tucking them into One Another.

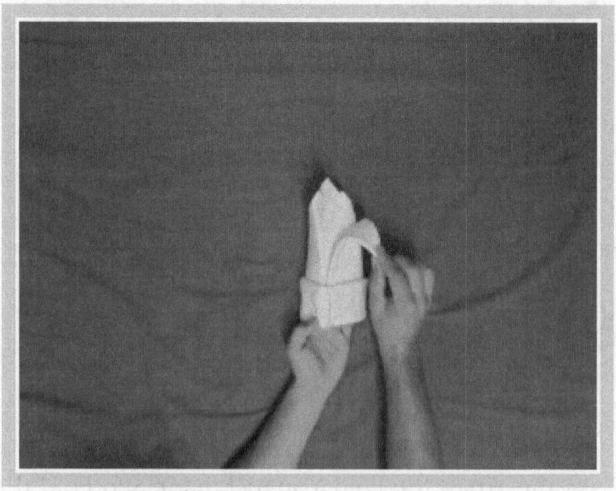

Ten the Napkin Around and Peal Down the Lose Flaps. It may take a While for Your Napkin Fold to Look Right but just keep at it. If Your Napkin isn't Holding Shape try Starching it Before Hand. You've Completed you Dinner Napkin Fold. Time to Position them on the Table and Wait for the Guests.

11

Origami

Origami , from ori meaning "folding", and kami meaning "paper" (kami changes to gami due to rendaku) is the traditional Japanese art of paper folding, which started in the 17th century AD at the latest and was popularized outside of Japan in the mid-1900s. It has since then evolved into a modern art form. The goal of this art is to transform a flat sheet of paper into a finished sculpture through folding and sculpting techniques, and as such the use of cuts or glue are not considered to be origami. Paper cutting and gluing is usually considered kirigami.

The number of basic origami folds is small, but they can be combined in a variety of ways to make intricate designs. The best known origami model is probably the Japanese paper crane. In general, these designs begin with a square sheet of paper whose sides may be different colors or prints. Traditional Japanese origami, which has been practiced since the Edo era (1603–1867), has often been less strict about these conventions, sometimes cutting the paper or using nonsquare shapes to start with. The principles of origami are also being used in stents, packaging and other engineering structures.

HISTORY OF ORIGAMI

The history of origami followed after the invention of paper and as a result of paper's use in society. Independent paper folding traditions exist in East Asia and Europe, and it is unclear whether these evolved separately or had a common source.

ORIGINS AND THE TRADITIONAL DESIGNS

The Japanese word "origami" itself is a compound of two smaller Japanese words: "ori", meaning to fold, and "kami", meaning paper. Until recently, all forms of paper folding were not grouped under the word origami, namely "tsutsumi", a kind of wrapper used for formal occasions. Before that, paperfolding for play was known by a variety of names, including "orikata", "orisue", "orimono", "tatamigami" and others. Exactly why "origami" became the common name is not known; it has been suggested that the word was adopted in the kindergartens because the written characters were easier for young children to write. Another theory is that the word "origami" was a direct translation of the German word "Papierfalten", brought into Japan with the Kindergarten Movement around 1880.

Japanese origami began sometime after Buddhist monks carried paper to Japan during the 6th century. The first Japanese origami is dated from this period and was used for religious ceremonial purposes only, due to the high price of paper. A reference in a poem by Ihara Saikaku from 1680, which describes the origami butterflies used during Shinto weddings to represent the bride and groom, indicates that origami had become a significant aspect of Japanese ceremony by the Heian period (794–1185). Samurai warriors are known to have exchanged gifts adorned with noshi, a sort of good luck token made of folded strips of paper.

In 1797 the first known origami book was published in Japan: Senbazuruorikata. There are several origami stories in Japanese culture, such as a story of Abe no Seimei making a paper bird and turning it into a real one. The earliest evidence of paperfolding in Europe is a picture of a small paper boat in Tractatusde sphaera mundi from 1490. There is also evidence of a cut and folded paper box from 1440. It is possible that paperfolding in the west originated with the Moors much earlier; however, it is not known if it was independently discovered or knowledge of origami came along the silk route. The modern growth of interest in origami dates to the design in 1954 by Akira Yoshizawa of a notation to indicate how to fold origami models. The Yoshizawa-Randlett system is now used internationally. Today the popularity of origami has given rise to origami societies such as the British Origami Society and OrigamiUSA. The first known origami social group was founded in Zaragoza, Spain, during the 1940s.

The Chinese word for paperfolding is "ZheZhi", and some Chinese contend that origami is a historical derivative of Chinese paperfolding.

MODERN DESIGNS AND INNOVATIONS

An Example of Modular Origami (Geometric Shapes Formed from Sonobe Units)

Friedrich Fröbel, founder of the kindergartens, recognized paper binding, weaving, folding, and cutting as teaching aids for child development during the early 19th century. As the kindergarten system spread throughout Europe and into the rest of the world, it brought with it the small colored squares that we know of today as origami paper. Josef Albers, the father of modern color theory and minimalistic art, taught origami and paper folding in the 1920s and 30s at the famous Bahaus design school. His methods, which involved sheets of round paper that were folded into spirals and curved shapes, have influenced modern origami artists like KunihikoKasahara.

The work of Akira Yoshizawa, of Japan, a prolific creator of origami designs and a writer of books on origami, inspired a modern renaissance of the craft. He invented the process and techniques of wet-folding and set down the initial set of symbols for the standard Yoshizawa-Randlett system that Robert Harbin and Samuel Randlett later improved upon. His work was promoted through the studies of GershonLegman as published in the seminal books of Robert Harbin's Paper Magic and more so in Secrets of the Origami Masters which revealed the wide world of paper folding in the mid-1960s.

Modern origami has attracted a worldwide following, with ever more intricate designs and new techniques. One of these techniques is 'wet-folding,' the practice of dampening the paper somewhat during folding to allow the finished product to hold shape better. Variations such as modular origami, also known as unit origami, is a process where many origami units are assembled to form an often decorative whole.

Complex origami models normally require thin, strong paper or tissue foil for successful folding; these lightweight materials allow for more layers before the model becomes impractically thick. Modern origami has broken free from the traditional linear construction techniques of the past, and models are now frequently wet-folded or constructed from materials other than paper and foil. With popularity, a new generation of origami creators has experimented with crinkling techniques and smooth-flowing designs used in creating realistic masks, animals, and other traditional artistic themes.

SADAKO AND THE THOUSAND CRANES

One of the most famous origami designs is the Japanese crane. The crane is auspicious in Japanese culture. Legend says that anyone who folds one thousand paper cranes will have their heart's desire come true. The origami crane (orizuru in Japanese) has become a symbol of peace because of this belief and because of a young Japanese girl named Sadako Sasaki. Sadako was exposed to the radiation of the atomic bombing of Hiroshima as an infant, and it took its inevitable toll on her health. She was then a hibakusha — an atom bomb survivor. By the time she was twelve in 1955, she was dying of leukemia. Hearing the legend, she decided to fold one thousand origami cranes so that she could live. However, when she saw that the other children in her ward were dying, she realized that she would not survive and wished instead for world peace and an end to suffering. A popular version of the tale is that Sadako folded 644 cranes before she died; her classmates then continued folding cranes in honor of their friend. She was buried with a wreath of 1,000 cranes to honor her dream. While her effort could not extend her life, it moved her friends to make a granite statue of Sadako in the Hiroshima Peace Park: a girl standing with her hands outstretched, a paper crane flying from her fingertips. Every year the statue is adorned with thousands of wreaths of a thousand origami cranes. A group of one thousand paper cranes is called senbazuru in Japanese.

TECHNIQUES AND MATERIALS

YOSHIZAWA–RANDLETT SYSTEM

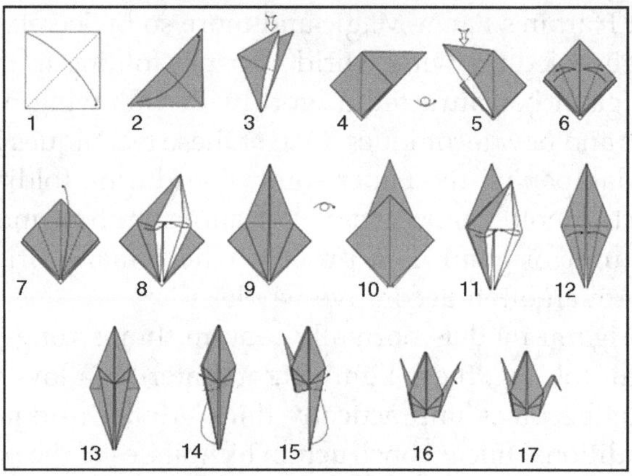

The Origami Crane Diagram, Using the Yoshizawa–Randlett System

The Yoshizawa–Randlett system is a diagramming system used to describe the folds of origami models. Many origami books begin with a description of basic origami techniques which are used to construct the models. There are also a number of standard bases which are commonly used as a first step in construction. Models are typically classified as requiring low, intermediate or high skill depending on the complexity of the techniques involved in the construction.

History

The concept of diagramming originated in the 1797 book "SenbazuruOrikata", the first origami book ever published. The diagrams in this book were very unclear, and often only showed the end result of the folding process, leaving the folder unsure how the model was created.

Later books began to devise a system of showing precisely how a model was folded. These ranged from an unwieldy set of symbols to a photograph or sketch of each step attempting to show the motion of a fold. None of these systems were sufficient to diagram all models, and so none were widely adopted.

In the 1950s and '60s, Akira Yoshizawa proposed a system of diagramming. He introduced its diagramming notation in his first published monograph, Atarashi Origami Geijutsu (New Origami Art) in 1954. He employed dotted and dashed lines to represent mountain and valley folds, and a few other symbols such as the "inflate" and "round" symbols. This system caught the attention of Samuel Randlett and Robert Harbin, who added a few symbols such as "rotate" and "zoom in", and then adopted it as the standard. The Yoshizawa–Randlett system was first described in Samuel Randlett'sArt of Origami in 1961. It was then accepted as the default throughout the international origami community, and is still in general use today.

Origami Symbols

Basic Folds

There are two main types of origami symbol, lines and arrows.

The arrows show how the paper is bent or moved. Lines show various types of edges:

- A thick line shows the edge of the paper
- A dashed line shows a valley fold. The paper is folded in front of itself.
- A dashed and dotted line shows a mountain fold (there may be one or two dots per dash depending on the author). The paper is folded behind itself, this is normally done by turning the paper over, folding a valley fold and then turning the paper back over again.
- A thin line shows where a previous fold has creased the paper.
- A dotted line shows a previous fold that's hidden behind other paper, or sometimes shows a fold that's not yet made.

Symbols for basic folds

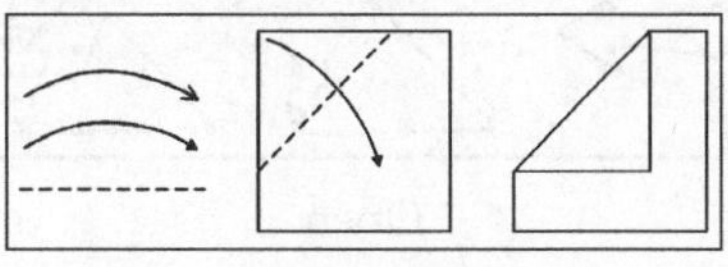

Valley Fold

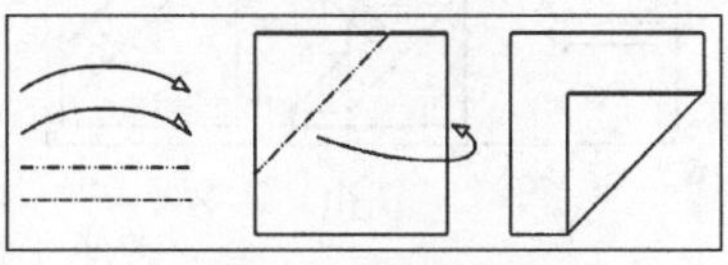

Mountain Fold.

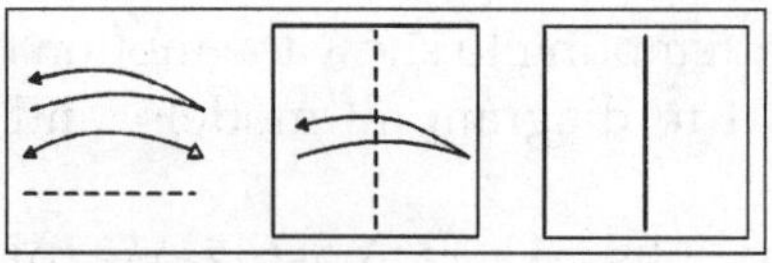

Fold and Unfold Valley.

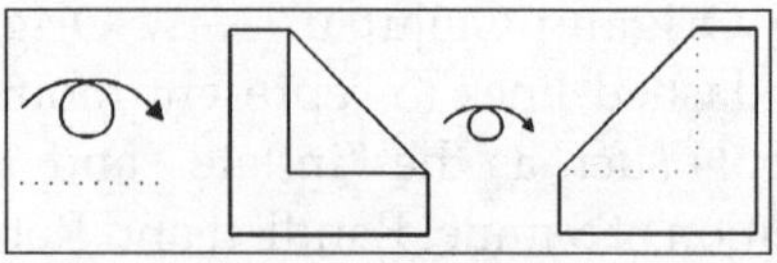

Turn Over and Invisible Line.

Common Operations

The operations shown here are all fairly common. The pleat folds and reverse folds are often done with the two creases at an angle. Reverse folds of a corner are typically used to produce feet or birds heads.

The sink fold is considered an intermediary to high skill. The version shown here is called an open sink and there is another version called a closed sink which generates a triangular pocket with no flaps showing. In simple cases the model can be partly unfolded and then folded with the sink in place.

Origami symbols

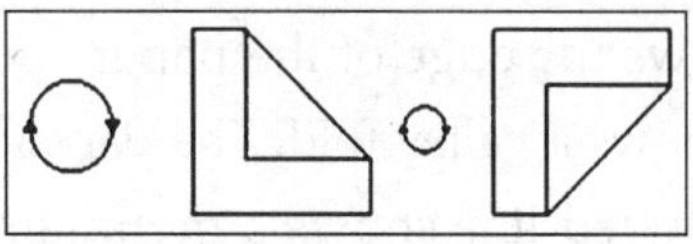

Rotate.

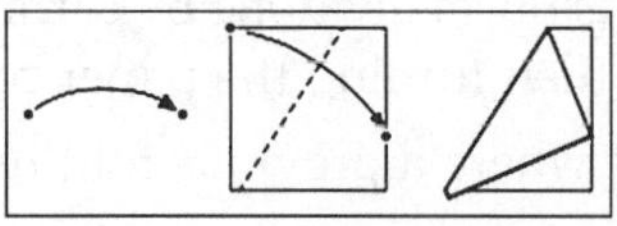

Put the Points Together

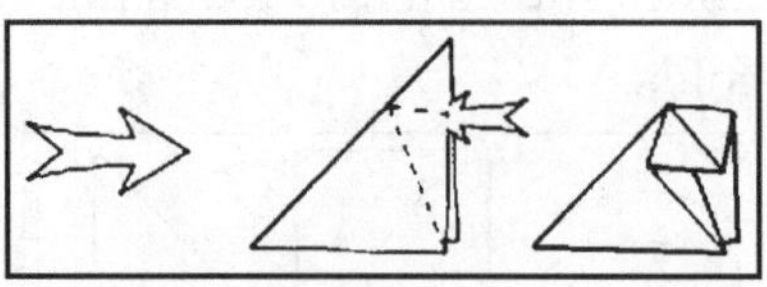

Open.

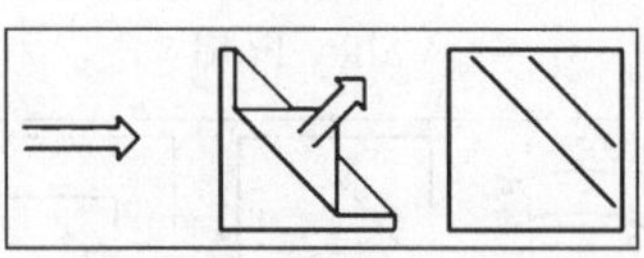

Pull.

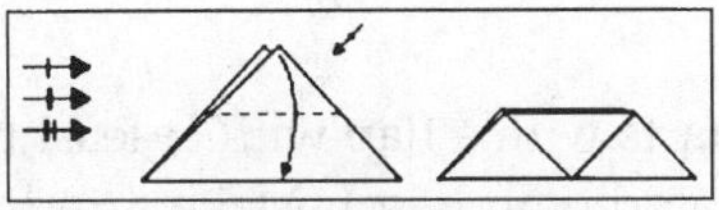

Repeat Action.

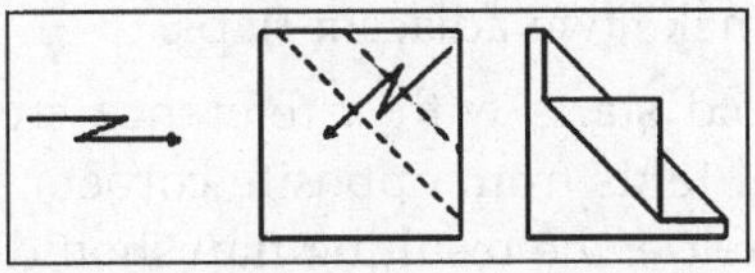

Pleat Fold, also called an Accordion Fold.

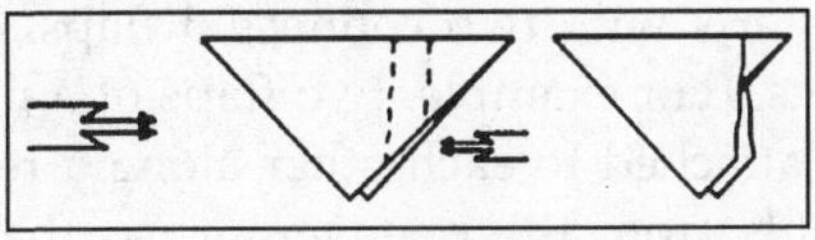

Inside Crimp Fold.

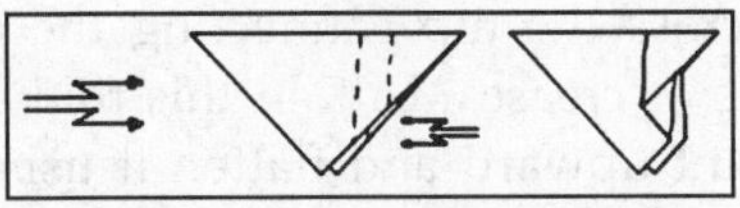

Outside Crimp Fold.

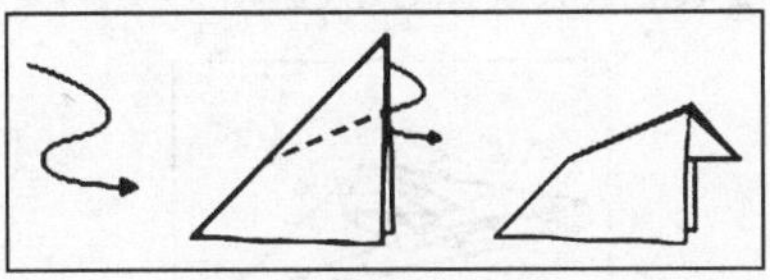

Inside Reverse Fold.

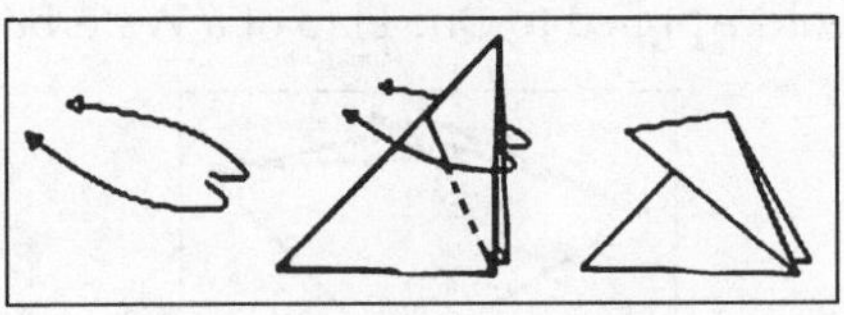

Outside Reverse Fold.

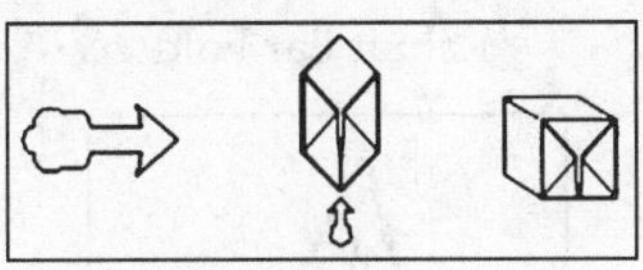

Inflate the Model.

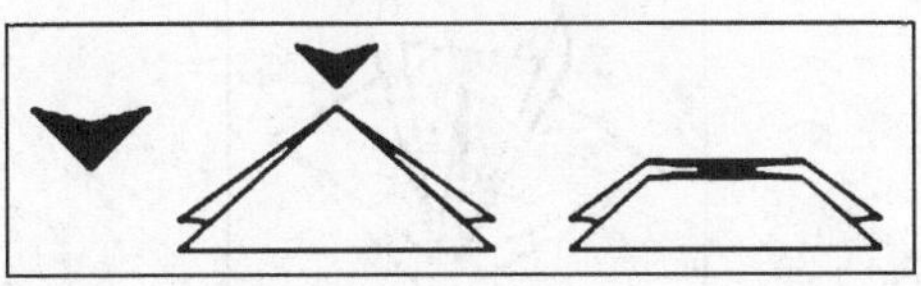

Sink a Corner.

Compound Folds

- A squash fold starts with a flap with at least two layers (for example, one flap of a waterbomb base). Make a radial fold from the closed point down the center of this flap. Open the flap and refold downward to make two adjacent flaps.
- A rabbit ear fold starts with a reference crease down a diagonal. Fold two radial folds from opposite corners along the same side of the reference crease; the resulting flap should be folded downwards so that the previous edges are aligned.
- A petal fold starts with two connected flaps, each of which has at least two layers. (For example, two flaps of a preliminary base). The two flaps are attached to each other along a reference crease. Make two radial folds from the open point, so that the open edges lie along the reference crease. Unfold these two radial folds. Make another fold across the top connecting the ends of the creases to create a triangle of creases. Unfold this fold as well. Fold one layer of the open point upward and flatten it using the existing creases. A petal fold is equivalent to two side-by-side rabbit ears, which are connected along the reference crease.

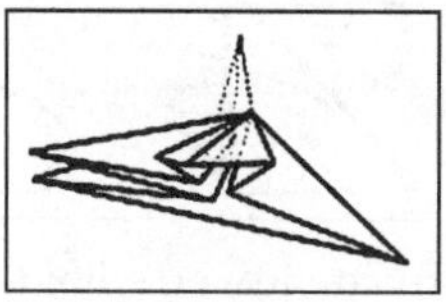

Squash Fold Applied to One Flap of a Waterbomb Base

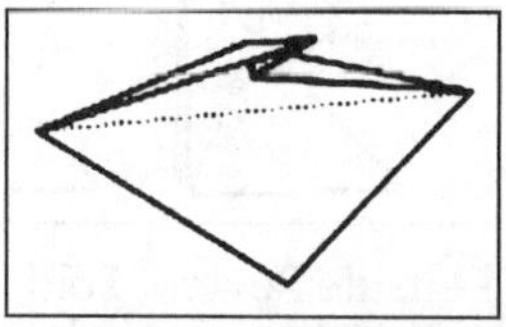

Rabbit Ear Fold

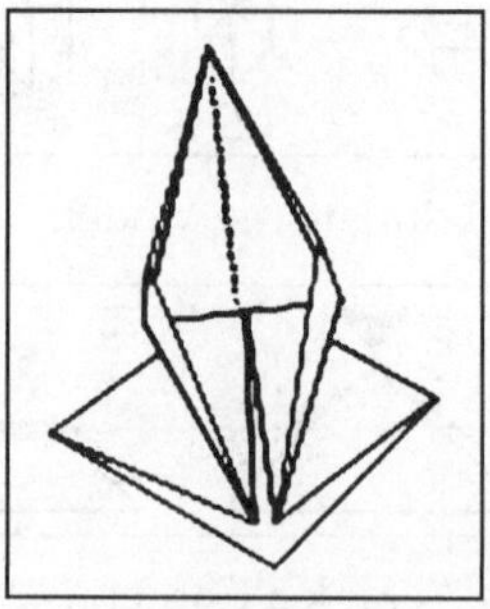

Petal Fold on One Half of a Preliminary Fold

Origami Bases

In origami, there is a series of several bases that many models are created with. In general, "base" refers to any folded paper that immediately precedes final folding and shaping of the model-to-be.

The ones listed below are generally accepted as the traditional origami bases:

- A blintz base is made by folding the corners of a square into the center. The resulting square can then be used as the starting point for any base or blintzed again. The resulting base will then have more points available for folding.
- The kite base is merely two valley folds that bring two adjacent edges of the square together to lie on the square's diagonal.
- The fish base consists of two radial folds against a diagonal reference crease on each of two opposite corners. The flaps that result on the other two corners are carefully folded downwards in the same direction. In other words, it consists of two side-by-side rabbit ears.
- The waterbomb base consists of two perpendicular valley folds down the diagonals of the square and two perpendicular mountain folds down the center of the square. This crease pattern is then compressed to form the waterbomb base, which is an isosceles-right triangle with four isosceles-right triangular flaps. The waterbomb base is an inside-out preliminary fold.
- The preliminary fold consists of two perpendicular diagonal mountain folds that bisect the corners of the square and two perpendicular valley folds that bisect the edges of the square. The paper is then collapsed to form a square shape with four isosceles-right triangular flaps. It is sometimes called the Square Base
- The bird base, or crane base, consists of a preliminary fold with both the front and the back sides petal folded upward.
- The frog base starts with a waterbomb base or preliminary fold. All four flaps are squash-folded (the result is the same in either case), and then the corners are petal folded upward.

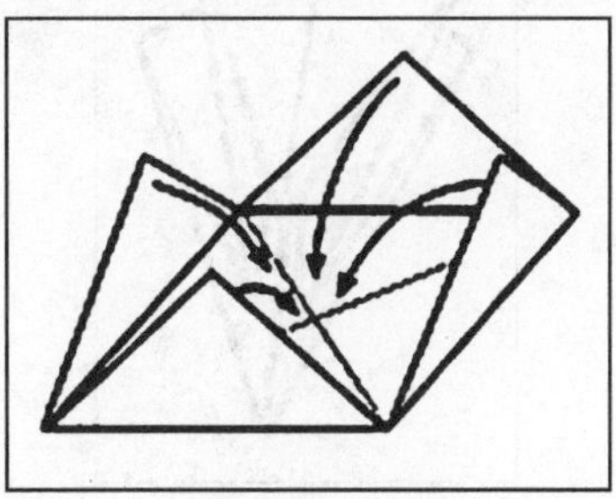

Blintz Base

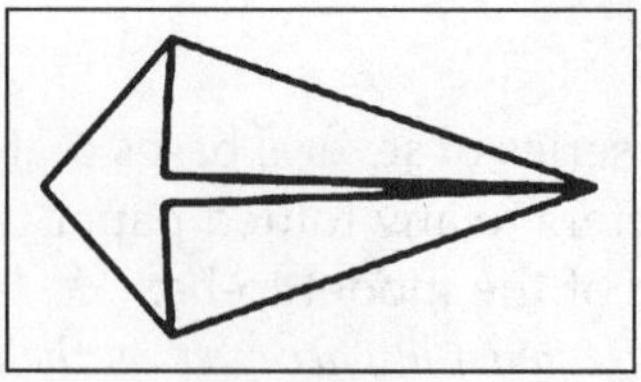

Kite Base

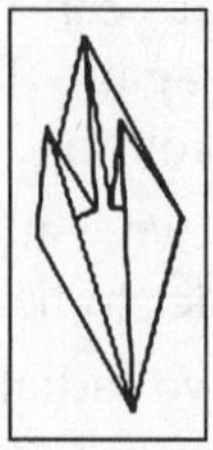

Fish Base

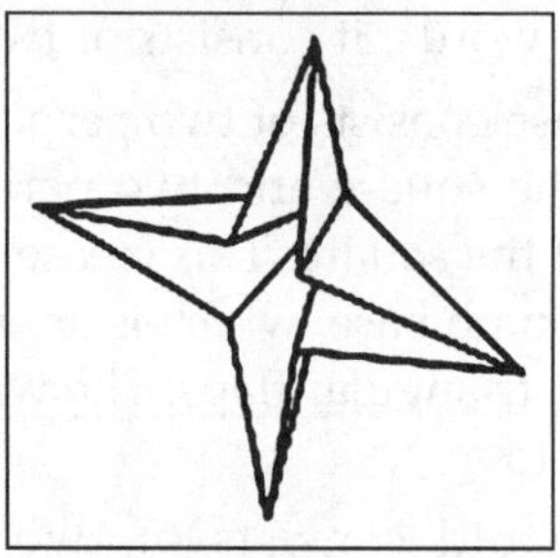

Water Bomb Base Before Flattening

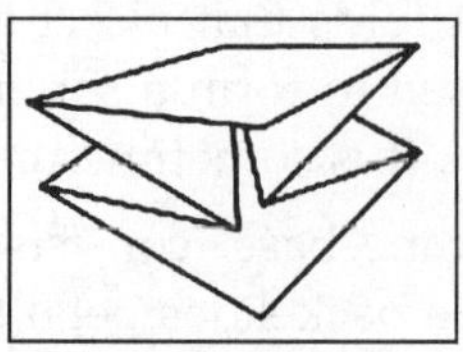

Preliminary Fold or Square Base

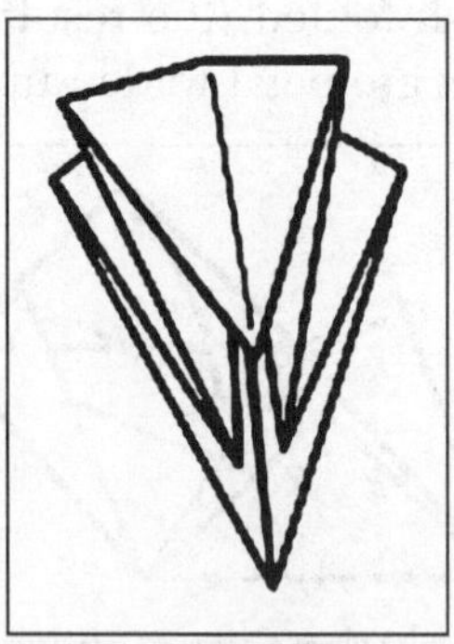

Bird Base

More Advanced Skills

- The Swivel fold is difficult to describe as the term is loosely defined and there are so many different versions that could be called "swivel folds". However, generally swivel folds involve a flap of paper "swivelling" at a certain point or vertex and another flap or edge of paper, connected to the first, dragged around that point or vertex.
- Most of the creases in a stretched bird base are present in the regular bird base. When forming this bird base, make sure to crease the triangle at the center corner through all layers. After forming the bird base, either partially unfold the paper, and/or "stretch" two opposite corners of the bird base. These two corners, their associated flaps, and the central square will all lie flat. The other two flaps will form a pyramid. Rabbit ear each flap that is in the pyramid, so that the model lies flat. All of the raw edges will lie along the centerline of the model. The stretched bird base is used in Lang's Bald Eagle, Greenberg's Eeyore, and some other high-intermediate and complex models.
- The open sink usually involves opening out the paper, and reversing creases to make a waterbomb base in the middle of the model.
- The open double sink is equivalent to making an open sink, and then open-sinking the point in the opposite direction. It is a sinkedanalog of the crimp fold. When made in a single step (after pre-creasing), it can be easier to make than a single open sink, because it does not require neatly reversing the point. The open double sink is used in many box-pleated models.
- The spread squash can similarly be considered the sinkedanalog of the squash fold. It is used to flatten a closed flap or twist fold. Instead of creating a long point to one side of the flap's base, the spread squash creates a wide splat around the flap's base. The spread squash is used in the eyes of Engel's Octopus, in Marie's Rose, and in some other intermediate and complex models.
- The closed sink simultaneously makes a locking flap inside of a sink. It is difficult because the paper cannot be opened out further than a triangle. This technique is illustrated in the Origami Forum's thread #462. The closed sink appears in some high-intermediate and complex models.
- The twist fold involves, as the name implies, twisting a section of the paper with respect to its original position. The section twisted will be a polygon; the numerous required support creases include pleat folds radiating from its corners. Marie's Rose demonstrates this on a pentagon.

- It is also possible to twist a single conical point indefinitely, collapsing the sides in a waterbomb-base-like fashion as one goes. (If this is tried with a non-conical point, such as the waterbomb base itself, eventually the fold will terminate in a spread squash.) This variant is used in many of Tomoko Fuse's modular boxes.

- Unsink, or sometimes open unsink, makes a concave pocket convex without fully unfolding the paper, or the opposite of an open sink. It is more difficult than the closed unsink below because there is no internal flap to grab onto to help unsink the paper, so the paper must be opened out and the area to be unsunk is pushed out (to be convex) from inside the model and from behind. It is a common fold in Lang's insects.
- The closed unsink inverts a closed sink without completely opening out the affected paper. In theory, it is "just" the opposite of a closed sink. In practice, it is very difficult, because the paper being "popped" into place usually must be pulled (not pushed), and because it involves simultaneously folding over a locking flap that is hidden inside the sink. However, it is easier to manipulate than an open unsink as there is an internal flap to pull to pop the unsink in place; in an open unsink there is nothing to hold. The closed unsink appears in some complex models, such as a few of Lang's insects.

ORIGAMI PAPER

Origami Paper and a Traditional Origami Crane

Origami paper is used to fold origami, the art of paper folding. The only requirement of the folding medium is that is must be able to hold a crease.

KAMI

This paper is the easiest to find and cheapest to buy. It is also the most basic: kami, or koi paper. Kami is thin and easy to fold. It is usually printed only on one side, with a solid color or pattern. These patterns can be as simple as a gradation from red to blue, or as complex as a multi-coloredkimono pattern of flowers and cranes with gold foil embellishments. Kami comes in several sizes, but standard sizes include 75 × 75 mm (about 3 × 3 inches), 6-inch squares and 10-inch squares.

ORIGAMIDO

Meaning the "Way of paper folding," this handmade paper is created by MichealLafosse specifically for origami. It is designed for thinness.

PAPER-BACKED FOIL

This medium is a slightly more expensive, flashier, paper that is good for retaining creases called paper-backed foil paper, Japanese foil, or simply foil. Foil paper is composed of a thin layer of foil adhered to an extremely thin sheet of paper. The most common colors are silver and gold, but any color is possible in foil paper including bright pink, blue and copper. In many multi-color packs, one sheet each of silver and gold paper is included. These are usually placed on the bottom end of the string if used in a thousand origami cranes.

WASHI

Washi is a thick handmade paper, available commercially but very expensive. Washi is a long-fibred paper but is also very soft. It does not hold a sharp fold due to the extremely long and thick fibres of the pulp. Inclusions of flowers, leaves, grass, seeds, string, ribbon, and other small decorative items are common for washi, adding to the random and handmade appearance of the finished craft. Washi is also accepting of ink, making it easy to print upon. Printed washi has a uniquely shiny, uneven and occasionally transparent texture. In origami it is not as commonly used as kami paper.

CHIYOGAMI

Chiyogami (literally "1000 generation paper") is an inexpensive alternative to washi paper. It is a traditional block-printed paper.

DOLLAR BILLS AND BANKNOTES

An Origami Snail that is made Out of a Dollar bill.

Banknotes may be used to fold models as well. Banknotes are common media for folding as the subject in the center of the banknote, like George Washington, can make a striking appearance on the finished model.

TYPES OF ORIGAMI

ACTION ORIGAMI

A Decorated Paper Fortune Teller.

Action origami is origami that can be animated. The original traditional action model is the flapping bird. Typically models where the final assembly involves some special action, for instance blowing up a waterbomb, are also classed as action origami. More rarely models like paper plane and spinners which have no moving parts are included. Some traditional action origami involved cuts but modern models typically are built with no cuts. Action origami are normally toys built to amuse but some are designed to inspire wonder.

Action Toys

Action toys include birds or butterflies with flapping wings, beaks that peck, and frogs that hop, as well as popular traditional models like the fortune teller. Paper poppers or bangers are models that make a noise when flicked down hard. Some action origami is designed to accompany a story whilst it is built.

Complex Models

Some models are far more complex than can be classed as toys. They are built to amaze and astonish. For instance Robert J. Lang's Bassist, Pianist, and Violinist is a set of action models where each one plays an instrument when pulled on appropriately. Jeremy Shafer has made a number of extraordinary action models including a Swiss army knife with tools that open out, a slithering snake skin, and flashers, one of which he demonstrated on The Carol Duvall Show.

Mathematical Models

Flashers are models with a regular pattern that can be folded up small and rapidly expanded. The miura fold is a similar idea that has been used in commercial applications. Versions on a regular pattern can for instance be used to make a human figure when folded up or a maze when opened.

MODULAR ORIGAMI

A Great Stellated Dodecahedron Made from Custom Papers

Modular origami or unit origami is a paperfolding technique which uses two or more sheets of paper to create a larger and more complex structure than would not be possible using single-piece origami techniques. Each individual sheet of paper is folded into a module, or unit, and then modules are assembled into an integrated flat shape or three-dimensional structure by inserting flaps into pockets created by the folding process. These insertions create tension or friction that holds the model together.

Definition and Restrictions

Modular origami can be classified as a sub-set of multi-piece origami, since the rule of restriction to one sheet of paper is abandoned. However, all the other rules of origami still apply, so the use of glue, thread, or any other fastening that is not a part of the sheet of paper is not generally acceptable in modular origami.

The additional restrictions that distinguish modular origami from other forms of multi-piece origami are using many identical copies of any folded unit, and linking them together in a symmetrical or repeating fashion to complete the model. There is a common misconception that treats all multi-piece origami as modular, but this is not the case.

More than one type of module can still be used. Typically this means using separate linking units hidden from sight to hold parts of the construction together. Any other usage is generally frowned upon. The word origami comes from Japan. "Oru" meaning to fold and "Kami" meaning paper

History

The first historical evidence for a modular origami design comes from a Japanese book by HayatoOhoka published in 1734 called RanmaZushiki. It contains a print that shows a group of traditional origami models, one of which is a modular cube. The cube is pictured twice (from slightly different angles) and is identified in the accompanying text as a tamatebako, or a 'magic treasure chest'. Isao Honda's World of Origami appears to have the same model, where it is called the 'Cubical Box'. The six modules required for this design were developed from the traditional Japanese paperfold commonly known as the Menko. Each module forms one face of the finished cube.

There are several other traditional Japanese modular origami designs, including balls of folded paper flowers known as kusudama, or medicine balls. These designs are not integrated and are commonly strung together with thread. The term kusudama is sometimes, rather inaccurately, used to describe any three-dimensional modular origami structure resembling a ball. There are also a few modular designs in the Chinese paperfolding tradition, notably the Pagoda (from Maying Soong) and the Lotus made from Joss paper. Most traditional designs are however single-piece and the possibilities inherent in the modular origami idea were not explored further until the 1960s when the technique was re-invented by Robert Neale in the USA and later by MitsonobuSonobe in Japan. Since then the modular origami technique has been popularized and developed extensively, and now there have been thousands of designs developed in this repertoire.

Types

Modular origami forms may be flat or three-dimensional. Flat forms are usually polygons (sometimes known as coasters), stars, rotors, and rings. Three-dimensional forms tend to be regular polyhedra or tessellations of simple polyhedra. There are some modular origami that are approximations of fractals, such as Menger's sponge. Macro-modular origami is a form of modular origami in which finished assemblies are themselves used as the building blocks to create larger integrated structures.

WET-FOLDING

Wet-folding Bull

Wet-folding is an origami technique developed by Akira Yoshizawa that employs water to dampen the paper so that it can be manipulated more easily. This process adds an element of sculpture to origami, which is otherwise purely geometric. Wet-folding is used very often by professional folders for non-geometric origami, such as animals. Wet-folders usually employ thicker paper than would usually be used for normal origami, to ensure that the paper does not tear.

One of the most prominent users of the wet-folding technique was ÉricJoisel, who specialized in animals, people, and mythological creatures such as fairies. He also created origami masks. Other folders who practice this technique are Robert J. Lang and John Montroll. The process of wet-folding allows a folder to preserve a curved shape more easily. It also reduces the number of wrinkles substantially. Wet-folding allows for increased rigidity and structure due to a process called sizing. Sizing is a water-soluble adhesive, usually methylcellulose or methyl acetate that may be added during the manufacture of the paper. As the paper dries, the chemical bonds the fibers of the paper tighter together which results in a crisper and stronger sheet. In order to moisten the paper, an artist typically wipes the sheet with a dampened cloth. The amount of moisture added to the paper is crucial, because too little will cause the paper to dry quickly and spring back into its original position before the folding is complete, but too much will fray the edges of the paper or will cause the paper to split at high-stress points.

PURELANDORIGAMI

Pureland origami is a style of origami invented by the Britishpaperfolder John Smith which is limited to using only mountain and valley folds. The aim of Pureland Origami is to make origami easier for inexperienced folders and those who have impaired motor skills. This means that many, but not all, of the more complicated processes that are common in regular origami are impossible; and so alternative manipulations have been developed to create similar effects.

KIRIGAMI

Kirigami is a variation of origami that includes cutting of the paper (from Japanese "kiru" = to cut, "kami" = paper). It is also called "Kirie" From "Kiru"= to cut, "e"= picture. Typically, kirigami starts with a folded base, which is then cut; cuts are then opened and flattened to make the finished kirigami. Kirigami are usually symmetrical, such as snowflakes, pentagrams, or orchid blossoms. A difference between kirigami and the art of 'pop up' is that kirigami is made out of a single piece of paper that has been cut into a design. Pop ups can be made of several pieces glued together. Mon-Kiri is the Japanese art of paper cutting.

TECHNICAL ORIGAMI

Technical origami, also known as origami sekkei is a field of origami that has developed almost hand-in-hand with the field of mathematical origami. In the early days of origami, development of new designs was largely a mix of trial-and-error, luck and serendipity. With advances in origami mathematics however, the basic structure of a new origami model can be theoretically plotted out on paper before any actual folding even occurs. This method of origami design was developed by Robert Lang, Meguro Toshiyuki and others, and allows for the creation of extremely complex multi-limbed models such as many-legged centipedes, human figures with a full complement of fingers and toes, and the like.

The main starting point for such technical designs is the crease pattern (often abbreviated as CP), which is essentially the layout of the creases required to form the final model. Although not intended as a substitute for diagrams, folding from crease patterns is starting to gain in popularity, partly because of the challenge of being able to 'crack' the pattern, and also partly because the crease pattern is often the only resource available to fold a given model, should the designer choose not to produce diagrams. Still, there are many cases in which designers wish to sequence the steps of their models but lack the means to design clear diagrams. Such origamists occasionally resort to the sequenced crease pattern (SCP) which is a set of crease patterns showing the creases up to each respective fold. Paradoxically enough, when origami designers come up with a crease pattern for a new design, the majority of the smaller creases are relatively unimportant and added only towards the completion of the crease pattern. What is more important is the allocation of regions of the paper and how these are mapped to the structure of the object being designed. For a specific class of origami bases known as 'uniaxial bases', the pattern of allocations is referred to as the 'circle-packing'. Using optimization algorithms, a circle-packing figure can be computed for any uniaxial base of arbitrary complexity. Once this figure is computed, the creases which are then used to obtain the base structure can be added. This is not a unique mathematical process, hence it is possible for two designs to have the same circle-packing, and yet different crease pattern structures.

As a circle encloses the maximum amount of area for a given perimeter, circle packing allows for maximum efficiency in terms of paper usage. However, other polygonal shapes can be used to solve the packing problem as well. The use of polygonal shapes other than circles is often motivated by the desire to find easily locatable creases (such as multiples of 22.5 degrees) and hence an easier folding sequence as well. One popular offshoot of the circle packing method is box-pleating, where squares are used instead of circles. As a result, the crease pattern that arises from this method contains only 45 and 90 degree angles, which makes for easier folding.

ORIGAMI-RELATED COMPUTER PROGRAMS

A number of computer aids to origami such as TreeMaker and Oripa, have been devised. Treemaker allows new origami bases to be designed for special purposes and Oripa tries to calculate the folded shape from the crease pattern.

ETHICS

Copyright in origami designs and the use of models has become an increasingly important issue as the internet has made the sale and distribution of pirated designs very easy. It is considered good ethics to always credit the original artist and the folder when displaying origami models.

All commercial rights to designs and models are typically reserved by origami artists. Normally a person who folds a model using a legally obtained design can publicly display the model unless such rights are specifically reserved, however folding a design for money or commercial use of a photo for instance would require consent. It can be difficult to contact individual designers for permission or payment therefore there is a drive to set up a group to ease such issues.

MATHEMATICS OF PAPER FOLDING

The art of origami or paper folding has received a considerable amount of mathematical study. Fields of interest include a given paper model's flat-foldability (whether the model can be flattened without damaging it) and the use of paper folds to solve mathematical equations.

HISTORY

In 1893 T. SundaraRao published "Geometric Exercises in Paper Folding" which used paper folding to demonstrate proofs of geometrical constructions. This work was inspired by the use of origami in the kindergarten system. This book had an approximate trisection of angles and implied construction of a cube root was impossible.

In 1936 Margharita P. Beloch showed that use of the 'Beloch fold', later used in the sixth of the Huzita–Hatori axioms, allowed the general cubic to be solved using origami.

In 1949 R C Yeates' book "Geometric Methods" described three allowed constructions corresponding to the first, second, and fifth of the Huzita–Hatori axioms.

The axioms were discovered by Jacques Justin in 1989. but overlooked till the first six were rediscovered by HumiakiHuzita in 1991. The 1st International Meeting of Origami Science and Technology (now International Conference on Origami in Science, Math, and Education) was held in 1989 in Ferrara, Italy.

PURE ORIGAMI

Flat Folding

Two-colorability.

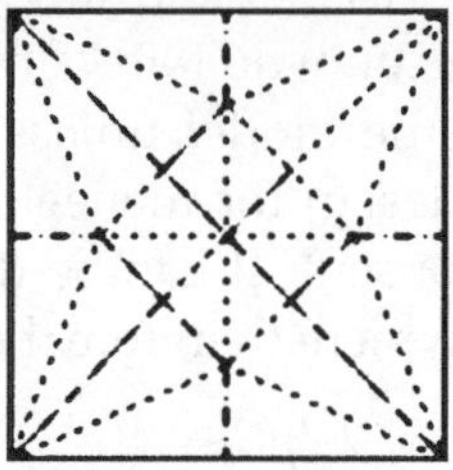

Mountain-valley Counting.

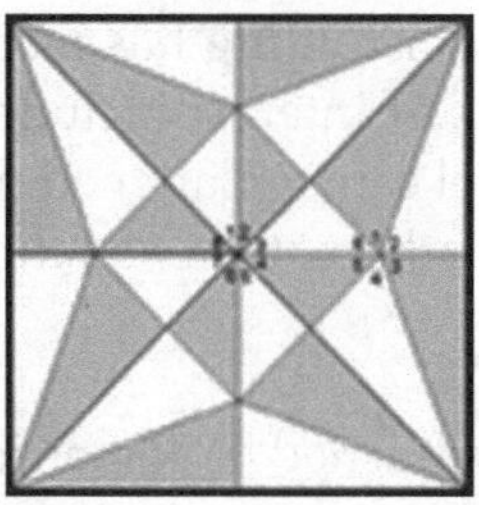

Angles Around a Vertex.

The construction of origami models is sometimes shown as crease patterns. The major question about such crease patterns is whether a given crease pattern can be folded to a flat model, and if so, how to fold them; this is an NP-complete problem. Related problems when the creases are orthogonal are called map folding problems.

There are four mathematical rules for producing flat-foldable origami crease patterns:

1. Crease patterns are two colorable
2. Maekawa's theorem: at any vertex the number of valley and mountain folds always differ by two in either direction
3. Kawasaki's theorem: at any vertex, the sum of all the odd angles adds up to 180 degrees, as do the even.
4. A sheet can never penetrate a fold.

Paper exhibits zero Gaussian curvature at all points on its surface, and only folds naturally along lines of zero curvature. Curved surfaces which can't be flattened can be produced using a non-folded crease in the paper, as is easily done with wet paper or a fingernail. Assigning a crease pattern mountain and valley folds in order to produce a flat model has been proven by Marshall Bern and Barry Hayes to be NP complete. Further references and technical results are discussed in Part II of Geometric Folding Algorithms.

Huzita–Hatoriaxioms

Some classical construction problems of geometry — namely trisecting an arbitrary angle, or doubling the cube — are proven to be unsolvable using compass and straightedge, but can be solved using only a few paper folds. Paper fold strips can be constructed to solve equations up to degree 4. The Huzita–Hatori axioms are an important contribution to this field of study. These describe what can be constructed using a sequence of creases with at most two point or line alignments at once. Complete methods for solving all equations up to degree 4 by applying methods satisfying these axioms are discussed in detail in Geometric Origami.

CONSTRUCTIONS

As a result of origami study through the application of geometric principles, methods such as Haga's theorem have allowed paperfolders to accurately fold the side of a square into thirds, fifths, sevenths, and ninths. Other theorems and methods have allowed paperfolders to get other shapes from a square, such as equilateral triangles, pentagons, hexagons, and special rectangles such as the golden rectangle and the silver rectangle. Methods for folding most regular polygons up to and including the regular 19-gon have been developed.

Haga's Theorems

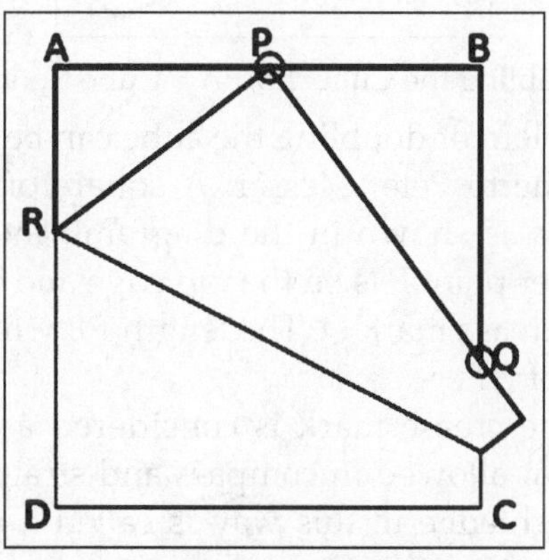

BQ is Always a Rational if AP is.

The side of a square can be divided at an arbitrary rational fraction in a variety of ways. Haga's theorems say that a particular set of constructions can be used for such divisions. Surprisingly few folds are necessary to generate large odd fractions. For instance/5 can be generated with three folds; first halve a side, then use Haga's theorem twice to produce first/3 and then/5.

The accompanying diagram shows Haga's first theorem:

$$BQ = \frac{2AP}{1+AP}$$

The function changing the length *AP* to *QC* is self inverse. Let *x* be *AP* then a number of other lengths are also rational functions of x. For example:

Table. Haga's First Theorem

AP	BQ	QC	AR	PQ
x	$\frac{2x}{1+x}$	$\frac{1-x}{1+x}$	$\frac{1-x^2}{2}$	$\frac{1+x^2}{1+x}$
/2	/3	/3	/8	/6
/3	/2	/2	/9	/6
/3	/5	/5	/18	/15
/5	/3	/3	/25	/15

Doubling the Cube

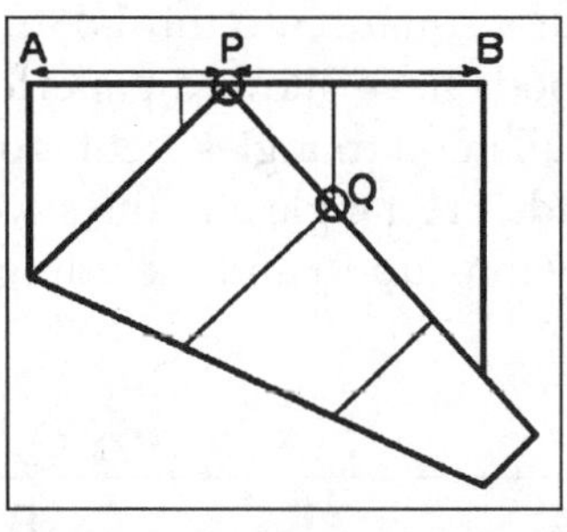

Doubling the Cube: PB/PA = Cube Root of 2

The classical problem of doubling the cube can be solved using origami, this construction is due to Peter Messer. A square of paper is first creased into three equal strips as shown in the diagram. Then the bottom edge is positioned so the corner point P is on the top edge and the crease mark on the edge meets the other crease mark *Q*. The length *PB* will then be the cube root of 2 times the length of *AP*.

The edge with the crease mark is considered a marked straightedge, something which is not allowed in compass and straightedge constructions. Using a marked straightedge in this way is called a neusis construction in geometry.

Trisecting an Angle

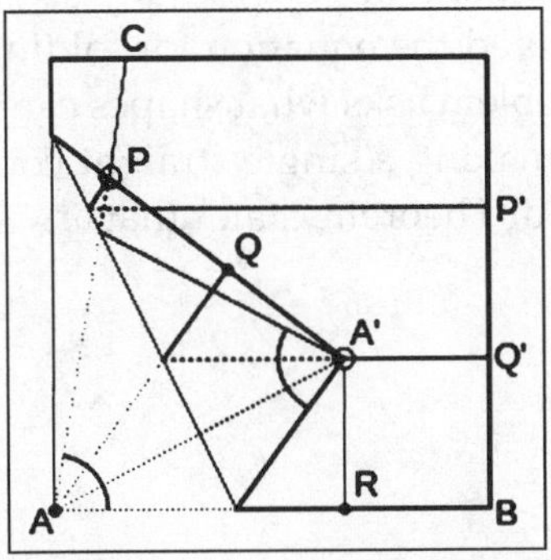

Trisecting the Angle CAB

Angle trisection is another of the classical problems that cannot be solved using a compass and unmarked ruler but can be solved using origami. This construction is due to Hisashi Abe. The angle CAB is trisected by making folds *PP'* and *QQ'* parallel to the base with *QQ'* halfway in between. Then point *P* is folded over to lie on line *AC* and at the same time point A is made to lie on line *QQ'* at A'. The angle *A'AB* is one third of the original angle CAB. This is because *PAQ, A'AQ* and *A'AR* are three congruent triangles. Aligning the two points on the two lines is another neusis construction as in the solution to doubling the cube.

RELATED PROBLEMS

The problem of rigid origami, treating the folds as hinges joining two flat, rigid surfaces, such as sheet metal, has great practical importance. For example, the Miura map fold is a rigid fold that has been used to deploy large solar panel arrays for space satellites. The napkin folding problem is the problem of whether a square or rectangle of paper can be folded so the perimeter of the flat figure is greater than that of the original square.

Curved origami also poses a (very different) set of mathematical challenges. Curved origami allows the paper to form developable surfaces that are not flat. Wet-folding origami allows an even greater range of shapes.

The maximum number of times an incompressible material can be folded has been derived. With each fold a certain amount of paper is lost to potential folding. The loss function for folding paper in half in a single direction was given to be,

$$L = \frac{\pi t}{6}\left(2^n + 4\right)\left(2^n - 1\right)$$

where L is the minimum length of the paper (or other material), t is the material's thickness, and n is the number of folds possible. The distances L and t must be expressed in the same units, such as inches. This result was derived by Gallivan in 2001, who also folded a sheet of paper in half 12 times, contrary to the popular belief that paper of any size could be folded at most eight times. She also derived the equation for folding in alternate directions.

The fold-and-cut problem asks what shapes can be obtained by folding a piece of paper flat, and making a single straight complete cut. The solution, known as the Fold and Cut Theorem, states that any shape with straight sides can be obtained.

Index